Understanding Digital Electronics: How Microcomputers and Microprocessors Work

PATRICK J. O'CONNOR

DeVry Institute of Technology
Chicago, Illinois

PRENTICE-HALL, INC., Englewood Cliffs, NJ 07632

Library of Congress Cataloging in Publication Data

O'Connor, Patrick J. (Patrick Joseph), 1947–
   Understanding digital electronics.

   Includes index.
   1. Microcomputers. 2. Microprocessors. I. Title.
TK7888.3.028 1984   621.3819'58   83-21206
ISBN 0-13-936964-3

Production supervision and
   interior design: *Shari Ingerman*
Cover design: *Lundgren Graphics, Ltd.*
Manufacturing buyer: *Tony Caruso*

Printed in the United States of America

10 9 8 7 6 5 4 3 2 1

ISBN 0-13-936964-3

Prentice-Hall International, Inc., *London*
Prentice-Hall of Australia Pty. Limited, *Sydney*
Editora Prentice-Hall do Brasil, Ltda., *Rio de Janeiro*
Prentice-Hall Canada Inc., *Toronto*
Prentice-Hall of India Private Limited, *New Delhi*
Prentice-Hall of Japan, Inc., *Tokyo*
Prentice-Hall of Southeast Asia Pte. Ltd., *Singapore*
Whitehall Books Limited, *Wellington, New Zealand*

Contents

Preface

This book is based loosely on a series of lectures given at the DeVry Institute of Technology to students in the Electronics Technician Program. The microprocessor and microcomputer are discussed in the T-5 Digital Systems, III course, the third of three trimesters in a digital electronics sequence. The goal of the technician program is not to produce designers, but individuals competent enough in the basic principles to service existing equipment. In the technician program, the emphasis in these courses is threefold:

1. To present the vocabulary, so that the student can comprehend and use the "buzzwords" of the field with a real understanding of the underlying concepts which these words embody.
2. To explain the principles of operation of components used in existing circuits and systems.
3. To describe safe handling procedures and failure modes for the logic devices likely to be encountered in the field.

It is now becoming apparent that technicians are not an isolated case. They are not the only people for whom a knowledge of the basic principles of computer operation is indispensable. Every technically-literate layman should be familiar with the basics. It is with this idea in mind that this book is presented to the general reading public.

NOTE:

There are a few things you should be aware of before beginning this book. It is a book about HOW THINGS WORK. To understand every detail of the explanations, you already should know a little about binary numbers, elementary logic gates, and Boolean logic. If you are not already familiar with these things, skim over the first three chapters. They are quite technical in places, and there may be things that you will not understand—but do not skip them entirely. There is a lot of useful information in them which is available to a person with no technical training. The rest of the chapters in the book, although spiced liberally with technical details, do not require much technical background to understand.

Patrick O'Connor

1

Bus-Oriented Systems: How the Parts of the Microcomputer Are Connected Together

There are two ways to build computers. Older models, and the very largest and fastest computers built today, are designed as MONOLITHIC machines. What that means is that the individual parts of the computer are connected so that a signal can travel from its source to its destination by the shortest path possible. There is a separate connection for each part of the computer, and signals are traveling in many directions and on many paths at once. This kind of design makes for very fast computing, but it is also very expensive. Another type of design, called BUS-ORIENTED design, connects all the parts of the computer to a common group of wires, called a BUS. Although parts of the computer must "take turns" using the shared signal-path, which makes the computer slower, it also makes the computer much less expensive, since there aren't as many paths and connections. In modern large-scale integrated circuit design, such as microprocessors and microcomputers use, the interconnections and signal paths cost more than the actual logic gates doing the "computing." Thus, there is a savings in cost, and personal computers (as well as other digital consumer circuits) are designed to use BUSES to carry all signals around the interior of the computer system. In another sense, bus-oriented design is a part of every computer's design. In large digital networks, where parts of the system must be co-ordinated precisely, buses are usually used to connect all of the parts of the system together.

In these systems, the buses provide the timing signals that keep all parts of the network "in step." We'll begin our discussion of computers by seeing how a simple calculator does a limited task. Later, we'll advance to a discussion of microprocessors and microcomputers, which are simply a "classed-up" and automatic version of the calculator.

1.1 BLOCK DIAGRAM OF A BUS-ORIENTED COMPUTER

Figure 1-1 is a block diagram of a computer showing three main blocks and three buses connecting them. Each bus coordinates a different sort of activity, and each block handles a special part of the functions of the computer.

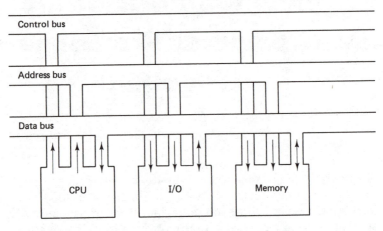

Figure 1-1   Block diagram of a bus-oriented computer

1.1.1 Address, Data, and Control Buses: Their Function

Micro- and minicomputers have three basic blocks attached to each other by connection to three buses. The **data bus** carries data—which are numbers that say what some part of the computer has to say to another part of the computer. The **address bus** carries addresses—numbers that say where the data is going to or coming from. The **control bus** is used by the CPU block to activate or deactivate other parts of the system. Control signals are not a binary code like addresses or data. Each one is an independent ON/OFF signal that controls one thing, such as the direction of data travel or the type of **peripheral**—an output or input device—that the CPU is communicating with.

1.1.2 CPU, Memory, and I/O Portions of the System

The three main blocks—the CPU, I/O, and memory blocks—are the central processing unit (CPU), the input and output devices (I/O), and the memory. We know that a memory is a section of the computer whose job is to store and retrieve binary numbers, but we haven't discussed yet why this is necessary, or what the other blocks do.

Let's begin our discussion of the computer by comparing it with something more familiar. You have all had experience with a pocket calculator. Imagine the calculator operation of adding "5 + 2 = 7." If you are operating the calculator, you begin by pressing the keys on the calculator keypad in the sequence "5 + 2 =." The keyboard is an **input device**. It is a source of two kinds of information used by the calculator. Creating inputs for logic gates, each key of the calculator makes a binary code that represents either a number like 5 or 2—a **data word**—or an operation like + or =—an **operation code** (opcode).

How does the calculator keep the number 5 on its display after you take your finger off the key—and for that matter, how does the 5 stay there while you're keying in the +? (The 5 goes away when you hit 2.)

The answer is that the calculator contains a memory section. It needs to store decimal numbers and whatever other **keystrokes** the keyboard user puts in. The + operation, for instance, can't be activated until both the 5 and the 2 have been keyed in—yet the + is keyed before the 2. A memory is needed here to hold the + operation until both the 5 and 2—the addend and the augend—are in the memory. Then the 5 and 2 are added by an **adder circuit**, and the result (7) replaces the last number on the display. This is an output operation.

There you have it. Although this is a calculator, not a full-bore computer, it has all the basic parts: there's an input device, a memory, an output device, and—the part that actually does the adding—a central processor (CPU). With these same parts, we could make a computer with the addition of only one more part.

The calculator's sequence of actions in 5 + 2 = 7 is mostly manual. You have to key in the addend, the augend, (the two operands), and the + sign (the opcode), and then the = sign (which is really an opcode for doing an output of what's been added so far). Nothing's automatic. The calculator won't go and get the numbers on its own and know what operation to do with them; it must be "stepped through" manually.

Computers can do all this automatically; the operations' sequence can be *programmed* in advance, and as long as the computer has been told in what order to push the buttons, it can complete the calculation by itself. A decoder uses the list of instructions—a **program**—to "push the buttons." The outputs of the decoder activate different circuits in the arithmetic and memory sections of the calculator—even the input and output devices. A programmable calculator is one that's able to store up a list of keystrokes—including data and opcodes—and carry out its list of instructions at the touch of a button. There is little real difference between a programmable calculator and a computer.

We'll describe the function of each part of the computer block diagram by comparison with the calculator doing "5 + 2 =."

1. CPU   (does the actual computing of 5 + 2)
2. I/O   (input gets 5 + 2 = and output shows 7)
3. Memory   (holds the data 5, 2 and opcodes +, =)

1.2 ADDRESS DECODING FOR MEMORY AND I/O BLOCKS

The address bus is used by the memory section of the computer to find where things are stored. Memory devices store information in rows and columns called X and Y. We can take it for granted that the inner workings of any memory device will include X and Y decoders, and we know that these use bits from the address bus to decode the row and column where the information we want is located. The total memory of a computer is usually much larger than any single memory device.

The first thing we'll look at is how the address helps us select which devices will be enabled out of the total memory, and how we put together these devices to make a memory bigger than any one device.

The second place where addresses are used by the computer is the I/O (input/output) section of the computer. In a computer, unlike a pocket calculator, there may be hundreds of input devices instead of just one (the keyboard) and there may be hundreds of output devices instead of just one (the LED or LCD displays). With hundreds to choose from, the computer needs a way to pick the device being operated. The same address bus used to select memory locations is also used to select which I/O device we want. We'll see how this is done in the following sections.

1.2.1 Expansion of 1K × 1 RAMS (2102) into a 1K × 8 Block

The circuit in Figure 1-2 shows eight memory devices (the 2102 random-access memory, or RAM) put together in a 1K memory for an 8-bit computer. The phrase "1K × 8" refers to the fact that 1K (1024) places in the memory can be selected by the address, and each place contains an 8-bit data word (binary number). Each 2102 is a 1K × 1 device, meaning that the 1024 places in the memory each contain a 1-bit data word.

Each memory chip has 10 address lines. These conductors have a number from 0000000000 (0) to 1111111111 (1023) put on them to select one of the 1024 locations. The memory chips are put together like core planes in a 3D core memory. All eight chips use the same address at the same time. Each chip's data input and output represent a different bit of the same word.

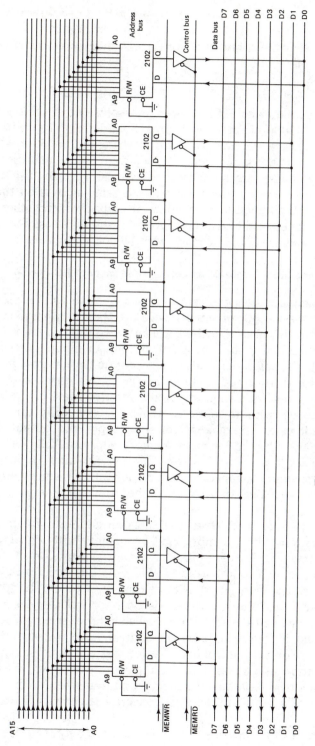

Figure 1-2 A 1K × 8 RAM using 2102's

For instance, if the 8 bits of a word stored in the memory are organized like this:

128	64	32	16	8	4	2	1
D7	D6	D5	D4	D3	D2	D1	D0

then each of the eight 2102 devices represents one of these bits. If we were storing a 01000000 in memory address 30, a 1 would be written into the 30-location of device D6, and 0s would be written in the 30-locations of all the other devices at the same time. All eight are on the address bus in parallel, and their addresses are all the same. We can get back the same 8 bits we stored at any time by going back to the same address on the address bus. With everything synchronized, all eight chips work together every time a memory write or read operation is done. It should be easy to figure out how a 1K $\times$ 16 memory could be made with 1K $\times$ 1 chips.

1.2.2 Decoding DSPs (Device-Select Pulses) for Memory of I/O Devices

When a computer uses the same address lines to call on memory location 30, output device 30, or input device 30, there is a problem deciding who the 30 is for. It's clear that there are only two ways to tell whether the code on the address bus is for a memory, output, or input. Either never use the same number for all three kinds of device (you have to give up some memory addresses for this) or add some extra signals to the system that tell whether the address is one for a memory, input, or output device.

If you go with the first approach, you've really thrown away some memory addresses in exchange for some input and output devices. Since most computers have a lot more memory addresses than I/O devices, this is usually no big loss. When it's done this way, the input or output devices are said to be **memory mapped**. There couldn't be a memory 30 and an I/O 30 together in this kind of scheme. The Apple II computer uses memory mapped I/O.

The other method (**true I/O**) uses all addresses for memory read or write operations when memory read or memory write signals are active, and uses the same addresses for input or output when I/O read or I/O write signals are active. These signals are found on a bus of lines called the control bus. In this case, there could be more than one "30" in the system.

Figure 1-3(b) shows a device decoder for input device 30 in a true-I/O system. It generates a strobe pulse called a **device-select pulse** (a DSP) when 30 is present in binary code on the address bus at the same time as memory read is active on the control bus. Notice that what's being done is a memory read operation at address 30. The input device "fakes" the computer into thinking it's read data out of a memory address when the information really comes out of a keyboard, an A/D converter, a punchtype reader—take your pick.

Figure 1-3(d) shows a device decoder for output device 30 in a mem-

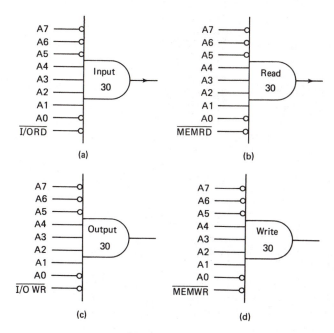

Figure 1-3 Device decoders for input: (a) true I/O (b) memory mapped I/O; and output: (c) true I/O; (b) memory mapped I/O.

ory-mapped system. The only difference in this device is the control signal. This time, the computer "thinks" it's writing into memory, when it's really sending data to an LED display, a printer, a tape recorder—take your pick.

Figure 1-3(a) shows a device decoder for input device 30 in a true I/O system. This system has control signals for I/O as well as memory devices so the decoder looks for a 30 on the address bus and an I/O read (input) signal. A memory operation at 30 would never have this control signal, so the input device doesn't replace memory 30.

Figure 1-3(c) shows a device decoder that generates a DSP for output device 30. The address is the same in every case, but the control signal is memory write (output) for the output device.

There is one other case where a decoder would have to be attached to address lines to provide a DSP. There's always someone who wants a computer to have a memory bigger than the biggest available device. For example, if the biggest available RAM chip is 16K × 8, someone wants a memory 64K × 8. This means the computer that uses the 64K × 8 memory will have more address bus lines (16) than the address inputs on the 16K × 8 device (14). The wanted memory is four times as large as the real device, so we need four of these devices. When 14 of the available address lines are attached to the 14 address inputs of each device, the two address lines "left over" have four states: 00, 01, 10, and 11. Left to themselves, the four 16K chips attached to the same 14 address lines would all write the same data in four places, and would never contain more than 16K of data (four copies of each byte). This is where a decoder comes to the rescue. By decoding

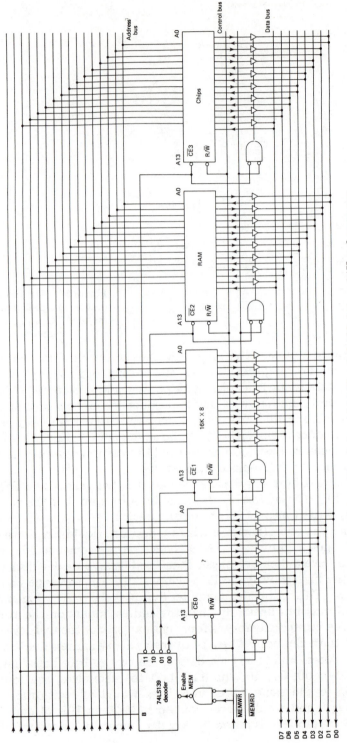

Figure 1-4 Expansion of 16 K × 8 RAMs into a 64K × 8 memory

the left over address lines as 0, 1, 2, and 3, the 16K of addresses that start "00XXXXXXXXXXXXXX" will enable only device 0 in Figure 1-4. The first 16K of data will be written there, and no place else, because it's the only device enabled. The addresses that start 01XXXXXXXXXXXXXX will affect only device 1. The device decoders for devices 2 and 3 will assure that only addresses 10XXXXXXXXXXXXXX and 11XXXXXXXXXXXXXX will be written in those devices, even though the four devices themselves have only the capability of "seeing" the XXXXXXXXXXXXXX part of the address. Since the decoder, and the four device-select pulses it generates, allow 14-bit devices to respond to 16-bit addresses, this is called **memory expansion**.

1.2.3 Expansion of the 2102 Circuit to 16K Using a 74154 Decoder

In Section 1.2.1 we spoke of expansion of a 1K × 1 memory chip into a 1K × 8 memory array. This type of expansion was an expansion of the word size on the data bus. A 2102 chip handles words of 1 bit apiece, but we wanted a 1K memory with words of 8 bits apiece. This required eight 2102s.

What we want to do now is to expand the address bus. Although there are 1024 addressable places in a 2102, we'd like to make a memory out of 2102s with 16K places in it.

In Figure 1-5, a 74154 decoder (a 1-of-16 decoder), is used to take the bits of a 16-line address bus and use them to select memory locations in an array of 2102s which only have 10 address lines. Think of the 16-line address bus as selecting memory locations with addresses made from the following binary code:

32,768		8192		2048		512		128		32		8		2	
	16,384		4096		1024		256		64		16		4		1
A15	A14	A13	A12	A11	A10	A9	A8	A7	A6	A5	A4	A3	A2	A1	A0

Using this code, numbers on the address bus can go from binary

0000000000000000 (0)   to   1111111111111111 (65,535).

With these numbers, 65,536 different locations could be selected, but this is 64 times the 1K (1024) places there are in a 2102 device. If we build our memory out of 2102s we'll have six address lines left over. What do we do with them?

Although memory devices with a lot more than 1K locations are available, there will always be someone who wants a memory bigger than the biggest available device. A **chip enable input** is provided on memory chips with memory expansion in mind. On the 2102, this enable input is active low.

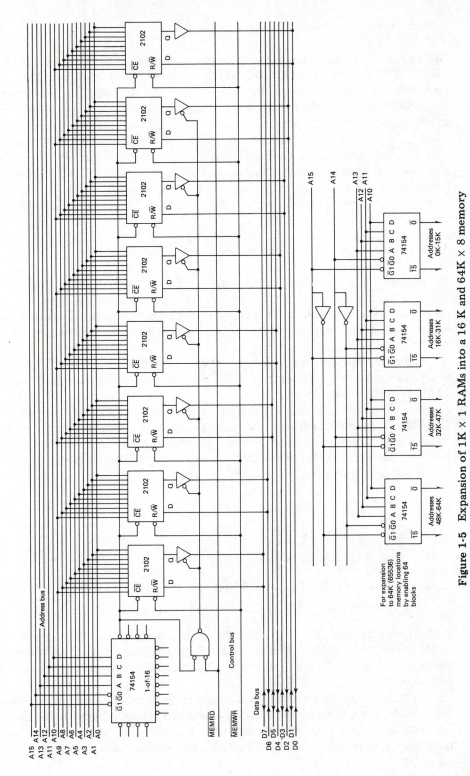

Figure 1-5 Expansion of 1K × 1 RAMs into a 16 K and 64K × 8 memory

There are 10 lines in the address bus that can go directly to all the 2102s. The remaining six lines go to a decoder, where two are used to enable the decoder (when both are LOW) and the rest are decoded by DCBA into numbers from 0000 (0) to (1111) 15. Each of these inputs is used to enable a different block of 2102s.

In this case, we've compromised. With 6 bits, the remaining address lines could be decoded into 64 different numbers. We've chosen to use a decoder that only "sees" the first 16 of these numbers, so we can only handle the first 16K of memory addresses with this one decoder. That's OK; computer designers don't always use the full memory capacity of a computer anyway.

Since only one output of the decoder is active (LOW) at a time, only one block of 2102s is enabled. There are a total of sixteen 1K × 8 blocks that can be enabled. The rest of the disabled chips will still have an output of some kind, and 15 disabled 2102s (whose outputs are all HIGH or LOW) are "fighting" with the output of the one enabled 2102 for control of each data out line. To avoid **bus contention,** *Tri-State* or open-collector logic was necessary in conflicts of this sort. That's why the outputs of each 2102 are attached to a Tri-State buffer which is disabled when the 2102 is disabled.

In this system, memory block 0 is treated as a single device—all its chips are enabled and disabled at the same time—as is true with block 1, 2, and all those up to 16. The decoder's DSP is the chip enable for each 2102 in the block. Memory addresses in the first K (0–1023) of the memory will be found in block 0, the second K (addresses 1024–2047) will be found in block 1, and so forth.

You'll notice that the decoder we used also has enable inputs like the 2102 chips. On the memory chips, the enable was for memory expansion. The enables on the 74154 are also for expansion, and a circuit can be made with four 74154s that can enable a total of 64 blocks. In this example, we only had one 74154, and enabled it when the A(15) and A(14) bits were LOW, but by adding a few inverters, another three 74154s could be activated when 01, 10, and 11 appear on these bits.

1.2.4 Memory Devices with Common I/O versus Separate I/O
(2114 versus 2102) for Bidirectional Busing

In Figure 1-6, you see a 16K memory made of 2114 memory devices which have a common I/O. In the circuits made with 2102s, there was a separate input data bus and output data bus, because there were separate output and input terminals on each 2102 chip.

On the 2114, the same terminal is used for the input and output of each bit. There are 4 bits in each address, so there are four data pins on the integrated circuit. These terminals are multiplexed. They alternately act as inputs and outputs according to the state of the WR control pin. This scheme

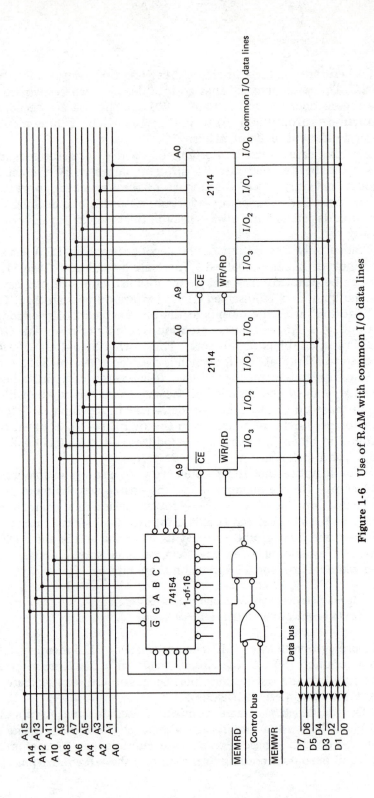

Figure 1-6 Use of RAM with common I/O data lines

is called common I/O because input and output are done at a common point (the name has nothing to do with the I/O of an input/output section of a computer). There is just one data bus—called a **common data bus** or **bidirectional data bus**—in this circuit. Since data goes into or out of the memory devices on the same wires, they are bidirectional, like a reversible express lane on a highway, which is southbound in the morning and northbound in the evening. Data don't travel both ways at the same time on a wire, but they can travel either way, alternately. Signals on the control bus are used to coordinate parts of the system to place data onto, or pick data up off, the data bus.

All of the buffers and separate-bus switching needed for the separate I/O 2102 devices are built in the 2114. Having a single data bus working all the time instead of a double data bus with only one half running at any one time, common I/O systems are more efficient than separate I/O data buses. Early microcomputers used the separate I/O scheme, but this has been largely replaced with common I/O in later designs.

1.3 OPEN-COLLECTOR AND WIRE-OR BUSING FOR COMMON BUSES

Attaching all the parts of a digital system to a common bus to synchronize them would be impossible without the ability to float outputs. In any bus-oriented architecture, many circuits share each conductor of the bus. If more than one circuit is sending at the same time, there will be conflict on the bus conductor. When one output wants to pull up and another wants to pull down, they can't both succeed. It's important for only one circuit to be sending and one circuit to be receiving at a time. When the sending circuit's output is driving the bus conductor HIGH or LOW, the rest of the outputs attached to the conductor must be floating.

In section 1.2.3, we mentioned that open-collector (O.C.) logic can solve this problem. Although the outputs of open-collector logic can't be HIGH, LOW, and floating all at the same time, adding a pull-up resistor to the bus conductor gives results that are just as good.

When one O.C. gate is enabled, its output is LOW and floating at times when other families of logic are LOW and HIGH. Suppose that five O.C. gates are attached to a bus line, three with their outputs driving the line, and two with their inputs driven by the line. When one driving gate is enabled, and the other two driving gates are disabled, the enabled gate pulls down on the bus line and makes it LOW because its pull-down output is stronger than the pull-up resistor we used. When the enabled gate is not pulling down, nothing else is either, and the pull-up resistor has nothing fighting with it— so the bus line is pulled up and becomes HIGH.

Of course, having O.C. outputs driving signals into the bus won't do any good unless there's only one enabled output. It doesn't matter how many O.C. inputs are enabled, they don't pull up or pull down on the bus

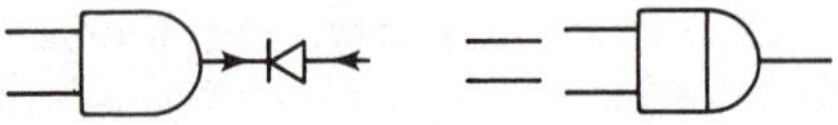

Figure 1-7 Adding a diode to make O.C. TTL from standard TTL

that's driving them like outputs do. Also, the amount of pull-up or pull-down from an input attached to the bus (the **fan-in**) doesn't change when its gate is disabled or enabled. That only affects the outputs. In common busing, the one important thing to remember is that if the gates driving the bus get into a "fight," there's trouble.

Preventing this kind of trouble is the job of the control signals that enable and disable the bus drivers. The logic designed into the system must be mutually exclusive. That means that you can enable one driver OR the second but not both (in a system with two drivers). Driving the bus with multiple open-collector outputs is called **wire-OR**. If more than one is enabled, the outputs are ANDed together, which is not good. The use of wire-OR logic with O.C. devices, it must be remembered, works only as well as the enabling and disabling circuits that control it.

A footnote in the "sneaky trick" department: If you add a diode to the output of a standard logic gate (shown in Figure 1-7), with the cathode connected to the gate's output and the signals sent from the anode outward, the gate acts just like an open-collector gate, with outputs LOW and floating. If you are doing a circuit "fix" or "kluge" that needs just one gate with a floatable output, and you have some spare gates of nonfloatable types, this is a nice trick to know (germanium diodes work better than silicon diodes for this).

1.4 TRI-STATE LOGIC IN BUS-ORIENTED SYSTEMS

If TTL Tri-State logic is used where O.C. logic was used in the preceding section, there will be no need for pull-up resistors. The Tri-State gate has an authentic HIGH, LOW, and floating condition at its outputs, so the enabled gate can either pull up or pull down on the bus while the other gates float. Of course, if the other gates don't float, their outputs have the same characteristics as standard TTL—two gates "fighting" will resolve their conflict by having the LOW output "win" and the HIGH output "lose," and if three or more gates are fighting, the fight may end with one or several gates being burned out as their pull-down transistors are "blown" by excessive pull-up current. As with O.C. logic, the gates' outputs must activate in a mutually exclusive way. The busing arrangement is only as good as the logic that keeps only one driver driving and the others floating. Several types of standard devices in the TTL family, including counters and latches, are also available in versions with "Tri-Statable" outputs, for use in bussed systems. The only easy way to make a standard TTL gate into a Tri-State version, when one isn't already available, is to add a Tri-State buffer to its output. There aren't any shortcuts like the one for O.C.

Many devices in the MOS logic category are also available in Tri-State varieties. In fact, since O.C. or Tri-State capability is essential to bus utilization, most large-scale integrated (LSI) circuits like MOS microprocessors have outputs that are Tri-Statable (floatable). Bus architecture is also found inside microprocessors and other LSI devices, and of course, enable/disable "float" logic is used in every buffer, latch, and register that attaches to these buses inside the chip.

Multiplexed busing. Another completely different approach to bus utilization is to multiplex together the drivers for the bus. Instead of having each output drive the same bus, each driver drives an input of a multiplexer. In this kind of scheme, a data bus with four driver devices would have a 1-of-4 multiplexer attached to each data bus line. All the multiplexers would share common address (select) lines, so that all the 2-drivers would be connected to the bus at one time, all the 3-drivers at another, and so on.

Some popular microcomputers, like the Radio Shack TRS-80 series, use Tri-State buffers for driver selection; others, like Apple computers, have multiplexers in the same places. There doesn't seem to be any advantage of one over the other; the two methods are equivalent and work equally well.

1.5 PRACTICAL CONSIDERATIONS IN BUS-ORIENTED DESIGN

Digital switching circuits sometimes have problems that show up when the circuits are clocked at full speed, but are not evident in static tests with a meter or logic probe. These problems are often caused by noise, extra pulses and spikes that appear on the 1 and 0 logic levels in the circuit. Sometimes, the noise makes itself evident when some gates on a board generate enough noise glitches to make other gates on the board switch incorrectly. In other cases, the noise radiates, and interferes with other circuits (RF interference).

1.5.1 Decoupling Capacitors

TTL devices switching ON and OFF in a very short period of time draw surges of current from the power supply. Even a very well regulated power supply cannot keep this switching from affecting the voltage near the switching chip. To smooth out the "spikes" in the voltage produced by this switching, every second or third TTL package should have a small ceramic disk capacitor (around 0.01 μF) attached to its 5-V and ground connections. This capacitor, called a **decoupling capacitor**, helps to soak up the noise pulses in the power net near the switching chip.

If a digital circuit board is glitching intermittently with no visible cause, but the board doesn't have much decoupling, try "tack-soldering" a few decouplers to the power leads of some TTL chips. If certain signal lines are causing false switching due to noise, another thing that sometimes helps is adding a pull-up resistor between the line and Vcc. This doesn't reduce the noise, but it makes the 1-level higher. Increasing the separation between the 1-level and the 0-level may "pull the noise up" out of the "gray area" that causes false switching in gates down the line. MOS circuits do not need as much decoupling as TTL, because they draw far less current. MOS LSI devices on circuit boards often use TTL buffers and gates, and run from the same 5-V supply, so these boards should still be decoupled in proportion to the number of TTL devices they contain.

1.5.2 Gridded Vcc and Ground

Figure 1-8 shows a circuit board design that uses gridded Vcc and ground. This arrangement helps to reduce RF radiation and it cuts down noise somewhat, too. You can see decoupling capacitors at some points in the circuit.

If a board without decoupling and gridded power is interfering with some circuit—like a TV—replacing the foil pattern on the board, or rewiring

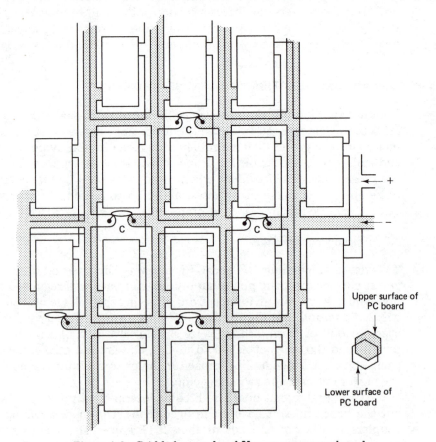

Figure 1-8 Gridded ground and Vcc on a memory board

all power conductors, is out of the question. Some things that might help are:

1. *Decoupling*. This is mostly a way to suppress noise but it does reduce RF radiation also.
2. *Faraday shielding*. Enclose the board in some kind of box or cage made of an electrical conductor and connected to ground. This soaks up radiation before it can "get out of the box."
3. *Filtering*. Add a filter to the antenna or power lines of the device being interfered with that blocks the frequency of the interference from the digital system. If it's a TV, and the filter also blocks out all the television channels, too bad.

1.5.3 MOS/LSI Handling Precautions for Static

MOS devices are especially sensitive to static damage when handled. A whole board full of MOS/LSI devices is just an accident waiting to happen for the inexperienced handler. Merely taking a printed-circuit board full of MOS devices out of its socket can "zap" the board! To safely handle MOS boards:

1. Work surfaces, such as tabletops, should be covered with a grounded, conductive surface. Special plastic or rubber materials are available for this, or a sheet of foil/sheet metal can be placed on the table top. Mats on the floor and static-reducing sprays are also sometimes used in the work area to reduce the buildup of hazardous charges.
2. The ground trace on the board, and a grounding strap around the handler's wrist, should be connected to the same ground as used in step 1 before the board is taken out of its socket.
3. Soldering iron tips can develop an induced voltage that is dangerous to MOS inputs. Ground the tip of the soldering iron before doing any soldering on the circuit board.
4. For shipping, MOS circuit boards should be wrapped in conductive plastic or wrapped in foil. This keeps all charges across the board equal. Static cannot damage MOS components unless voltages are different from one place on the board to another.
5. Unwrapping or unpackaging of MOS/LSI—wrapped as described in step 4—should be done only after you give the charges on your body and the board/conductive wrapper a chance to equalize. Holding the board and wrapper in your hand for 10 to 15 seconds before you unwrap the board should be enough.

In many designs, TTL buffers, drivers, and gates are attached to all MOS inputs and outputs—"fully buffered inputs and outputs"—on a circuit board. This provides a measure of static protection, since the TTL devices provide low-impedance discharge paths for static to ground. Fully buffered boards are still not static-proof, however, and should be handled with the same precautions as all-MOS boards, just for your peace of mind.

1.6 BUS-ORIENTED INPUT/OUTPUT

The I/O section of the computer is its link with the outside world. Although the computer uses its memory section to store and recover data and instructions, the data and instructions had to get into the computer from somewhere in the first place. The input devices are the source of information put into the computer. When the computer processes the data and comes up with a result of some kind, it's the output devices that are the destination of these results, used to display them in some way to the user.

An input device is one that puts data into the data bus, and an output device is one that takes data out of the data bus. The data on the bus is used by the CPU. You can picture data flow in the system like traffic on an expressway. For instance, suppose that a news report says "Outbound traffic is heavy on the expressway, but inbound traffic is light" and you're going from O'Connor's house to the downtown area. Does "outbound" mean outward from O'Connor's house or outward from downtown? Usually, news reports are based on what everybody in the city agrees is the most important part. O'Connor's house is not the most important part of the city to its citizens; the downtown district is. If you're going outbound from O'Connor's house and inbound toward downtown, the inbound lane (the one with the lighter traffic) is the one you'll use.

Similarly with the computer, the input and output are named according to the important "downtown" part of the computer system. The CPU (central processing unit) is the "important" part of the system; everything inbound or outbound goes into or out of the CPU. To decide what's an input or an output, you only have to ask yourself the question: Does it provide data that's for the CPU (input) or display data that's from the CPU (output)?

1.6.1 Decoding of Device Number

We've already described this. All we'll add here is that the job of the device decoder is to identify whether the number on the address bus is the device number of the I/O device, and whether the code on the control bus is for an input or an output operation. This can be done by a system of gates, a prefabricated decoder chip, or by the decoder that is a built-in part of a multiplexer.

1.6.2 Relevant Control Signals

We've discussed this before, too. The only things we need to recap here are that two forms of I/O exist, the memory-mapped I/O design and the true I/O.

In the memory-mapped scheme, it's how we design the hardware that determines what addresses are I/O devices and which are really memory. The control signals that distinguish input from output are the same ones that distinguish memory read from memory write. The memory read signal is used for input and the memory write signal for output when the memory happens to be an I/O device. The only way to know what's a memory operation and what's I/O is to know which addresses are mapped as memory locations and which are used for I/O.

In the true I/O scheme, all addresses for I/O devices are also legitimate addresses for memory locations. To tell them apart, I/O operations cause input (I/O read) and output (I/O write) signals to appear on the control bus while memory operations produce memory read and memory write signals. There's no chance of confusing memory operations with I/O operations because they produce completely different signals on the control bus.

1.6.3 Input Ports (Buffers)

We're introducing a new vocabulary term here, the **input port,** which has a different meaning from input device. An input device might be something like a typewriter keyboard equipped so that it generates an 8-bit ASCII code whenever a key is pressed. The input device creates the data in a digital form. An input port, on the other hand, is the device that interfaces (communicates) the data to the data bus. There may be many kinds of input devices converting data from real-world signals into digital code, but once converted, the code is brought into the data bus through the same kind of input port in every case.

Figure 1-9 shows a system with four input devices and four input ports connecting them to the data bus. All four input devices have a data word for the bus, but the four data words of information can't be put on the bus at the same time. Instead, the devices must take turns so that one device "talks" to the CPU at a time. The CPU controls this. It is the CPU that originates the addresses and control signals used in this diagram. A program in the CPU that contains input instructions is responsible for enabling each input port, letting that port "drop" its data word onto the data bus. In this diagram, we imagine that the instruction "input a data word from port 3" is being carried out by the CPU at this moment. The results are fourfold. The CPU:

1. Originates an address (00000011).
2. Puts out an active (LOW) "IN" signal on the control bus.

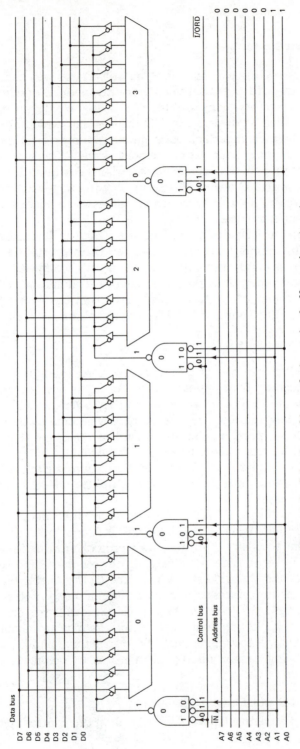

Figure 1-9 Selection of input devices using buffers as input ports

3. The port 3 decoder is a gate with the logic: "If IN is LOW and address lines (1) and (0) are HIGH, with all other address lines LOW, make the output of this gate LOW.

4. This gate enables the Tri-State buffers between the input device and the data bus and these buffers place a data word on the bus.

The other decoders only enable their port buffers for other conditions. They are not enabled right now, and their floating condition does not interfere with the HIGHs and LOWs put on the bus by port 3.

Every input port in this diagram is a Tri-State buffer enabled by a DSP from a device decoder. It doesn't matter if the data word for the CPU is generated by a keyboard, a punch tape reader, or a cassette player: once the data word is in digital code, a buffer must stand between the word and the bus. We already discussed the mutually exclusive nature of each input—and we can see that the decoders in this diagram work according to this rule; only one port at a time is ever enabled.

1.6.4 Output Ports (Latches)

An output port is the interface between the data bus and an output device. This means, as you might guess, that an output port enables data to pass to a particular output device from the data bus. When an output operation is taking place in the computer, data are placed on the data bus by the CPU for pickup by an output device. The task of the output device is to display the digital code in some form that's useful in the outside world.

You might be led to believe that an output port is just an input port turned around. That's not so. A buffer can't be used for an output port for a very important reason. The display devices normally attached to computers (printers, numeric displays, video monitors) work much more slowly than the computer itself. An output command in a program might put a number on the data bus for a millionth of a second or so before the computer moves on to the next operation. This is not enough time for a printer to print a letter, or a person looking at a numeric readout or video monitor to read the number displayed there (even with help from Evelyn Wood!). The number sent to the output device must stay a lot longer than a millionth of a second to get anything done.

Do we slow down the computer to the speed of the output devices? This doesn't work, because even if we did slow the computer down, only one data word can be on the data bus at a time, and a system with hundreds of output devices would display a number at each device for a second or so once every few minutes. This is not a good way to work with computers. What we need instead is an output port that will remember the word sent to it while the computer goes ahead to other tasks. Memory in the output port would let it keep applying the data word to its output device until it gets its job done, even as the data bus carries other numbers to other ports.

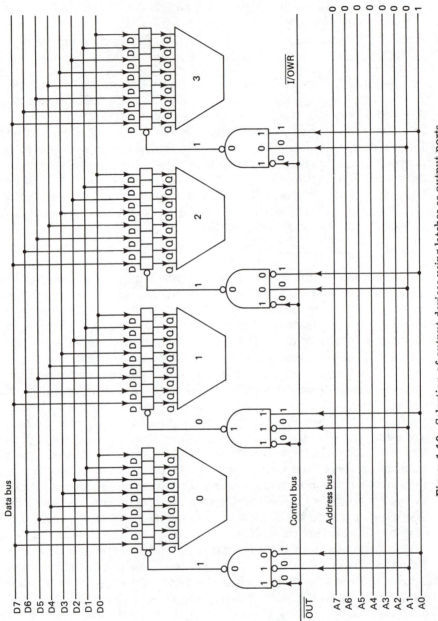

Figure 1-10 Selection of output devices using latches as output ports

The ideal device to use in this case is a latch, shown in Figure 1-10. Each of the four output ports in the picture is an 8-bit latch strobed by a clock pulse. In the diagram, we imagine that the computer is doing an "output a data word to port 1" operation. The port 1 decoder has the job of recognizing when a 00000001 appears on the address bus at the same time as the OUT signal is active. When the decoder sees a 1, it sends a LOW signal to strobe the latch. The latch then picks up the word on the data bus, and keeps it active at its outputs until another "output to port 1" strobes it again at some later time.

Since a latch has a memory capability, it will keep the data word at its Q outputs until a new data word is sent to the same port. The outputs of of the latch can keep pushing the word at the output device while the computer proceeds to use the data bus for other tasks. The word in the port will not be affected by these changes on the data bus because the strobe (clock pulse) is not active.

As before, it's the job of the device decoder to make sure that this port gets data for only one set of conditions, and all the other device decoders should be mutually exclusive and strobe their ports for different conditions.

Unlike the input situation, however, there could be more than one output device/output port combination with the same code—if multiple displays of the same data at different locations were desired. Since the output port doesn't place any data on the common bus, there's no way two different sets of bits would appear on the same conductor to "fight" with one another. It's only input devices that must be enabled one at a time only— but output devices usually are organized along the same lines, since the multiple-display arrangement mentioned above is rarely needed.

1.6.5 An Input Port for 8-Bit Data

The input ports seen in Figure 1-9 are suitable for interfacing input devices to an 8-bit microcomputer (the most common word size for micros). It's typical of the interfacing scheme used in computers like the Altair 8800 or the Radio Shack TRS-80. Another circuit that does the same job with multiplexers is shown in Figure 1-11. It's like the scheme used in the Apple II, although the Apple uses a memory-mapped arrangement instead of having a separate I/O read signal generated by its CPU.

In Figure 1-11, four 74LS253 dual 1-of-4 MUX circuits are used to select which data word will reach the data bus. The select inputs A and B are attached to address lines (1) and (0). By themselves, A and B can only "see" what address lines (1) and (0) are. This is fine for decoding device codes 00, 01, 10, or 11 (0, 1, 2, or 3), but cannot tell 00000111 (7) or 00001111 (15) from 00000011 (3) if only two of the eight address lines are connected. The remaining six address lines and "IN" control line are attached to an OR gate with seven inputs. If all seven inputs are LOW, the output of the OR is LOW.

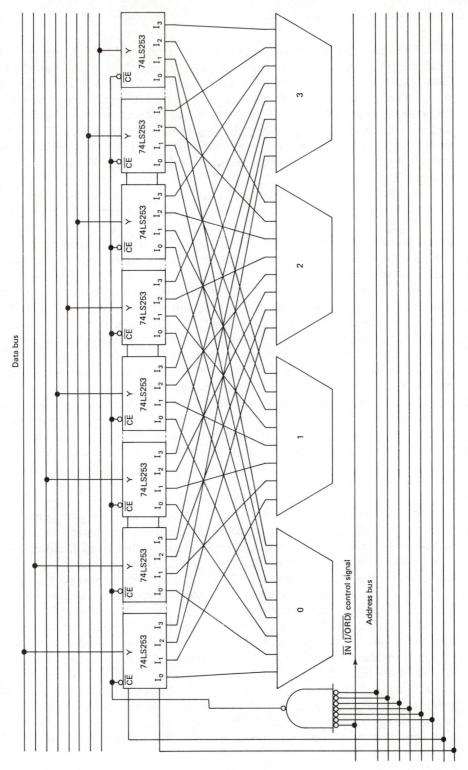

Figure 1-11 Selection of input devices using multiplexers

24

Since it's used as the enable for the MUXes, the only time the MUX circuits can work correctly is when the addresses are really 0, 1, 2, or 3, and the device is an input.

In this example, each multiplexer is Tri-State logic with the capacity to float when disabled. We can assume other multiplexers are available on the bus for other combinations of address and I/O signals.

1.6.6 An Output Port for 8-Bit Data

The output ports in Figure 1-9 are suitable for any output device that converts digital code into a display or some sort of action. The four 8-bit ports shown are operated as a true I/O circuit. Data is sent to these ports using "OUT" output instructions to port 0, 1, 2, or 3.

The same four ports are operated in memory-mapped I/O systems using instructions that write in memory location 0, 1, 2, or 3. To make Figure 1-9 into a memory-mapped circuit, change the control bus signal in the diagram from "out" to "memory write."

1.6.7 Parallel I/O Port ICs
(Intel 8212, Motorola 6821 PIA, Intel 8255)

The I/O ports shown in the preceding sections of this chapter are **parallel I/O ports**. The data they input and output is transferred 8 bits at a time at eight different points, so they are **parallel data**. To make the input port, for example, we need an 8-bit buffer and a decoder to enable it. An output port needs an 8-bit latch and a decoder to strobe it.

One single-package device that has parts of both an input and an output port is the Intel 8212 buffer/latch. It contains eight Tri-State output flip-flops, strobed by a gate network. Two modes of operation permit use of the 8212 as an input or output device. Two inputs called device-select permit strobing of the latch or enabling of the Tri-State buffers with either active-HIGH or active-LOW logic. A strobe input strobes the latch in input mode, while the buffers are controlled separately. A reset input is also present for clearing the bits in all latch flip-flops.

Since this is a level-triggered latch, the flip-flops of the latch can be "clocked" so that data simply pass through the latch and are then stopped or passed by each flip-flop's Tri-State output. In this mode, the 8212 can be used as an 8-bit buffer in an input port. If the latch clock is "strobed"—turned ON and OFF again after a short time—the latch will store the bits at its inputs during the ON time. In this mode, the 8212 can be used as an output port. In addition to these functions, the 8212 also contains an input and output for use with interrupts, which we'll discuss in a subsequent chapter.

The Motorola 6821 Peripheral Interface Adapter (PIA) is another device that can be used as an I/O-port-in-a-chip. It has two 8-bit bidirectional registers and roughly double the buffer and latch contents of the 8212, plus a much more sophisticated control system that allows, for instance, definition of each bit in each register as an input or output bit. For replacement of the circuits in Figures 1-8 and 1-9, the PIA is maybe a bit too much. Its advantage is that the CPU can control or reconfigure the PIA in ways that the circuits in Figures 1-8 and 1-9 would have to be mannually rewired to accomplish. Sophisticated software control is the major difference between the 6821 and 7400-series TTL implementation or the 8212 LSTTL/MSI (low-power Schottky TTL, medium-scale integration). It may be an advantage, where rapid redefinition of port structure is required, or it may be a disadvantage, if the port is always going to stay the same and simpler software is desired. Every time a system with a 6821 is powered up, the complex reinitialization procedure for defining all port functions must be done, whether or not any startling changes in configuration are anticipated. (A large number of programmers and designers of our acquaintance are not convinced that all the "flashy" features of the PIA are worth it. We'll leave it to your imagination what they think the letters "PIA" stand for.)

The Intel 8255 Programmable Peripheral Interface (PPI) is similar in nature to the Motorola PIA, but with a control complexity somewhere in between the 8212 and 6821. As with the 6821, it contains two bidirectional, software-definable registers, but also contains an additional "split" register permitting two 4-bit interfaces.

All of the devices described in this section are designed to run from a single 5-V TTL-type supply, and generate TTL-compatible signals suitable for driving TTL or TTL/Schottky devices. The 8212 is itself a TTL/Schottky device; the others are MOS/LSI.

1.6.8 I/O Interface Adapters
(Serial I/O Ports, UARTs, Intel 8251, Motorola 6850)

In addition to the parallel devices just described, there are also serial I/O devices, which send data to or from the computer, one bit at a time. To output to a serial device, you need a transmitter to convert parallel data into serial data. Similarly, to receive data from a serial device, you need a serial-to-parallel converter. A device that can both receive and transmit serial data is called a UART.

Two such devices are the Intel 8251 USART (called a PCI—a Programmable Communication Interface—by Intel) and the Motorola 6850 UART (called an ACIA—an Asynchronous Communications Interface Adapter—by Motorola). They are very similar in structure and control, although the 6850 is somewhat simpler, having only an asynchronous mode of operation, whereas the 8251 has both synchronous and asynchronous modes of operation.

One job of both circuits is to take parallel data from the data bus and transmit it serially (bit by bit on one line). In this mode, the UART is being used as an output port with 8-bit SDM (space-division-multiplexed) data converted to TDM (time-division-multiplexed) data. The output device most commonly connected to this type of port is a **modem** (modulator/demodulator), which is used as a modulator when it's doing output things.

The other job of both circuits is to receive serial data arriving from another location and convert them to parallel data for the data bus. In this mode, the UART is being used as an input port with 8-bit TDM data converted to SDM. The input device that provides the serial bit stream to the UART in this mode is usually a modem, operated as a demodulator.

These LSI packages contain all the circuitry necessary to do both of these jobs simultaneously (full duplex) through separate paths, and also contain check circuitry for detection of transmission errors through parity detection and other tests. Circuits inside the UART also respond to signals that tell whether the circuit at the other end of the link is ready to receive/transmit, and generate signals that say whether *this* circuit is ready to transmit/receive. This sort of cross-communication, called "handshaking," is discussed in detail in a subsequent chapter.

QUESTIONS

1.1. Which bus of a computer makes it possible to transfer inputs (like 5, +, 2, and =) from the input device to the memory?

1.2. Describe how the control bus signals I/OWR, I/ORD, MEMWR, and MEMRD control transfer of data to I/O or memory devices in a bus-oriented computer.

1.3. What is the difference between true I/O and memory-mapped I/O?

1.4. Describe how a device decoder makes it possible to make a 64K RAM out of 16K RAM chips.

1.5. Describe the difference between memory devices with common I/O and separate I/O (see Figures 1-5 and 1-6).

1.6. Draw a schematic showing how you would convert a TTL 7432 OR logic gate to Tri-State logic.

1.7. Why is Tri-State logic preferable to open-collector logic?

1.8. Describe what "decoupling" is and why it's needed.

1.9. Since most bus-oriented systems contain one or more MOS devices, handling precautions for MOS circuit boards were included in this chapter. What problem does MOS logic have that makes it necessary to take these precautions?

1.10. Describe a way to determine what parts of a computer system do inputs and what parts do outputs.

1.11. Describe the difference between an input port and input device.

1.12. Describe the difference between an output port and an output device.

1.13. Draw the schematic of an input port that will enable input device 13 to put its data on the data bus (use a four-line address bus to the device decoder).

1.14. Draw the schematic of an output port that will latch data for delivery to output device 10 (use a four-line address bus in this schematic).

1.15. Why are latches used in output port design? Why isn't an output port just an input port "turned around"?

1.16. Input devices must be enabled onto the data bus through their input ports one at a time only. Does this rule apply to output devices as well?

1.17. The Motorola 6821 PIA is useful where rapid redefinition of port structure is required. Describe two situations where this might be necessary.

1.18. Describe, briefly, what "serial I/O" means.

2

Peripherals: I/O Devices (Input)

In Chapter 1 we saw the layout, in broad terms, of a bus-oriented digital computer. We divided our computer block diagram into three main divisions: the CPU, memory, and I/O (input/output). Since memory devices were described somewhat in Chapter 1, the memory part of Chapter 1 already had a foundation to build on when we described how the memory was interfaced to the buses of the computer system. The I/O section, however, had no background, and we simply dealt with the I/O ports that connected these devices to the computer. From what you read in Chapter 1, you could find out very little about the devices themselves.

In the next two chapters, we plan to go outward from the buses and ports in the computer system to the peripheral devices. The word *peripheral* means "around the outside". In a data processing center, the processor is usually a box in the middle of the room with other boxes arranged around it, connected to it by cables, but outside the housing of the CPU itself. These boxes are the computer's eyes and ears, and also its muscles and power of speech. We've already discussed what input and output mean in terms of the computer system. This chapter will deal with input devices.

The task of an input device is to convert an "outside" signal—which is not digital and may not even be electrical—into a binary digital word. An input port will place this data word on the data bus if its number comes up on the address and control buses.

We have already seen the details of how input ports accomplish their job. Now we will see how the input devices create the data words that pass through the ports when the computer calls for them.

Three categories of input devices will be discussed: manual switch devices, document reading devices, and sensors.

2.1 BINARY INPUT (BIT SWITCHES)

Let's say you want a simple way to enter numbers into a computer. It may be that the numbers are commands for the computer or merely numbers the computer uses in some calculation. Whatever they are for, the input device's task is to make each number available to the computer in a code its port can put directly on its data bus. Since most microcomputers use an 8-bit binary code, the input device in Figure 2-1 has eight bit switches.

What it does isn't complicated. In one position (up) the switch is open, and its data wire is pulled up to a HIGH logic level by a pull-up resistor. In the other position (down) the switch is closed, and connects its data wire directly to a LOW logic level. Since the path to the 0 level (ground) is a much better conductor than the 1-kΩ resistor, the pull-down is stronger, and the logic level is LOW. There are eight switches, one for each bit of the data bus. If each of these data wires is connected to one bit of an input port, it will input any data word you put on the switches. Of course, to use this input device, you need to put data bit by bit onto the switch panel, and know the exact binary code for every word you want to input to the machine.

This input device is not a very good one from the human factors standpoint. The hardware is easy enough to design, but a mess to operate. You must make eight switch entries for each new word you want to enter. You

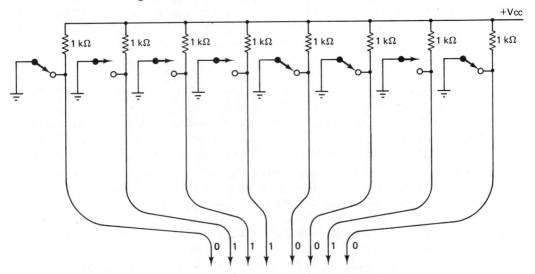

Figure 2-1   An 8-bit binary input device (bit-switches)

have to know the bit code for each word, even if all you want to enter is the letter A, or the binary code for the number 4. It's the slowest, most error-prone method of entry there is.

The earliest models of microcomputers used this method of entry. Bit-switch panels are cheap, and don't take much hardware or power to interface. The human factors problem made this a case of "penny wise and pound foolish," however. Later designs included numeric and alphabetic keyboards as a built-in part of the unit, and companies that continued to make nothing but boxes with bit switches went *bankrupt*.

2.2 NUMERICAL INPUT (KEYBOARDS)

For human convenience, keyboards are a big improvement over bit-switch panels. They need more hardware, true—but have advantages for speedy, error-free operations that far outweigh their greater complexity and higher cost.

2.2.1 Octal Keyboard with Hardware Encoding

This is a keyboard somewhat like the panel used for code entry to the Heath-kit H-8. The idea of an encoded keyboard is that each key is a switch, and each switch closure produces not one, but a whole group of binary digits (a code). In our example (Figure 2-2), the eight keys are attached to a three-wire bus (that has binary 4, 2, and 1 place values) by diodes. Each set of diode connections passes a code from the key to the bus. In Figure 2-2(a), each switch puts a logic 0 on the diodes, and they conduct the 0s to the places where a 0 appears in the 3-bit code for that key's octal number. For instance, the 0 key's diodes conduct 0s to all three wires, giving a code of 000 binary for this key, while the 5 key conducts a 0 only to the 2-wire, producing a 101 code. The wires that don't receive a 0 through a diode are 1s because there are pull-up resistors on each wire. No diodes are needed on the 5 key, or on any key that makes only one connection. It is when two or more bus wires are connected to a key, like the 0, that diodes are necessary, so that the key can conduct to the bus wires, but they don't conduct to one another.

In Figure 2-2(b), each switch puts a logic 1 on the diodes, and they conduct the 1s to the places where a 1 appears in the code for the key's octal number. In this example, imagine that the 7 key is pressed. The diodes are pointed in a direction that will conduct the 1 to all three bus wires, making 111. If the 5 key is pressed, 1s will be conducted to the 4 and 1 wires, giving 101 as the code for a 5. The wires that don't receive a 1 through a diode are 0s because there are pull-down resistors on every wire. The conduction path

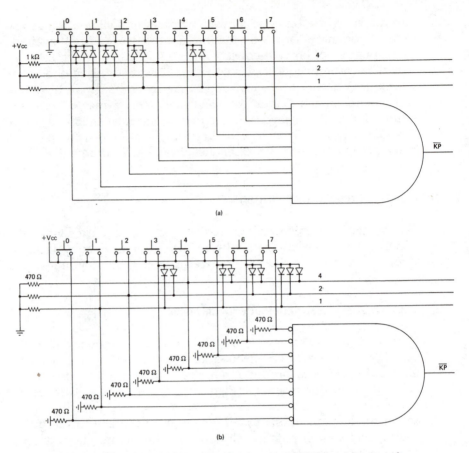

Figure 2-2 (a) Active LOW and (b) active HIGH octal keyboards

for the 1s is a better conduction path than the pull-downs, so when a diode *does* conduct, the voltage will be HIGH, but otherwise, the voltage is LOW.

The keyboard (usually called a **keypad**) in Figure 2-2(a) uses an active-LOW design, because each key produces its code by applying LOW levels to the bus. Figure 2-2(b) is an active-HIGH design, since each key produces its code by applying HIGH levels to the bus.

Look at the 7 on the active-LOW keypad. There is nothing connected to the bus to make a 7 in this case. There is a 7 on the bus of the active LOW keypad if no key is pressed, because the pull-up resistors put 1s on all the bus wires that aren't pulled down. How does the computer know if a 7 is real or if it's just a number on the bus between key presses?

All the keys produce a signal that goes to a gate. This gate produces the $\overline{\text{KP}}$ (key pressed) signal. In both Figure 2-2(a) and (b), the keypressed gate produces a LOW output if any one of the keys is pressed. When the signal

is active, it's the keyboard's way of saying to the computer "Hey! Over
here! I've got a live one for you—this is the real thing!"

Let's assume that our keyboard is used as an input for a microcomputer
with 8-bit input ports. You might ask: "How is this keyboard, which
produces 3-bit numbers, supposed to be connected to an 8-bit data bus?"
There are two answers. One solution is to add a shift register to the circuit
that can save up each 3-bit key code, until an 8-bit number is built up with
several keystrokes. This is called the hardware solution to the problem.
Another way to save up the keystrokes until an 8-bit word is entered is by
program. The computer receiving the data can take in 3 bits at a time,
shifting over the bits every time another key is struck.

The hardware solution is shown in Figure 2-3. If a key is pressed, the
keypressed signal shifts the last 3 bits over one level in the shift register. In

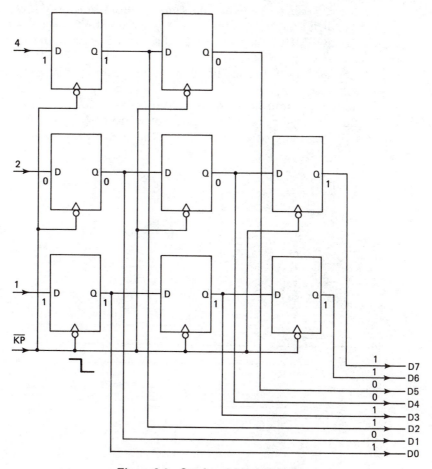

Figure 2-3   Octal-to-8-bit shift register

our example, we imagine that the key sequence 315 has been pressed on the keypad, and the 5 is still on the bus, although the keypressed signal has clocked it into the front end of the shift register already. The 8-bit number 315 converts into (from octal to binary) 11,001,101. This number is available on an 8-bit bus which can be attached directly to an input port.

Another circuit for the hardware solution to the octal keyboard is shown in Figure 2-4. This circuit uses keyboard scanning, which is the most common way of identifying and encoding keys on larger keyboards. Even on this very small keyboard, you'll see that the scanning approach reduces the number of diodes in the matrix encoder and cuts down the number of inputs needed for the keypressed gate.

The eight keys of our keyboard have been organized into two rows of four keys each. On the bottom row, the codes for the 0123 keys are shown in binary. On the top row, the codes for 4567 in binary are shown. Notice that for each pair of keys on the same column, both key codes end in the same two digits. For instance, 1 and 5 are on the same column, and their codes 001 and 101 both end in 01. This fact is critical in the design of the encoder used here.

Let's see how this encoder works by imagining what happens when the 5 key is pressed.

The 5 key connects a row wire to one of the four column wires. The J-K flip-flop is toggling a 0 back and forth from Q to not-Q. When the 0 reaches Q, the 5 key connects that 0 to the column wire that 5 and 1 are on.

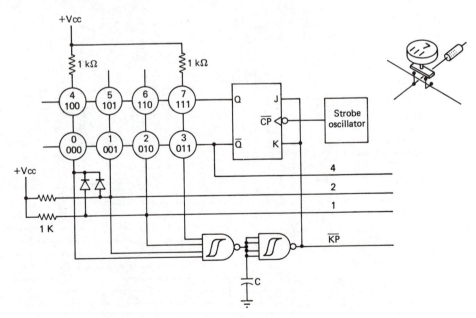

Figure 2-4   Octal keyboard with synchronous scanning

That connection passes the 0 to one of the wires on the 421 bus (the 2 wire). While this is happening, there is a 1 on the not-Q output of the keyboard strobe flip-flop, which is also the 4 output on the bus. The remaining wire on the bus is floating, and its pull-up resistor makes its logic level a 1. This means that at this instant, the number on the 421 bus is 101—a 5 in binary code—but will this number stay there if the flip-flop keeps toggling? The answer is "no," but the flip-flop won't keep toggling. While all this is happening, the *keypressed decoder* is receiving the same 0 on the column line that made the 2 bus line LOW. This 0 will make the output signal, $\overline{KP}$, go LOW after a small delay while the C capacitor charges up. The keypressed signal does two things. It goes on to the shift register or input port of the computer, and it goes to the J and K inputs of the flip-flop, making it stop toggling and "freeze" at its present state. When the key is released, and the 0 on the keypressed line becomes a 1 again, the toggling—which is used to scan the two rows of the keyboard—will resume.

Key Debounce.   There is a reason for the capacitive time delay put into the keypressed signal. At first, when the key is pressed and the contacts meet, they will bounce for a while. The code on the 421 bus will switch from 101 to 111 and back again as the contacts bounce. The KP signal doesn't become active until the capacitor charges and the voltage rises above the upper trip point of the Schmitt trigger logic gates. If the capacitor is large enough, this time delay is long enough for the bouncing key to stop and the 101 to stabilize on the bus. At a few milliseconds after the 5 key is pressed, the KP signal switches active, and by that time, the 101 on the 421 bus is steady.

You can see that all the other numbers on the keyboard will work also. A combination of two actions makes this possible. The row information—what row the key is on—contributes the 4-bit of the 421 data word. The column information—the 0 on one of the column lines—provides the encoder with enough information to generate the remaining two bits of the data word.

2.2.2 Hexadecimal Keyboard with Hardware Encoding

In Figure 2-5, you can see that the method used for an octal keyboard in the last section can be extended to a hexadecimal keyboard with twice as many keys. The only differences in this circuit and the octal keypad in Figure 2-4 is the line decoder used to scan the row, and the "freezable" clock oscillator for the flip-flop. Because the oscillator can be frozen at a particular place, the count can be stopped when the KP signal appears. Using the output of the oscillator as one bit of a 2-bit counter with double-rail outputs, we can get this combination of oscillator plus flip-flop to count in modulus 4, with the sequence 0, 1, 2, 3, 0, 1, 2, 3, ... Since we can stop the oscillator at any moment when the KP strobe goes LOW, the scan stops

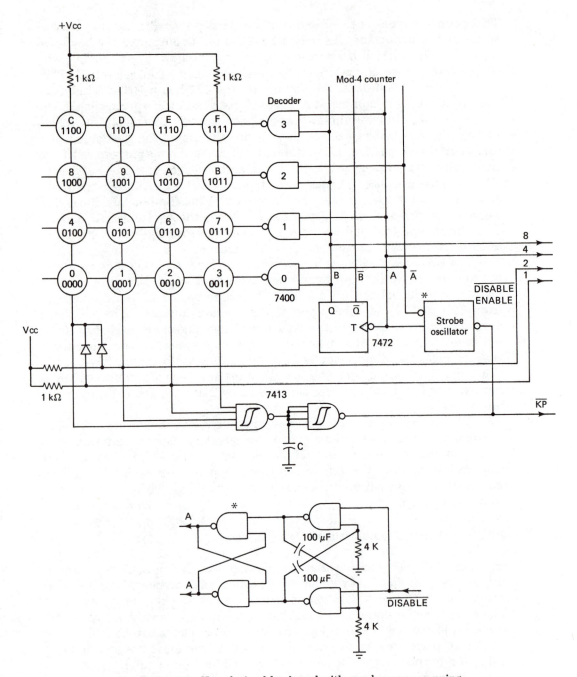

Figure 2-5 Hexadecimal keyboard with synchronous scanning

just like the scan for the octal keyboard in Figure 2-4, as soon as the key has been found and the debounce delay is completed.

2.2.3 Decimal Keyboard with ROM Encoding

We have just seen several ways to scan and encode a keyboard. In particular, we have a lot of versions of the octal keyboard we started with. Although we discussed four different methods of keyboard encoding in preceding sections, there is yet another important way to convert a key closure into a binary code. In Figure 2-6 there are two versions of a decimal keypad that takes the closure of one key and converts it into a 4-bit BCD code for the number on the key. The first keypad is organized as a row of 10 keys which provide 10 inputs to a ROM. The second is arranged in two rows of five keys, providing five inputs to the ROM, and with a scanner switching a 0 from one row of keys to the other. The scanner provides an additional bit of input for the ROM, making 6 bits in all.

What do they do? In the first ROM, the 10 inputs are the address lines for a 1K × 4 ROM. There are 1024 places inside the ROM with a permanently burned-in number in each place. Assuming that we only press one key at a time, there are only 10 of these 1024 places that we'll actually use. This is a very wasteful method of keyboard encoding. We use less than 1 of every 100 addresses in this design.

When a 5 is pressed on the keypad, for instance, the address 1111101111 is put on the address lines. We've burned in the code 0101 at that location in the ROM, so the four outputs that appear on the data lines of the ROM are 0101. Although the ROM is a memory device, we're using it here as an encoder. Since the contents of each location in the ROM are nonvolatile and permanent, the ROM will remember a 0101 every time a 5 is pressed, even though the power has been turned off for a while. In this regard, the keyboard ROM is used as hardware more than software.

We said that using a 1024-location ROM is wasteful when we only need to encode 10 keys. The second design is more efficient. The ROM being used has six address lines, and 64 places where 4-bit numbers are stored. Each key that's pressed generates row and column information. The row number is a 0 or a 1, and the column number is a LOW on one of the five column wires. In this design, if the 5 is pressed on the keypad, the column wires will be 01111 and the row wire will be a 1. Address 101111 is address 47, and our 64 × 4 ROM had better have a 0101 stored there, or our keyboard won't work. Similarly, the other nine keys of the keyboard will address nine other locations, each with the key's code stored in it. This ROM encoder is still wasteful. From 64 locations, we get 10 useful numbers. That's 5.4 useless locations to every useful one.

For larger keyboards, the ROM method is more efficient, and is often used. A 10-digit decimal keypad is just too small to take advantage of this

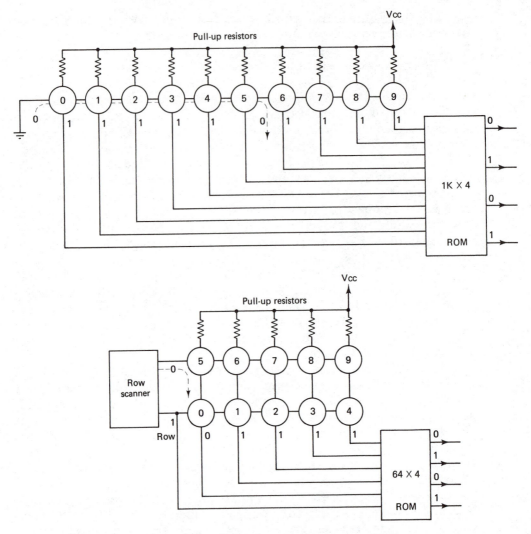

Figure 2-6 Keyboards with encoder ROMs

method of encoding. Keyboards with 64 and 96 keys are frequently de-signed with ROM encoders built in. For smaller keypads, a diode matrix encoder is more efficient than a ROM.

You may have wondered why all our keyboard designs have used active-LOW logic when we introduced both active-HIGH and active-LOW types at the beginning. This is no accident. Since most computer logic is designed to be TTL compatible, its inputs regard a disconnected line the same as a 1. We don't want a disconnected line or plug to act as an *active* signal (or a whole bunch of active signals). There could be major trouble if HIGH was the active state of logic devices in a computer. A plug accidentally kicked loose would turn on all the devices it was supposed to control—and there might be several fighting for control of the data bus at the same time. When this happens, some gates usually get burned out somewhere, and that's not a good design. Instead, computer circuits should be designed so that a disconnected plug makes everything play dead and float. That's why active-LOW logic and active-LOW enables are used in as many places as possible where TTL or TTL-compatible devices are used.

2.3 ALPHAMERIC INPUT

"Alphameric" is a contraction of two words, "*alpha*betic" and "nu*meric*." An **alphameric** (sometimes, **alphanumeric**) **keyboard** is one that has both numbers and letters on it. This is the type of keyboard usually found on data terminals. It is normally laid out like a typewriter keyboard, and the key operations usually produce some code with both letter and number capability, such as ASCII or EBCDIC code. The EBCDIC keyboard is largely obsolete; even IBM is s-l-o-w-l-y adapting to ASCII code. There are two basic kinds of alphameric keyboard: hardware encoded and software encoded. Let's briefly review what is meant by the terms **hardware** and **software**. A flip-flop is hardware. The resistors, transistors, and wires the circuit is made of are its hardware. To change any part of it requires a rewiring job. In the case of integrated circuits this is virtually impossible. The flip-flop circuit is "graven in stone" and is not going to change easily—hence the name hardware. If the flip-flop is set so that is Q output is HIGH, the 1 at Q is software. It is stored in the hardware, but is not a part of it. The wiring is not changed by altering the 1 to a 0, and the alteration doesn't require a major rewiring job. If power is turned off, the 1 or 0 will be lost. It's temporary, "soft" information, easily changed or lost—hence the name "software." If we think of the circuit and the wiring as hardware, and the 1s and 0s as software, there shouldn't be much confusion about which is which.

What's a ROM? Well, the 1s and 0s are permanently wired in, so they seem to be hardware, but they're also logic states (HIGH and LOW), so they seem to be software. The ROM falls into a gray area—not bird and not beast—and is usually called **firmware**. ROM programs stored inside a computer are sometimes called software instead of firmware, but we've never seen them called hardware. Are you still confused? So are we.

2.3.1 ASCII Keyboard (Fully Encoded)

In Figure 2-7, we're cheating a little. The box in the diagram marked "magic" might be a diode matrix, a ROM, or a gate array. This hardware encoder converts the row and column information from the keyboard into 8-bit

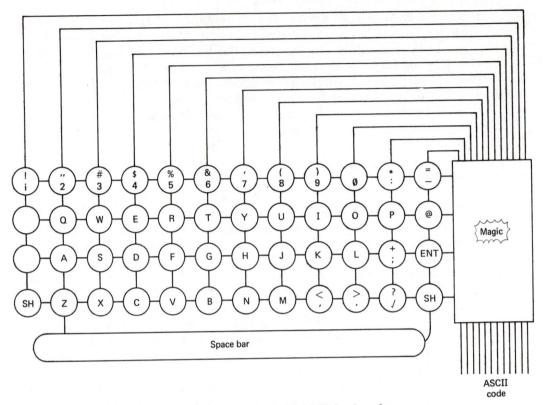

Figure 2-7 A "smart" ASCII keyboard

ASCII code. The ASCII code is passed on to the computer through an (input) I/O port.

Even if this port is memory mapped, the keyboard data will only occupy one byte of memory where a memory address has been replaced by the buffers of the keyboard input port.

The advantage of this type of keyboard is that it takes up very little of the computer's memory space for ports or a keyboard-scanning program, and provides very fast conversion of keystrokes into code, without taking any of the computer's time for the process. The disadvantage is that the keyboard encoder circuitry is expensive and takes up extra power and board space as compared to the software-encoded type.

This type of keyboard is used on the Apple II computer.

2.3.2 ASCII Keyboard (Software Encoded)

In Figure 2-8 we see a keyboard with no encoding of its own. The computer scans a row on the keyboard by reading a certain address in memory.

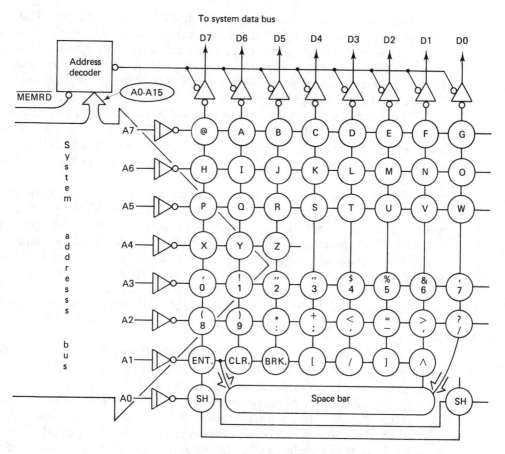

Figure 2-8 A "dumb" ASCII keyboard

The address bus provides eight signals which are used by the program (the software) in the computer to scan the keyboard row by row. A single 1 is put on one of the eight address lines to see if a key is pressed on that row. The 1 is converted to a 0 by the inverting buffers used to pass the address bits A(7) through A(0) to the keyboard rows. If a key is pressed, the 0 on the row wire (notice that the keyboard is strobed with active-LOW signals) appears on one of the column wires. These are passed to the data bus through inverting buffers—and the lone 0 becomes a single 1. The computer program identifies from the 1 which key has been pressed, and extracts a suitable code for that key from a table stored in the computer's memory. Then it reads another address that is the next row down on the keyboard, and continues until all rows on the keyboard have been read. This is repeated every time the computer "looks" at the keyboard.

This software-encoded keyboard design has one advantage. The hardware is simpler and cheaper than a hardware-encoded keyboard. The software that runs the keyboard-scan program takes up little space in the computer's operating system, and costs almost nothing. Data the computer gets from this keyboard can only tell it the row and column the key is on. The rest is done by the computer program.

This is a memory-mapped keyboard. Addresses where the eight rows of the keyboard are located (256 of them) are off-limits for use as ordinary memory by the computer. The keyboard is wired in at these locations. Part of the memory has been sacrificed so that the keyboard requires less hardware to make it operate.

The advantages of software encoding are the reduced cost of the simpler hardware (all that's needed is two buffers with gate logic for enables), and the lesser power requirement and smaller board space this provides. The disadvantages are the extra time it takes for the computer to run a keyboard-scan program every time it wants to see what key's been pressed, the keyboard-scan program that takes up memory space we could have used for other programming, and the large amount of memory space that must be "lost" to fit the undecoded keyboard into the memory map.

This is the kind of keyboard used in the Radio Shack TRS-80 microcomputer.

In the trade-off of hardware costs versus software costs these two styles of keyboard come out about even. The added expenses of hardware decoding (extra parts, more board space, more power consumption) are balanced by the inconveniences of software decoding (less available memory, slower conversion time). In the marketplace, where dollars and cents is most important, the software-encoding scheme gives the vendor a slight advantage in price (and few people can hit keys fast enough to notice the speed difference). A fully encoded (hardware encoded) keyboard attached to a true I/O port, however, would give the programmer more room to work in, and this is a selling point for the serious business or scientific user. It's hard to say which one of these schemes will win out in the long run—if either one does—and it appears we'll have both of them around in different machines for some time to come.

2.3.3 Difference between "Smart" and "Dumb" Input

For the two types of keyboard described in the last two sections—and for input devices in general—the names "smart" and "dumb" are used. A **smart keyboard** has its own "smarts"—that is, it has its own on-board decoding—and doesn't need to use any of the computer's smarts to convert the keystrokes into ASCII. A **dumb keyboard** has the bare minimum of logic ("smarts") on the board with the keys, and depends on the computer program to have the smarts to convert each key (row and column) into an ASCII code.

In a larger sense, smarts come from the encoding and logic circuitry that's on board the input device. If all the code conversion work is done at the input device before data are put into the input port—if the data are all digested before they're sent to the computer—the input device has the smarts. A dumb device lets the computer do more (or all) of the converting work, and doesn't have any capability on board to do anything the computer could be doing instead. Since the smarts are already a built-in part of the computer, building input devices with smarts that duplicate a lot of the functions of the computer adds extra cost. The cost of smart peripherals is not always easy for the buyer to live with. A dumb peripheral that utilizes the computer's smarts can be purchased for less money, and unless the computer system it attaches to is "I/O-bound," it will appear to work the same way the smart one does. It may be that the smart designer is the one who uses the dumb peripheral.

2.4 MAGNETIC (I/O) STORAGE DEVICES

At the beginning of this chapter, we split the I/O device world into three parts. Keyboards, keypads, and switch panels fell into the category of direct input devices. They allowed generation and use of the input in "real time." The rest of the input world we called document-reading devices and sensors. We'll begin our discussion of **document-reading devices** with magnetic storage (tape, disk, magnetic card, magnetic bubble, etc). We might also consider these as forms of auxiliary memory, since they are used to store information that takes up too much space for the computer's main memory. It is possible, through the use of these mass-storage devices, to transfer chunks of information into and out of the real computer memory so that the virtual memory (the size the memory appears to be) is hundreds of times larger than the main memory actually is.

2.4.1 Tape

Several different schemes for recording 1s and 0s on tape exist. One simple system uses a north magnetic polarity on the top surface of the tape for a 1, and a south magnetic polarity for a 0. More complex methods better adapted to the response of magnetic r/p (record/playback) heads are used, but in all cases, the reading (this is a chapter on input devices, after all!) takes place like this:

A layer of plastic coated with a ferromagnetic oxide like ferrite has magnetic fields on its ferrite surface. This surface passes by the r/p head, which is made of a good magnetic-field conductor. A coil of wire is wrapped around this magnetic-field conductor, and as the field in the head changes, the changing field induces a voltage in the coil, which is amplified and wave-shaped by the electronics in the tape-drive mechanism to digital logic levels before being input to the computer.

In some machines, **saturation recording** is used. The 1s and 0s are recorded as magnetic fields that completely saturate the ferrite magnetically. Each bit is usually represented by one region of magnetization, although the borders between magnetized regions may be used as bits instead.

In other machines, two tones or frequencies are used to represent the HIGH and LOW logic levels. As you might expect, the high frequency usually stands for the HIGH logic level, and the lower frequency stands for the LOW logic level. This system of recording is called **audio recording**. The frequencies used are generally in the middle (a few kiloHertz) audio range, and are recorded as sinusoidal, nonsaturated magnetic-field variations, instead of saturated pulses.

Figure 2-9 shows three methods of recording on tape. If we imagine

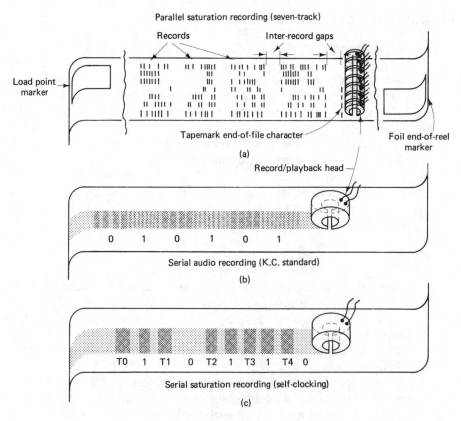

Parallel saturation recording (seven-track)

Records   Inter-record gaps

Load point marker

Tapemark end-of-file character

Foil end-of-reel marker

(a)

Record/playback head

0   1   0   1   0   1

Serial audio recording (K.C. standard)

(b)

T0 1 T1 0 T2 1 T3 1 T4 0

Serial saturation recording (self-clocking)

(c)

Figure 2-9 Magnetic tape data formats

that magnetic fields are visible as dark spots on the tape, Figure 2-9 illustrates the types of recording discussed in the next three sections.

Reel-to-Reel Seven-Track and Nine-Track Formats. The most popular mass-storage medium in large data processing centers are **saturation-recording tape drives** that record data in multiple tracks simultaneously. Early IBM machines that used BCDIC code (a six-level code) were able to store each byte on a seven-track strip (six for the code plus a parity bit). A seven-track tape drive has a record/playback head which records 7 bits at once to store a byte, then as the tape moves by, the next byte and the next are stored in strips of bits on the tape.

Later machines that use 8-bit EBCDIC or ASCII code record nine tracks on a strip 1 bit wide and 9 bits deep (8 bits of code plus a parity bit). All of these machines have certain things in common.

A standard-size reel of tape is about 25 cm in diameter and holds 800 meters of tape. Bytes are read from the tape at a few hundred to a few thousand bits per centimeter. U.S. tape recording densities are described in bits per inch (BPI). At 6400 BPI (2520 bits per centimeter) a reel of tape like this holds 192 million bytes of data.

Blocks of bytes recorded as a group are called **records**. A data processor recording data from a box of punchcards onto tape might record each card as a separate record, separated from the last card and the next card by an **inter-record gap** (IRG). The end of the box might be the end of all the records in that file of data. On tape, this point would be identified by recording a special end-of-file character called a **tapemark**. At the beginning (**load point**) and end of the reel, permanent foil reflectors—also called **tapemarks**—identify the points at which rewinding or further recording must stop. These reflective foil markers are sensed by photocells that "see" light from a small lamp bounced off the foil strips.

The tape-transport mechanism can move the tape in both forward and reverse directions at speeds up to several feet per second, yet can stop the tape in a fraction of an inch at the end of a record, file, or reel. It is possible to start and stop the tape within these short distances because the whole reel of tape isn't started and stopped as every record is read. Two loops with several decimeters of slack tape are held (on either side of the r/p head) under tension by a partial vacuum behind vacuum doors. When the tape is moved, one loop is shortened, and the other loop gets longer. Only the slack tape has to move, and the small inertia of a few decimeters of tape (compared to the whole reel) makes it easy to start and stop the tape in short intervals of time. Eventually, when one loop gets too short and the other gets too long, pressure sensors activate the drive and advance or rewind the reels until the loops are equalized. The IRGs between tape records provide startup time and braking time for the tape as each new record is read. When a tape drive is reading tape, even though the tape appears to move smoothly through the heads (it isn't; it's jumping ahead a fraction of a centimeter—a record—at a time), the reels appear to jump forward or back in steps of several decimeters.

Tape is much cheaper per byte of storage space than other magnetic media, and a reel of tape stores data in a smaller volume than any other type of machine-readable document. A 25-cm reel of tape, for instance, holds as much data as (at 6400 BPI) you could fit into 1200 boxes (about 6000 kg!) of punchcards.

Cassette: Serial KC standard (audio) recording. Microcomputers that cost a a few hundred to a thousand dollars aren't likely to use parallel multitrack digital recorders like those just discussed. Those cost tens of thousands of dollars. You're more likely to find a small computer using a cassette recorder that sells for under a hundred dollars. These recorders have only one r/p head that records one track. Most of them aren't suited to overdriving the heads for saturation recording. They also can't handle the bodaceous data rates computer tape is normally expected to handle (100K to millions of bits per second). Cassette tape recorders used with microcomputers record data one bit after another—serially—instead of 7 or 9 bits side by side.

In 1976, a convention of microcomputer and small-computer users devised a standard recording scheme used by several manufacturers. Since the conference was convened by *BYTE* magazine in Kansas City, the standard developed there is called the **BYTE standard** or **Kansas City Standard** (KC standard). Although it is by no means the only technique used for recording on small-computer cassette recorders, KC standard is representative of a number of other recording schemes. Here's how it's organized:

1. A logic 0 is recorded as four cycles of 1200-Hz sine-wave voltage. (a **space**)
2. A logic 1 is recorded as eight cycles of 2400-Hz sine-wave voltage. (a **mark**)

You can see that both a 1 and a 0 take 1/300 of a second, permitting data recording at a rate of 300 baud (300 BPS).

This is an audio-recording standard. The 1s and 0s are identified by tuned circuits or a phase-locked loop (PLL), and converted to logic levels in the input device. The serial-to-parallel conversion can be done either by software or by a UART.

Cassette: TRS-80 tape (saturation) recording. Cassette tape can be saturation recorded. One method of doing this is used by Tandy in their TRS-80. It is, in fact, the same method IBM uses to record on disks. A train of magnetic pulses is recorded on a single track of tape, serially. Two kinds of pulses are recorded, clock pulses and data pulses. A data pulse position is found between every two clock pulses. If there's no data pulse between two clock pulses, the data bit is a 0. If there is a data pulse between two clock pulses, the data bit is a 1. The recorded magnetic information is waveshaped by an op amp circuit in the computer and then input through a buffer. The computer program sorts clock from data pulses and converts the data from serial to parallel form.

Saturation recording has the advantage that bits can be recorded at a faster rate than KC standard—only one pulse has to be recorded per bit instead of 4 or 8—but the disadvantage that only one pulse has to be lost to lose the whole bit of data. The KC standard audio will be more reliable—but much slower—than saturation recording.

Cassette recorders used with small computers don't have the sophisticated direction-control and end-of-reel detection capability of the commercial drives for the big mainframes. The record, playback, and rewind/fast forward functions are all manual. About the only automatic thing you can do with these recorders is turn them on and off through the remote jack. Many computers don't even have provisions for this much control (or the control doesn't work very well).

The amount of data that can be recorded on a cassette is not as large as on a reel, partly because the data are recorded serially instead of one byte at at a time, and partly because lower frequencies and data rates are used on audio tape. Even so, a 60-minute cassette recorded at 500 baud can hold 225,000 bytes.

2.4.2 Disk

"Hard" disk (disk packs and Winchester disk). Disks and drums were invented as high-speed mass-storage devices for data processors in the late 1950s. Their main advantage over tape is that they are random access as opposed to the serial access of magnetic tape. An example of random access is a phonograph record. If you want to listen to the first cut on a record, then the last, then one in the middle, it's easy to do this on a phonograph by just picking up the tone arm and setting it down somewhere else. To do the same thing with a tape recording—you can't do the same thing with tape. Since the tape recording is all in a straight line you have to fast forward and rewind through all the intervening tape to get to the parts you want to hear. On a phonograph disk, since it's two-dimensional, the needle doesn't have to fast-forward through the groove to get where you want it. You just jump over the part you want to skip.

This feature of phonograph disks made a group of engineers at IBM think of doing the same thing with a magnetic recording disk for mass data storage. Unlike phonograph records, disks can be erased, recorded, and re-used. Like phonograph records, both the top and bottom surfaces are used.

In large data-processing systems, groups of platters called "packs" are spun on a common shaft and read by a comblike arrangement of r/p heads in a holder called an **access arm**. On a drive with six platters, there will be 10 usable surfaces (the top and bottom surfaces are protective covers) so the access arm will have 10 r/p heads. Figure 2-10 shows a disk pack with 10 surfaces, 100 tracks, and 20 sectors per track. These three dimensions define a system of *cylindrical coordinates* that allows access to any record on the disk. The surface number is selected by enabling just one of the 10 r/p heads on the access arm. The track number is selected by moving the access arm in toward the center of the disk or out toward the edge. Once the r/p head is positioned at a specific track, all we do to get a particular sector is just wait for it to come around on the disk, since the disk is spinning.

In some ways a **disk pack** is like a 3D memory. It has three dimensions, and is accessible at almost any location in (nearly) the same amount of time. The time it takes to find any piece of data on a disk is a combination of the time it takes the access arm to reach the desired track, and the time it takes the disk to rotate to the desired sector. Enabling the r/p head to select the surface takes no time on this scale. For instance, suppose that the disk pack in Figure 2-10 is rotating at 1500 rpm and the access arm is moved from track to track by a stepper motor that takes 100 steps per second. In a worst-case situation, the access arm would have to seek across all 100 tracks to find the right one (1 second), but in a typical case, the access arm only has to move one track at a time (10 ms). Again in a worst-case situation, the disk would have to complete one full revolution to reach the sector desired (40 ms), but a typical seek would find its target in half a revolution (20 ms) around the disk. Enabling the r/p head would take less than a microsecond

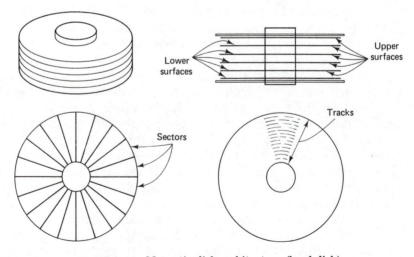

Figure 2-10 Magnetic disk architecture (hard disk)

(0.001 ms).   On the whole, in our hypothetical example, it would take an average 30 ms to reach any record on the disk, but could take as long as 1.04 seconds.

Is this significantly faster than tape? Suppose that we have a 25-cm reel (800 meters) of tape moving at 1 meter per second while a specific record is being searched for. If the tape mechanism can read data as it flies by at this speed, looking for a specific record number, how long would it take to find one of the records on tape? In the worst case, there are 800 meters of tape, and the next record might be 800 meters away from the last. That would make the worst-case time to find a record 800 seconds (13 minutes 20 seconds). An average record might be the next record over, but if tape is used for random access—not trying to read the records in the order they were recorded—the next record wanted would average 400 meters (6 minutes 40 seconds) away. For the worst case, tape is almost 800 times slower than the worst-case disk-seek operation (random access), and in the typical random-record disk seek, tape is 13,000 times slower.

The name **hard disk** or **rigid disk** comes from the fact that these platters are made of metal (usually aluminum) coated with ferrite—the same magnetic material on tapes—and recorded/played back with r/p heads very similar to those in a tape drive. Disk packs are fairly easy to change, but are more expensive, and have less capacity, than tape. Our example disk pack has 100 tracks $\times$ 10 surfaces $\times$ 20 sectors. That makes a total of 20,000 records on the pack (records are sometimes called sectors, too—just to confuse things). Suppose that each record contains 512 bytes. (On the innermost track, this is just slightly above the 6400 BPI we used on our tape example earlier.) The total content of the disk pack would be 10,240,000 bytes. This is larger than the main memory of many computers, but a lot less than the 192 million bytes on a 25-cm reel of tape recorded at the same BPI density.

Disk packs are precision-machined devices. The r/p heads float above the surface of the disk on a cushion of compressed air at a height of a few millionths of a centimeter. If the disks are warped or have irregularities in the surface that bump up more than this amount, the heads will "crash" and damage the disk. A head crash will usually gouge some of the ferrite off the disk surface (making it unrecordable) and damage or destroy the heads themselves. Dust (and even the particles of cigarette smoke) is made of particles big enough to get caught between the heads and the disk surface, causing scratches and damage to the disks. Most disk drives blow filtered air across the surface of the disks to keep them free of dust. A "clean room" environment is not absolutely necessary for disk drives, but is recommended.

As you could no doubt guess, disk packs cost a lot more than tape reels. A new disk pack would cost in the hundreds of dollars, whereas a reel of computer-grade tape would be in the tens of dollars.

Winchester disk drives are hard-disk drives for small/microcomputers, that usually have just one platter, which may not be removable. Winchester drives have higher recording densities than the disk pack discussed in our hypothetical example. Early units of this type had 30 megabytes on a surface with 30 sectors on a track. The designation 30-30 for this unit reminded someone of a 30-30 hunting rifle (a Winchester), and this name was coined for the disk and its drive.

Floppy disk. Popular in the microcomputer/small computer area, **floppies** are smaller, cheaper, slower, and have less precision (so they require less careful handling) than hard disks. A typical floppy is either $5\frac{1}{4}$ inches (about 13 cm) or 8 inches (about 20 cm) in diameter. The name "floppy" comes from the material (flexible plastic) on which the ferrite is bonded. Figure 2-11 shows a typical ($5\frac{1}{4}$ inch) floppy. The basic features are indicated on the diagram. Unlike the hard disk, floppies are enclosed in an envelope with a low-friction lining, and only one disk is placed on the drive at a time. Disks are removable and easily changed. The drive spindle in the disk drive is a tapered plug with a shoulder that grabs the disk and holds it by friction (when the disk is put into the drive and the door closed) so that it can turn without slipping. **Diskettes**—another name for floppies—are spun at 360 rpm. An indexing hole in the disk is read by photocell to identify its rotational position. There may be a hole at the beginning of each sector on

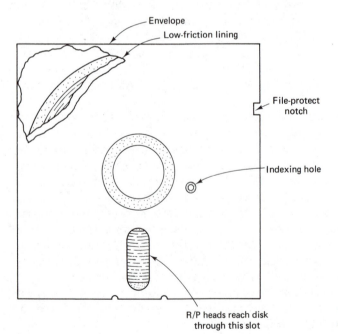

Envelope
Low-friction lining
File-protect notch
Indexing hole
R/P heads reach disk through this slot

Figure 2-11 Magnetic disk architecture (floppy disk)

the diskette (hard-sectored) or just one hole at the beginning of the first sector, with consecutive sectors identified by magnetic information recorded on the disk (soft-sectored). A single r/p head is usually all there is in a floppy drive, but both sides of each disk are recordable, so double-sided drives with two heads do exist.

The slower speed and lower bit density of floppies makes head crash less of a problem. Machine tolerances are less critical on floppies, and the "clean room" problem is less of a difficulty. The disk in our example has 35 tracks with 10 sectors on each track. Each record is 256 bytes long, so there are a total of 89,600 bytes on one surface of this disk, and 179,200 bytes on the entire diskette. As with the example of a hard disk pack, this figure is just one of a wide variety of possible track and sector configurations.

File protect.   Magnetic media like reel-to-reel tape, cassette tape, and floppy disk can be **file protected**. That is, the recording on the disk or tape can be protected against being overwritten by a later recording. Cassette tapes have two plastic tabs on the back end of the cassette which, when broken out, prevent recording on the cassette. Floppy disks have a square notch on the side of the disk that can be covered with tape to inhibit recording on the disk. Data-processing reels have a rubber ring which can be removed to inhibit recording. In all of these cases, the reason for doing this is to keep important programs or data safe from accidental destruction by being recorded over.

2.4.3 Bubble Memory

Bubble memory is a possible replacement for disks in computer mass-memory systems. Unlike disks, bubble memory chips are all solid-state, no-moving-parts technology, so there's none of the wear associated with drive spindles access arms and heads. The bubble can be read faster than disk, because no mechanical transport is necessary to move the bits past the reading mechanism. Single one-wafer devices (about 1 inch square) can now store 8 million bits, (1 million bytes), compared to the floppy in the preceding section, which stores less than one-fifth of that.

The compactness, speed, and mechanical simplicity (no motors, heads, or drive needed) of bubble memory suggests that these integrated circuits will replace floppies and fixed-hard disk in many applications. They will probably be configured (designed) to be transparent to the disk user—they'll look just like the disk they replaced to the programmer—but will be built into the system design in a much simpler way. Perhaps the bubble memories will interface into the computer as plug-in cartridges, looking something like tape cassettes as they are snapped into and out of a holder.

Disk drives and tape players read magnetic documents. These are simple and readily available media for data storage and retrieval, but the first machine-readable documents were not magnetic. The earliest machine-readable documents used by data processing machines were punchcards, and they are still in use a century after Herman Hollerith developed them to tabulate the census of 1890. Hollerith punchcard readers and punched-tape readers work in about the same way, so the working principles described in the card section will not be repeated in the tape section.

2.5.1 Punchcards

Hollerith cards. The Hollerith code and Hollerith card layout are described in Appendix A, so we won't repeat that information here. A **card reader** is shown in Figure 2-12. As the card passes between the *brushes* (electrical conductors actually made in the form of brushes with steel bristles) and the *contact roll*, the cardboard keeps the brushes and roller apart. When a hole punched through the card passes between the brush and roller, the brush drops through the hole and makes an electrical contact with the voltage on the contact roll. This is a logic 1 (on early data-processing equipment, +40 V was used), which can be input into the computer through an input port and processed into whatever code the computer needs to use.

Hollerith made his cards the size of a dollar bill (1890 issue)—$3\frac{1}{4}$ by $7\frac{3}{8}$ inches. Dollar bills have gotten smaller in all dimensions—especially value—since then, but the old "computer card" is soaked in so many years of tradition that its size didn't change when the currency did. The other dimension of a punchcard is 0.0065 inch—to a very high degree of precision.

Since punchcards are usually fed to the computer's card reader in stacks (decks), a mechanism is required for separating cards from the stack and feeding them into the brush block one at a time. This card-feeding mechanism depends on the exact physical dimensions of the card. The bottom card on the stack is pushed from the *hopper* into the *throat* of the card reader by a *feed knife*, which catches the card with a squared-off metal blade thinner than one card (0.0040 inch). The throat is a space between the *feed roller* and the *throat knife* that is just a bit wider than one card, but not wide enough to admit two cards (0.0080 inch). The card slides through the throat while the card above it is held by the throat knife, and gets fed into the brushes, where it is read. Other rollers continue to move the card until it ends up in a *stacker*.

The same job can be done in a noncontact way using photodetectors to see flashes of light that pass through the holes in the card from a light underneath the card. Both types of reader are shown in the diagram.

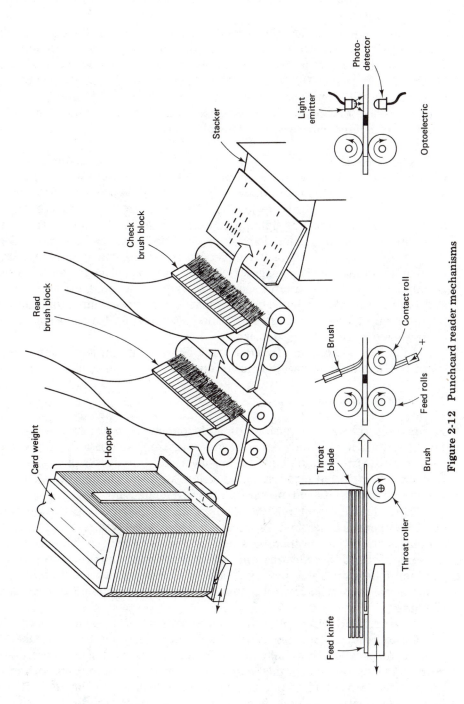

Figure 2-12 Punchcard reader mechanisms

Card weight

Hopper

Read brush block

Check brush block

Stacker

Light emitter

Photo-detector

Optoelectric

Brush

Contact roll

Feed rolls

Throat blade

Throat roller

Brush

Feed knife

Problems with card readers usually involve "card jams" that occur when cards are stacked poorly (all the edges don't line up) or when the edges of the cards get worn—dog-eared—to the degree that their edges are frayed and become wider than 0.0080 inch. Hot, damp weather will also cause cards to swell up with moisture beyond this critical threshold and jam in the reader. This is one reason why computer rooms are air-conditioned and de-humidified in large data-processing installations.

96-Column cards.   Based on the Hollerith code, but actually encoded in BCDIC instead of Hollerith, 96-column cards make six holes do the same job as the 12 in a Hollerith column. Although there are more data bits on each card, 96-column cards are smaller than Hollerith cards, because they are organized as three rows of 32 columns on a single card (Figure 2-13). The holes are round and smaller than those on a Hollerith card, and presumably a higher-precision type of reader is needed for them, but their compactness and higher storage density suggest that they should replace Hollerith cards in all applications. This doesn't seem to be happening—perhaps because, as I said before, the old Hollerith card is soaked in tradition, and data-processing people aren't going to change established systems just for the sake of com-pactness and higher storage density.

Like the 80-column Hollerith card, 96-column cards are the size and shape of a common twentieth-century currency—the plastic charge card.

2.5.2 Punched Paper Tape

Figure 2-14 shows two versions of code punched on paper tape. As with punchcards, a hole stands for a 1 and everything else is a 0. The code in Figure 2-14(a) is Baudot code, a five-level code discussed in Appendix A. In Figure 2-14(b), an eight-channel version is shown which uses BCDIC with added odd-parity bits and an end-of-line (EL) character.

The punching and reading equipment for paper tape is often found on Teletype machines and terminals. Paper tape was used in telegraph communications before there was data processing at all, which accounts for the use of Baudot code on some older machines, and the association of punched tape with Teletypes. It is also the most popular medium for input to industrial numerical-control systems, and computer-numerically controlled machines.

The basic principle of reading punched tape is the same as that of the punchcard reader. Brushes, pins, or starwheels may be used to make elec-trical contact when they fall into the holes, and optical sensors are used in current-generation noncontact high-speed readers. The only important dif-ference between a reel of punched tape and a deck of punchcards is that the tape is one continuous document, whereas the punchcard deck is broken up into unit records none of which is more than 80 (96) characters long. If you

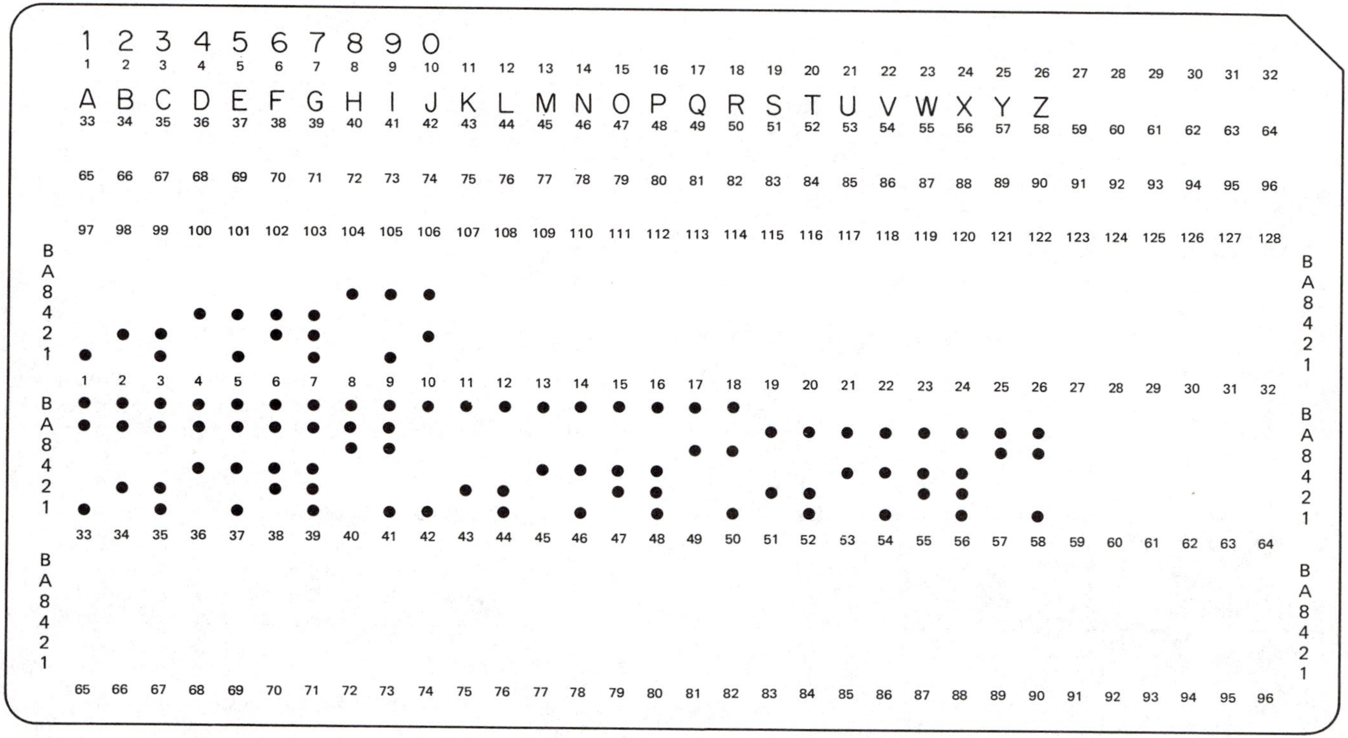

Figure 2-13 96-column punchcard format

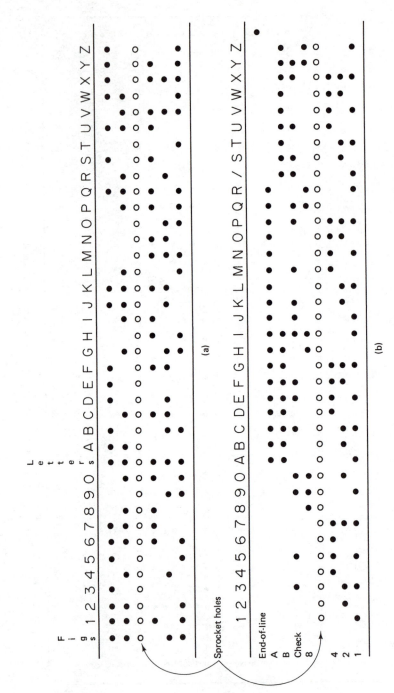

Figure 2-14 (a) 5-level and (b) 7-level punched paper tape format

56

make a mistake in a deck of punchcards, you've only got to duplicate one card with the mistake corrected, and throw out the old card in the deck, replacing it with the new one.   Changing the order of instructions in one-command-per-card programming languages like FORTRAN or BASIC is as easy as shuffling the order of cards.   With punched tape, however, if you make a mistake after 500 meters of tape, too bad!   You have to duplicate the entire 500 meters, correct the error, and throw out the old tape, or try to splice in a corrected section of tape to fix the error, a messy and unreliable procedure.   As for shuffling the order of commands by swapping cards, there's no way to do this with a reel of tape, except by cut and splice, or redoing the whole reel!

The good thing about tape is that being one continuous form, tape doesn't require a complicated feeding system like a punchcard reader's, and thickness or humidity aren't critical factors.   You'll also never have the sad job of trying to put a 1000-card program back in order after knocking the deck off the top of a table.   Tape readers are cheap, simple, and fast compared to card readers.   They're even found on small computer/microcomputer systems.   A really simple optical punchtape reader can be gotten for under a hundred dollars, whereas card readers with deck-feeding capability cost many thousands.

2.6 OCR/BARCODE READER

These are becoming very popular as data-entry input devices for *point-of-sale* (POS) *terminals* (what we used to call cash registers) at retail stores. Both OCR—**optical character recognition**—wands and *barcode readers* identify a product at the checkout counter, simplifying the clerk's job.   OCR wands contain a grid of photodetectors arranged to identify the shapes of alphameric characters on labels.   Most of this work is done by the smarts of the main computer or a microprocessor built in to the POS terminal.   OCR readers usually can read only one type of type font (character set), called OCR characters, but some programs are now smart enough to read several standard typewriter fonts as well as special OCR labels.   The idea of making machine-readable print on paper that is also people-readable began with magnetic-ink OCR characters on bank checks, read by magnetic sensors.   As the type of sensors that could read ordinary ink became cheaper and more reliable, the bank check reader moved out to department stores as the POS terminal.

At the same time, barcode readers using only one photosensor to read light and dark bars on a special label (UPC or *Universal Product Code*) began to appear in grocery stores, and a wide variety of products were required to carry these labels.

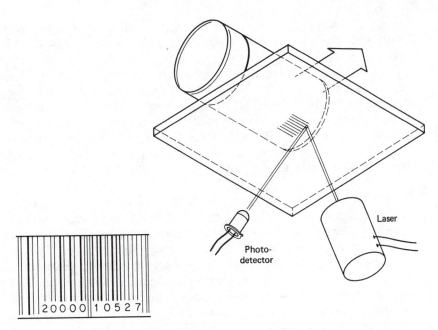

Figure 2-15   Barcode reader mechanism

    In both cases, the sensor picks up a pattern of changing light and dark spots as 1s and 0s, which are buffered into the computer from an input port. After that, some really hairy programming is required to digest these into useful alphameric information inside the computer.

    Ultimately, printed labels are a lot simpler to make than punchcards or punchtape, and the reader/sensors are much simpler than those needed for either punched document. One design for a barcode reader is shown in Figure 2-15 together with the barcode itself. OCR fonts and sensors are not standardized and we've made no attempt to cover the field with a chart or diagram.

2-7 A/D CONVERTERS USED WITH SENSORS

2.7.1 Graphics Input: Light Pens, Tablets, Joysticks, and Video Digitizers

These input devices are used to enter position information into computers. Their position usually controls the position of something else, like the position of a spot of light on the video screen or the place where a dot will print on a sheet of paper.

A **light pen** in use appears to be operating or controlling the video screen. It is usually used to draw onto the video screen or to move objects around on the screen. Although it appears that the light pen is some sort of output controller associated with the video, it is in fact the simplest of input devices. All the light pen tells the CPU is "light on" or "light off." Clever programming uses this one-bit data buffered in through an input port to locate the position of points of light on the screen. More clever programming is used to hunt, track, and follow the light pen around the screen with a point of light. A picture can be drawn on the video display, and its points digitized directly into the memory of the computer while this program is running. Without a suitable software driver program, the light pen does nothing.

A **tablet** is used like a pad of paper you draw on with a *stylus*—a pencil-like instrument. The stylus may—or may not—be an electrical contact. As it is moved across the tablet, a grid of wires under its surface detect the position of the stylus and send two numbers X and Y to the input ports of the computer. A drawing can be placed on the tablet and traced with the stylus to put its lines and curves into the computer as a set of numbers that describe the position of the points on the picture.

A **joystick** is a control handle used to steer things around on a display. It consists of variable resistors or switches that vary with position in two degrees of rotation. The variations in resistance are converted by an A/D converter into numbers that indicate two dimensions of position. Originally, the joystick was a steering handle in front of the pilot in a fighter plane that stuck up from between his legs. We'll let you guess why the pilots gave it that name.

Video digitizers take the signal from a television camera and sample the voltage at intervals of time. The voltages are converted from analog to digital, and each digital number—called a *pixel* or picture element—is stored in memory for future recovery and redisplay, printout, or *image processing*, in which certain aspects of the picture are sought out and enhanced.

2.7.2 Digitized Instruments: Sensors for Measurement and Data Logging

Any measurable quantity that can be converted into an electrical signal by a transducer can be input to a computer. An A/D converter will take the electrical voltage and turn it into a digital-coded number. When the number is input to the computer, it can be buffered in through an input port and used by the computer program, provided that the programmer knows what quantity is being measured and what the number means.

Figure 2-16 uses a digital thermometer as an example of an input device. The *thermistor* is a resistor whose resistance goes down as its temperature goes up. The oscillator's frequency increases as the resistance goes

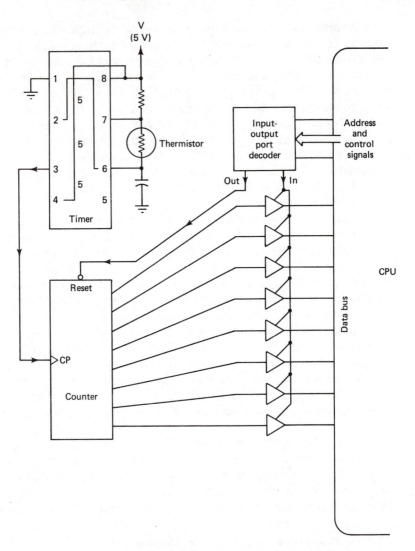

Figure 2-16   Direct A/D input device

down. The counter will count pulses from the oscillator. That's the whole input device. To use it, the computer program must reset the counter, let it count for a specified amount of time, then input the number in the counter and subtract a number from it to adjust for zero Celsius or zero Farenheit.

"So why," you ask, "should I use a computer to take temperatures?" "I can take a thermometer out with me and record temperatures on a pad of paper perfectly well myself."

By way of an answer, we'll ask another question; what would you do if you needed a temperature reading every thousandth of a second from 10 thermometers spaced every 10 meters outward from an underground nuclear weapons test until the sensors vaporize? Read the thermometers yourself and write them down on a pad? Not likely! This is a job for a computer.

Any time you need a lot of readings taken in a very short time, and remotely if necessary, digital data transmission and automatic (computer) data logging are called for.

2.8 DMA CONTROLLER

DMA stands for **direct memory access**. Although we've included DMA with other input devices, a DMA peripheral is not an ordinary input port at all. It's an input device that puts its data directly into the memory of the computer. The **DMA controller** takes over the functions of a CPU and generates data, address, and control signals itself. One of the control signals is called a *DMA request* (*bus request* and *hold* are other names for the same signal). When the peripheral has a data word ready for the computer, it generates a DMA request that causes the address, data, and some control signals from the CPU to float at the end of the next machine cycle. As soon as the CPU has gone "on hold" and everything's floating, a DMA granted signal is sent back to the requesting device from the CPU (this signal is also called *hold acknowledged* or *bus acknowledged*). The requesting device now has the "go-ahead" signal and can enable all its buffers that were *tri-stated* and holding back on address, data, and a memory write signal. Since these signals are enabled onto a bus that is floating already, they take over the system and the data are written into the memory at whatever address is placed on the address bus by the DMA controller.

In our example (Figure 2-17), a keypad generates a data word and a keypressed signal every time a key is pressed. The keypressed signal creates a DMA request and advances the address counter in the keyboard assembly. When a DMA granted signal returns from the CPU, the (memory) control signals, address, and data buses are floating, and when the buffers in the DMA keyboard are enabled, a memory write signal appears on the control bus, the address in the keyboard's address counter appears on the address bus, and the encoded character from the keyboard appears on the data bus. In our example, the address counter has counted to 0000000000001100 (12) and a 01000001 (the letter A) is pressed on the keyboard. The DMA request is the output of the keypressed flip-flop, set by the keypressed signal. When the DMA granted signal appears, in addition to enabling the 12 onto the address bus and the A onto the data bus, the DMA granted also resets the keypressed flip-flop so that the DMA request goes away after a delay of one clock pulse. The key will have to be released and another key pressed before the DMA request signal becomes active again.

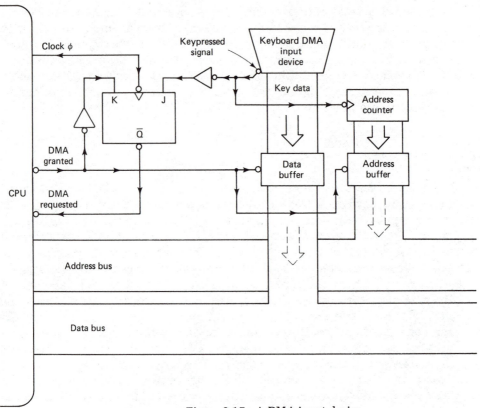

Figure 2-17 A DMA input device

The memory receives the 12 and the A and the memory write signal on the buses. This immediately causes the memory to write an A in memory location 12.

Meanwhile, the computer has been "playing dead." It's stuck at the end of its last machine cycle, ready to begin the next machine cycle, but unable to do so until the next clock pulse delay time is over. When the delay time passes, the A has been written into address 12, and the computer picks up where it left off as though nothing had happened. As far as the computer is concerned, there was a sudden puff of smoke and an A appeared! This is called a **cycle steal**, and the DMA controller that does it has done a cycle stealing DMA operation.

2.9 UARTs, MODEMS, SERIAL I/O FOR TELECOMMUNICATIONS

We have discussed UARTs and Modems in the previous chapter. The important thing to remember about these serial I/O devices is that they are "just another I/O device" where they connect to the I/O ports of the computer. As far as the computer is concerned, it comes to a port attached to a modem and picks up a byte of data just like it was from a keyboard. The fact that this byte of data might have come from the other end of the continent doesn't impress the computer at all!

Obviously, telecommunications is not a one-way process, and the data-set formed of acoustic coupler, modem, and UART is not just an input device. Just as obviously, there must be an input device among the things inside the dataset. To recap from previous chapters, the input part of the dataset takes serial FSK audio data from the acoustic coupler, the modem demodulates the FSK frequencies into two voltage levels, logic 1 and logic 0, and the UART collects the data bits one by one, converting from serial to parallel. The parallel data can now be gated onto the data bus by the input port.

2.10 AUDIO INTERFACE (MICROPHONE)

Finally, in the realm of audio interfaces, we'll discuss a slightly "blue sky" idea that is catching on. A microphone can be used as a detector (as it is in the acoustic coupler in the preceding section) for digital data, but it can also input music, sounds, and even human voice. With suitable analog-to-digital conversion, codes identifiable to the computer can be generated by spoken words.

With a suitable interface (and this is the complicated part) a microphone, a music-digitizer or voice-to-typewritten output converter could be imagined. The actual hardware and software reality is a bit short in these departments, but computers—even very small computers—that understand the spoken word are already available.

QUESTIONS

2.1. What is the task of an input device?

2.2. Redraw the bit-switch input device in Figure 2-1 to show how the switches would be set for the number 01000001.

2.3. Redraw either Figure 2-2(a) or (b) to handle a 10-key keyboard (with keys numbered 0 through 9.

2.4. What is the purpose of the Schmitt trigger logic in Figure 2-4?

2.5. Could a ROM be used in the place of the diode encoder for the eight-key octal keyboard in Figure 2-2? Would the ROM be used efficiently?

2.6. Why do we prefer active-LOW signals in TTL keyboards?

2.7. What are hardware, software, and firmware?

2.8. Which is faster, a hardware-encoded input device, or a software-encoded input device?

2.9. What is the difference between a smart I/O device and a dumb I/O device?

2.10. Describe the difference between saturation recording and audio (linear) recording.

2.11. Write definitions for the terms "inter-record gap" and "tapemark." What is the difference, if any?

2.12. What is the major reason microcomputer manufacturers use serial audio or saturation (single track) recording instead of multitrack reel-to-reel recording?

2.13. KC standard tape data are recorded at a lower density than multitrack (saturation) recording. (True or False?)

2.14. Magnetic tape is like a one-dimensional recording (on a straight line). To access information, you must travel up and down the line, past all the bits, to find the one you want. You have also heard of 2D (two-dimensional) and 3D (three-dimensional) RAMs and core memory. Which kind is most similar to a magnetic disk pack?

2.15. Which provides faster access to randomly distributed records on a magnetic recording, tape or disk?

2.16. A floppy disk is made of flexible material. (True or False?)

2.17. What would you do to file-protect a cassette tape?

2.18. How many characters are needed to fill a Hollerith punchcard?

2.19. Why are there check brushes in a punchcard reader?

2.20. Describe three reasons why punchcards might jam in a punchcard reader.

2.21. How many bits of data encode a character in 96-column, 80-column, and 90-column cards?

2.22. List one advantage, and one disadvantage, of punched paper tape compared to punchcards.

2.23. What sort of sensors are used to read OCR symbols and UPC code?

2.24. Which of these would be the easiest way to digitize a drawing that's already done, to store it in a computer's memory? (a) Light pen; (b) tablet; (c) joystick; (d) video digitizer; (e) OCR reader.

2.25. Describe how a DMA input device stores numbers in a computer's memory.

2.26. A digital tape recording is played back from the tape into a computer. If it's a monaural tape recorder, the input port connecting the recorder to the computer is probably a: (a) serial I/O port; (b) parallel I/O port.

2.27. Voice-recognition input equipment is a form of: (a) D/A input device; (b) A/D input device.

3

Peripherals: I/O Devices (Output)

In Chapter 1 we discussed output ports. What is done with the digital code once it is latched in the output port is the job of the I/O device. Whether it is a display, a document-generating machine (even one that makes documents for another computer to read), or a controller—that activates some sort of machine on computer command—the output device is the computer's way of talking to the outside world. In this chapter we split output devices into **displays**, which produce some visual effect to indicate the digital state of the output port, and **electromechanical devices**, which use the digital signal to control some sort of motion.

3.1 BINARY READOUTS (LED PANEL)

This is the output-device equivalent of a bit-switch panel. There is one LED lamp attached to each bit output of the output port's latch. Figure 3-1 shows that all there is to this sort of device is a light, a resistor (optional in configuration a), and a connection to the power supply ground (−) or Vcc (+) terminal for each bit of data. The LEDs which are the output device merely make the bits latched in the output port visible. What is displayed is the same information taken from the data bus, without any modification other than being converted from voltage into brightness.

In Figure 3-1(a), the HIGH states of the latch's Q outputs make the anodes of the lamps positive. The cathodes are grounded, so they are more negative than a HIGH anode, and the LEDs attached to HIGH Qs light. LEDs

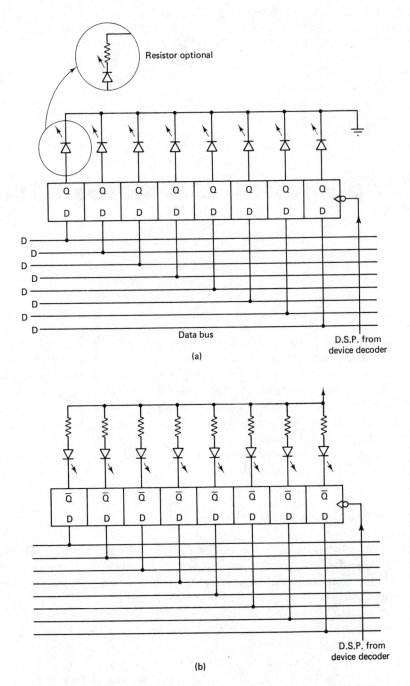

Figure 3-1 (a) active HIGH and (b) active LOW binary output devices

attached to LOW Qs have the same LOW voltage on anode and cathode, and don't light.

In the case of Figure 3-1(b) the $\overline{Q}$ output of each bit is used to drive the LED's cathode, while the anode is attached through a resistor to a voltage that's always HIGH. When a HIGH bit is taken from the data bus, the not-Q output (and the cathode) becomes LOW. This LOW makes the LED light, since its anode is more positive than its cathode. When a LOW bit is taken from the data bus, the not-Q output is HIGH. This HIGH voltage at the LED's cathode is just as HIGH as the anode and the LED's are dark, since the cathode must be at least 2 V less positive than the anode before the LED will light.

The result, either way, is that the binary readout shows a snapshot of what was on the bus at the instant an output operation was done. As with all other output devices, the bit panel continues to show the same data until its output port is strobed again.

This type of display is simple, but it requires the user to read directly the binary code used inside the machine. In Chapter 2 we described smart and dumb peripherals, with the smart peripheral having its own smarts and the dumb peripheral having the smart work done for it by the CPU. The binary LED display, and its input counterpart, the bit-switch panel, have no smarts of their own, but do not depend on the smarts of the CPU either; they must be used by a smart user.

3.2 SEGMENTED DISPLAYS

To display numbers and letters from binary output, rather than lights in ON and OFF states, a smarter output device than the binary LED readout is necessary. This method of displaying numbers and letters (segmented displays) is used in calculators and digital clocks. We've discussed it before, so we'll simply detail two ways these devices can be used.

3.2.1 LED Seven-Segment (Numeric)

Figure 3-2(a) shows a familiar seven-segment display and a **character set** that can be formed by these seven segments for the decimal numbers 0 through 9.

One method of using this display is shown in Figure 3-3, where a decoder is combined with the display to make the actual output device. The combination of a binary-to-seven-segment decoder/driver with the seven-segment readout gives a device that can be operated directly from the binary bus yet display two digits of decimal, provided that BCD numbers are placed on the bus. All current microprocessors include an instruction in their **instruction set** that transforms binary codes into BCD numbers.

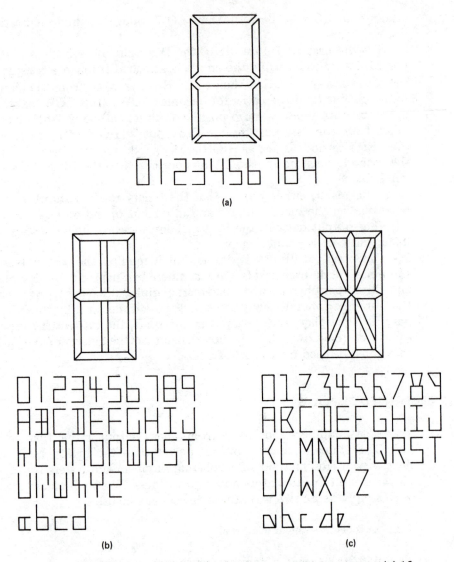

Figure 3-2   Segmented readouts: (a) 7 segments; (b) 9 segments; (c) 16 segments

The other method of using the seven-segment display is to attach its LEDs directly to the bit outputs of the output port latch. Then, special codes are sent on the bus that display in the shapes of the character set. For example, the code 01111111 can be put on the data bus for the number 8. To do this instead of using the normal binary codes, a special program (called a *display driver*) has to be running in the computer when this display is used. The combination of seven-segment readout plus display-driver program works

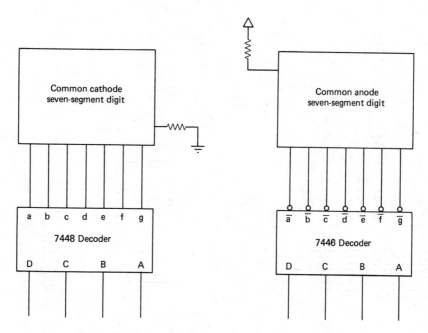

Figure 3-3   Decoder-drivers for segmented readouts

like the combination of the decoder/driver circuit and display. We can say in this case that the software (driver program) replaces the hardware (decoder/driver). The circuit for this "dumb" version of the output device is shown in Figure 3-4, along with a software block-diagram (a **flowchart**) of what the display-driver program has to do.

3.2.2 LED Nine-Segment and 16-Segment (Alphameric)

Figure 3-2(b) and (c) show displays with more segments and more characters in their character set. As more segments are added, the number of types of characters it is possible to make with a segmented display goes up. With nine or more segments, it's possible to define a whole alphabet as well as the numbers of the seven-segment display, and these can be called **alphameric displays** for that reason. There are drivers, both hardware and software, for these types of display. These devices, and their interface to the output port, differ from those in Figures 3-3 and 3-4 only in having more LEDs and more wires.

3.2.3 Dot-Matrix Displays

We said that as more segments are added, the number of different characters that can be formed out of them gets larger and larger. This is true not only

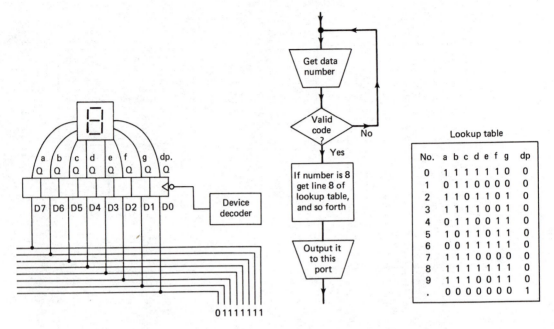

Lookup table

No.	a	b	c	d	e	f	g	dp
0	1	1	1	1	1	1	0	0
1	0	1	1	0	0	0	0	0
2	1	1	0	1	1	0	1	0
3	1	1	1	1	0	0	1	0
4	0	1	1	0	0	1	1	0
5	1	0	1	1	0	1	1	0
6	0	0	1	1	1	1	1	0
7	1	1	1	0	0	0	0	0
8	1	1	1	1	1	1	1	0
9	1	1	1	0	0	1	1	0
.	0	0	0	0	0	0	0	1

Figure 3-4 Software used to replace a decoder-driver

for the absolute number of characters (with 16 segments, over 65,000 combinations of lit and unlit segments are possible), but also for the precision with which familiar shapes can be represented using these segments. For instance, a 2 represented in seven-segment displays looks like a backwards, square S, but with 16 segments, it is a lot more recognizable as a 2. The 5 × 7 **dot-matrix display** in Figure 3-5 makes very recognizable shapes for every alphabetic or numeric symbol, and handles a number of punctuation marks as well. There are a total of 35 LED dots in this display. Although

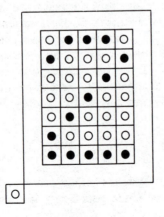

Figure 3-5 A 5 × 7 matrix display

it's possible to produce over 34 billion different patterns with this device, that's not the point. The shapes you want to make—no matter what they are—can probably be found among these 34 billion patterns, and a pretty good fit can be made to any alphameric or punctuation character.

3.3 LCD SEGMENTED DISPLAYS

LCDs (**liquid-crystal displays**) are passive light transmitters or light reflectors that do not emit any energy. Since they do not emit light energy—in fact, they're visible only if illuminated from elsewhere—they don't consume much energy to run. In fact, they consume almost no energy, which is what makes LCDs desirable in applications like digital wristwatches, where the unit must run from small batteries for a year or more.

As regards character set and character formation, the LCD is just like the LED display. The working theory, however, is much different. To understand how LCDs work, you must first understand what polarized light is.

Normal light, such as daylight or electric light, is *unpolarized*. That means that the waves of electromagnetism that make up the light vibrate any way they please, and a beam of **unpolarized light** is made of waves vibrating in all sorts of different directions at once. Now imagine a sort of filter with slots in it that only let through light that vibrates in one direction. Waves vibrating in the other directions don't get through the slots. This is shown in Figure 3-6. The filter is called a *polarizer*, and is actually made from crystals whose molecular lattice structure forms the slots in sizes small enough to be important to a light wave. Once you pass normal light through this filter, you have only the part of it that was *polarized* in the direction the filter was aligned. The **polarized light** can pass through another polarizer only if it is aligned in the same direction. If the polarized light or the second polarizer is rotated, less and less light gets through the second filter (called an *analyzer*) until, when the light waves and the polarizer are exactly crossed, no light at all gets through.

In a digital wristwatch display (reflective type), as shown in cross section by Figure 3-6, the light coming into the top of the picture is polarized by the polarizing filter (the top layer in the diagram). The polarized light is reflected from a mirror layer on the bottom back up and out through the polarizer again, to the outside world. If nothing else happened to the light, it would always get back out because the reflected light is still polarized in line with the polarizer. The space between the polarizer and mirror is filled with a nematic liquid crystal which does nothing to the polarized light passing through it, except when an electric field lines up the molecules of the *LC material* (which is why it's called a liquid crystal). Transparent electrodes placed just under the polarizer can produce an electric field in the LC material when a small voltage is applied to them. Three electrodes are

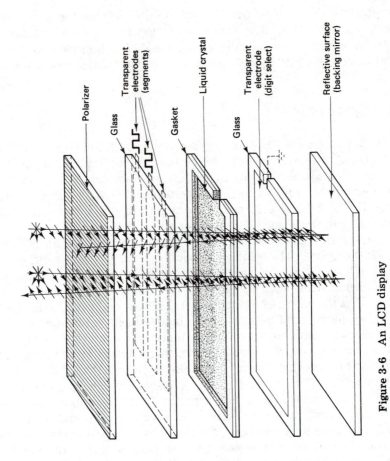

Figure 3-6 An LCD display

Polarizer

Glass

Transparent electrodes (segments)

Gasket

Liquid crystal

Glass

Transparent electrode (digit select)

Reflective surface (backing mirror)

Unpolarized light

Polarizer

Polarized light

shown in the picture, two with voltages, and one without. The electric field rotates the polarized light so that on the bounce it's crossed to the polarizer, and can't get out through the same filter it got in. From the outside, the two electrodes with voltages look dark—because there's no light getting out from those areas—and the electrode without voltage looks transparent—since the light bouncing off the shiny bottom layer can be seen. The whole effect of the charged and uncharged electrodes is to form characters out of dark segments where the voltages are, as compared to the LEDs, which are lighted where the voltages are. The background, with no electrodes, is shiny all the time, because there's no rotation of the polarization angle to block the light.

The seven-segment LCD display is typical of these displays. Its electrodes are shaped just like the LED displays. Unlike LEDs, very little current flows between the electrodes in an LCD, because the LC material is an insulator, something like oil or grease chemically. The electrodes form a capacitor, which consumes virtually no true power, except for a small leakage current. The currents used for LEDs are a few milliamperes per diode, but the current for LCDs is less than a thousandth of that. Of course, this means that battery lifetimes, largely determined by the current LEDs draw in devices like calculators, can be extended (thousands of times!) by using LCD readouts instead. Like capacitors, though, LCDs are slow to react, and the switching of segments is slow enough to drag visibly. Also, the LC materials used in a lot of these applications don't work well at all temperatures. In a wristwatch, where the device is strapped to a human wrist, it's kept warm, and functions OK. When the LC material gets cold, its responses slow down and the constrast between lighted and dark segments changes. Also, you need some source of light to see the LCD by, whereas LEDs are self-illuminated. Finally, LCDs have short life spans compared to LEDs, because their complex organic chemistry tends to break down—but the life span is several years anyway, and is likely to be long enough to match the obsolescence life span of most digital devices. In the next few years, look for LCDs to take over in many of the digital applications where LEDs are presently used.

3.4 GAS DISCHARGE/INCANDESCENT/MECHANICAL DISPLAYS

Displays that are similar to the LED/LCD segmented types but use older technology include fluorescent/gas plasma discharge tubes, incandescent displays, and mechanical or electrochemical displays.

Fluorescent displays are basically electron tubes or vacuum tubes lined with a phosphor that shines when struck by an electron beam or beam of energized secondary particles generated in a rarefied gas. The name "fluorescent" indicates that these are similar in nature to a fluorescent lamp, although the beams of charged particles that excite the phosphor can be steered or switched by electrodes you won't find in your kitchen fluorescent tube. Some pocket calculators use these instead of LED segmented displays. They are blue or green, and usually brighter than LEDs, but they eat up batteries at an even faster rate.

Gas plasma discharge tubes come in a variety of forms, some organized like segmented LED displays and others quite different. One type popular before LEDs came on the market was called a *Nixie* tube. This device was basically a neon glow-lamp with a grid-shaped positive electrode and 10 negative electrodes made of wires in the shape of the decimal numerals. Since a neon lamp's negative electrode glows when a dc voltage is applied to it, the number of your choice could be displayed by connecting its negative electrode to the negative voltage and leaving all the other number electrodes floating. The shaped-wire electrodes wear thin, and 10 of them could be stacked one behind the other in a glass envelope the size of a miniature vacuum tube. Voltage between the positive and negative electrodes was about 80 V. As you can imagine, controlling 80-V displays with 5-V logic devices took quite special integrated circuits, and a separate 80-V supply for the readouts. Being quite complicated to make, Nixies cost several dollars per digit, and being glass vacuum tubes (low-pressure neon, really), they break when they're dropped. LEDs are fairly indestructible in this regard, and cost less, and run from the same 5-V supply as everything else—so they've replaced Nixies for all display applications in present-generation equipment.

If you're servicing older units with funny orange-shaped digits that walk back and forth as they change, we suggest caution when you're testing the live circuits. Circuits that run on a single 5-V supply can't do much to you, but you can catch a nasty tickle from an 80-V Nixie-driver power supply.

Incandescent displays are basically Edison light bulbs with filaments shaped like numbers or segments in a segmented display. The filaments carry currents large enough to get them hot, and they glow. Being less efficient than either LEDs or fluorescent displays, these really eat up batteries. Nobody uses them in pocket calculators, but they're found in cash registers (point-of-sale terminals) and other plug-in applications where low power consumption is not essential. They are bright and easy to read. Since they emit white light, they can be covered by colored filters and be viewed in any color. Incandescent displays are available in a variety of voltages, and being filament devices, they aren't very particular whether the voltage they get is dc, ac, smooth, or noisy.

Fluorescent displays and incandescent displays contain filaments that burn out. The lifetime of a filament device is limited by this factor. The fluorescent devices are additionally limited by charged-particle etching of the phosphor until it is burned away in high-current, high-brightness devices.

Mechanical/electromechanical displays use the bits of the output port (or a decoder) to switch on currents to electromagnets. The electromagnets move displays mechanically (for example, flipping light-colored segments over to their dark side). Interfacing electromagnets and electromechanical devices are described in detail later in the chapter.

3.5 CRT DISPLAYS/VIDEO DISPLAYS

These are what almost everybody calls *TV* or *monitor displays*. There are really two basic types, *raster scan* and *random scan*. Both are called **CRT (cathode ray tube) displays** because they use the picture-tube display device familiar from TV sets and oscilloscopes. Cathode rays are a quaint Victorian term for electrons, the negative charge carriers in all circuits. In a CRT, a focused beam of electrons is formed and aimed at the front of the tube from a section in the back called the *electron gun*. Where the beam strikes the front of the tube, it produces a bright spot because the face of the tube is coated with a phosphor. The beam is deflected or steered to various places on the face of the tube by either electrostatic or magnetic fields (oscilloscopes usually use electrostatic deflection, but televisions invariably use magnetic deflection). Both types of tube and their deflection circuits are shown in Figure 3-7.

3.5.1 Vector-Graphics Display (Random Scan)

Random scan is used by CRTs in oscilloscopes. The electron beam is moved in two dimensions by forces that steer the spot of light so that it traces the outline of a figure on the phosphor. For every two-dimensional shape, there is a combination of two waveforms (one in the X direction and one in the Y direction) that move the electron beam around in the outline of the shape. The figure formed by the beam when it is steered by these two waveforms is called a *Lissajous pattern*. Figure 3-8(a) shows how a Lissajous pattern

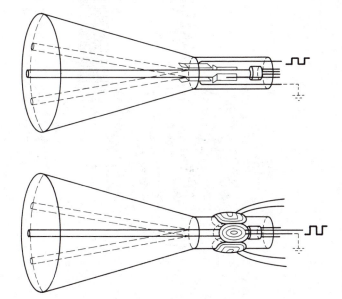

Figure 3-7   Two methods of CRT beam deflection

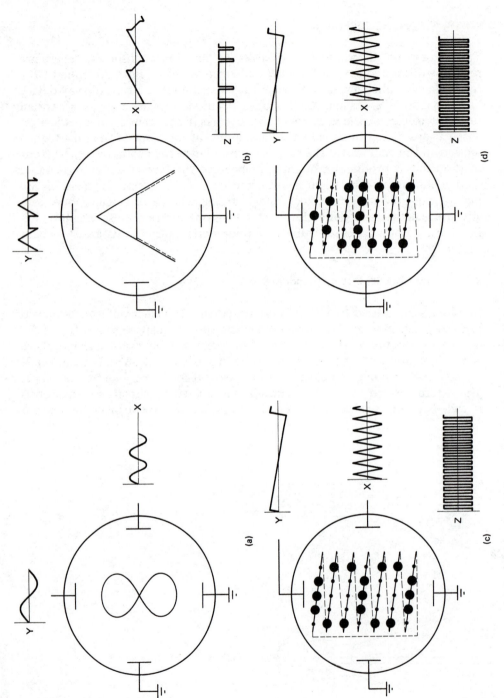

Figure 3-8 Random-scan and raster-scan displays: (a) Random-scan 8; (b) Random-scan A; (c) Raster-scan 8; (d) Raster-scan A

for the number 8 forms the character on the screen. To produce the waveforms, an output port attached to an A/D converter must be fed numbers
very quickly to move the beam in an 8. The 8 must be retraced often enough
in a second to give the impression of a continuous, stable figure 8 on the
screen—about 30 times a second—which is very quickly in human terms, but
no big deal to digital logic circuitry.

   In Figure 3-8(b), the Lissajous pattern for an A is shown. A third
waveform for *spot brightness* (called *Z-axis modulation*) is responsible for
"blanking" the beam (dotted line) while it is traced up to the crossbar of the
A from the lower right-hand corner. A combination of X, Y, and Z-axis modulation signals can form any character, whether it is continuous or made of
segments like a dotted line. Blanking is also used as the beam moves from
one letter to another when it is tracing out a line of letters.

3.5.2 Raster-Graphics Display (Raster Scan)

Raster scan is the method used in television picture generation. It is sometimes called "video" for this reason, although many raster displays are not
standard video at all.

   Figure 3-8(c) and (d) are raster displays of the number 8 and the letter
A. Notice that the figures are all made of dots like a dot-matrix readout.
The X and Y waves are the same for both figures; only the Z-axis modulation
is different. Basically, each character is formed by blanking the beam until
the raster (the pattern scanned by the X and Y waveforms) reaches the right
point on the screen, then turning the beam ON at that instant. The raster
scans every point on the screen, so it's just a matter of time before the scanning action reaches every point in an 8 or an A where a dot should be. The
character set is the same one used in an earlier section for the 5 × 7 LED matrix. Timing generation and synchronization between the raster and the Z-
axis modulation is accomplished by triggering the scanning action of each
line in the raster with a pulse from a counter (called a *horizontal sync pulse*).
A chain of counters (called a *video divider chain*) is responsible for synchro-
nizing just how many dot times appear before a new line is scanned. Each
dot time is a moment at which a bit can be transferred to the Z-axis modulation control to make a *dot* (ON) or *undot* (OFF). The video divider chain
also increases the downward position of each scan line below the last until
a certain count (for TV, 525 lines, but for monitors, it's often 512 or 256
lines) of lines is reached. Then the counter responsible for vertical position
resets and the next scan line appears again at the top of the screen.

   Who transfers each dot or undot to the Z-axis modulator? The answer
varies. It could be the computer's output port feeding serial data directly
from the data bus—but the computer has to run horrendously fast to do this
and have time for anything else. More generally, the character generator is
a ROM programmed with dots addressed by the count in the video divider

chain and an ASCII from a memory device's outputs (the memory is called *video RAM*) or an output port of the computer. The raster display that gets its ASCII codes from a part of the memory (video RAM) is a memory-mapped I/O device, because, to see the characters on the video, one has merely to place them in the video RAM part of the memory. The TRUE I/O approach to video is inconvenient in raster display for the same reason that feeding dots one by one from a serial output port is inconvenient—the CPU just wouldn't have time for anything else, running at microprocessor speeds. Most microprocessors are too slow to keep up with this task at all unless a limited number of characters per line (such as 32) is used. Limiting the number of characters per line reduces the number of dots and thus the frequency of dot transmission.

Random scan and raster scan each have advantages and disadvantages for certain applications. Random-scan graphics permit very high resolution line drawing, but as the number of lines on the screen gets larger, the scan gets slower and slower. Raster-scan graphics uses familiar and inexpensive television technology and is ideally suited to text (lots of letters and numbers on the screen) display, but is not capable of producing the high-precision quality line drawings of random scan. The number of figures on a raster-scan display has no effect on the speed (frame rate) of the display. The hardware used for raster scan—a television circuit with a video divider chain and character-generator ROM—is cheaper than the hardware for a vector graphics (random scan) display—a set of D/A converters and decoders for the X, Y, and Z signals.

3.6 HARDCOPY (PEOPLE-READABLE DOCUMENTS)

Hardcopy is a term that refers to devices that produce some sort of permanent document you can take with you as their output. Two types of documents (hardcopy) are possible; there are documents that can be read by people and documents that can be read by machines. The **people-readable documents** fall into two classes; *printouts*—which are alphameric documents printed on paper—and *graphic plotting*, which is also printed on paper—but is in the form of pictures rather than words. The **machine-readable documents** come in a variety of types we've discussed before. We'll devote a little space to how these documents are written, but not to how they're read (that's in Chapter 2).

3.6.1 Impact Printers

These are the most familiar types of ink-on-paper printing devices. Many of them are available as office typewriters, but when they are used as output devices for computers, they become printers (or sometimes, *lineprinters*).

Some are only used as printers in computer systems—these are found in large data-processing systems. We'll begin with these printers. They handle a high volume of output and are popular peripherals for business data processors.

Formed-character printers.   Formed characters are made by striking the paper with an embossed character (a raised piece of metal in the shape of a character) through an inked ribbon. Each character is written by a separate metal or plastic shape.

Drum printer.   This is one of several types of *speed printers* that print a line at a time, rather than a character at a time, and are appropriately called **lineprinters.**

In Figure 3-9, the working mechanism of the **drum printer** is shown. Part d is the *drum*, a metal cylinder embossed with raised letters. It is rotated by the motor, and as it rotates, a portion of it arranged as a shaft encoder is read by a group of photodetectors, p (each of these has a self-contained light source and photocell for detecting reflected light). The photodetector array provides a position signal that identifies what row of letters is under the *print hammers*, h. In this case, it happens that the letter G is lined up with the hammers.

When a voltage 1 is applied to one of the *print magnets* m, it *energizes*, as shown for magnet 5. The armature of the electromagnet pulls on a *print wire* w, which makes a *hammer* strike the paper. There are two hammers shown in the picture striking the paper. A hammer drives the paper against an inked ribbon, which strikes a letter on the drum as it flies by. In this example, there are two places on the current line where a G is being printed. When the drum has made a complete revolution, the whole character set on the drum has passed by the line, and hammers have been triggered to print every character on the line. The paper can be advanced to the next line by the *tractor* t, which is like a drive sprocket.

The drum printer can print whole lines every time the drum revolves. Maximum speed is a few thousand lines per minute. The limit on how fast this can be done is the speed with which the electromagnet-driven hammers can strike the paper and bounce off the drum. If the drum is moving too fast, the printed characters will smear in the direction of drum rotation. Improper hammer adjustment can also result in lines of print where the letters stagger up and down along the line (vertical misregistration).

If the drum becomes worn, the whole drum must be replaced, rather than just the characters that are worn, because the drum is a solid unit. Cost for drum printers is in the ten-thousand- to hundred-thousand-dollar price range. The standard number of characters printed across a line for printers in the business/data processing area is 132. Drums with 132 characters on a line cost around $3000 to replace. The expense of drum replacement and constant electronic/timing adjustments for hammer firing make the drum

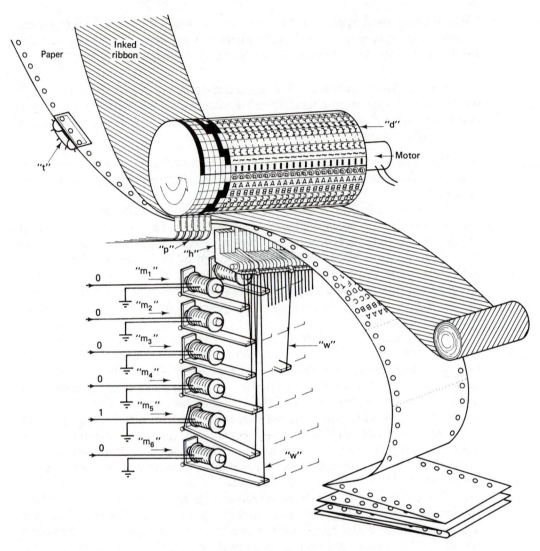

Figure 3-9   Drum printer

less desirable than some other types of speed printers. Over the next few years, drum printers will be gradually replaced by the horizontal moving-font printers describe in the following sections.

The drum printer was used in early printing telegraph mechanisms designed in the 1850s.

Chain (train, band, and belt) printers.   The drum printer discussed in the preceding section had one alphabet of embossed characters for each *print* *position (*each place where a character would print on a line). The characters moved in the direction of paper motion, which made the drum a *vertical moving-font* printer.   Figure 3-10 shows the mechanism of a **chain printer**. It is typical of **horizontal moving-font printers**, which also include *train printers, belt printers,* and *band printers*. All of these types have several full alphabets of embossed characters moving around a track across the line being printed.

In the example (Figure 3-10), a hammer behind the paper at each print position is fired as the character for that print position passes it. Exact timing is needed to hit the character on the fly. The *chain* c carries letters past the *hammers* h, which are fired as magnets m pull on wires w connected to the hammers. A *drum encoder* (shaft encoder) d keeps track of the position of the chain.

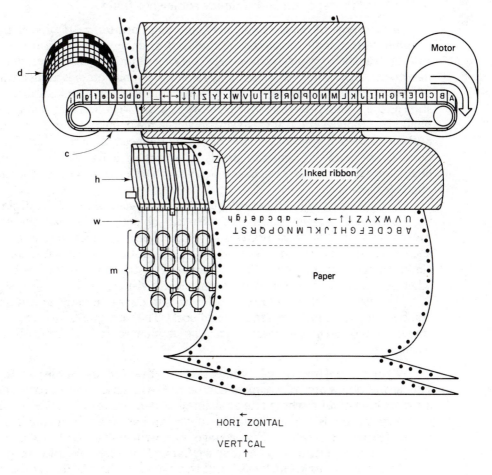

Figure 3-10   Chain printer

Except for the chain itself, this mechanism is identical to the drum printer.

In the chain printer, type slugs carrying one or two letters each are held together (in a chain). Train printers also have type slugs carrying embossed characters, but the characters aren't connected together. The type slugs push each other around a track (like a train). Belt and band printers have a ribbon of embossed characters which are not made of separate type slugs. Since all of these pictures move type past the paper horizontally, they're called horizontal moving-font printers.

Like drum printers, chain printers are speed printers. They print a complete line in the time it takes for a single character set to pass by a print position. The speed of chain printers is in range from a few hundred lines per minute to a few thousand. Belt and band printers tend to be at the low end of the speed range; chain and train are somewhat faster.

Advantages of chain, train, belt, and band printers. If type characters become worn, single slugs can be replaced in chain or train printers, and a belt or band with replaceable petals carrying embossed characters has been designed. This ability to replace single slugs or characters is a big advantage of these printers over the drum. In word-processing applications, for instance, the e and t become worn before the q. With a chain, train, belt, or band, you replace the e instead of the whole mechanism (as you would with a drum). Even if the entire band has to be replaced, as is the case where the band is not made of separate petals, the cost of a band with four or five character sets embossed on it is much less than a drum with 132 complete character sets.

If the timing adjustment of the print hammers is slightly off, the resulting horizontal misregistration is much less objectionable than the vertical misregistration that drum printers develop. Look at the two lines of letters shown at the bottom of Figure 3-10. They both have the same degree of timing error, yet the error in horizontal registration can hardly be seen, whereas the error vertical registration is clearly visible.

The price of chain and train printers is in the same range as drum printers; belt and band printers are lower in cost. The important cost savings with these printers is in the maintenance/adjustment cost, and replacement of worn parts.

Typewriter (traditional type-basket). Invented by Sholes in the late 1860s, the **typewriter** mechanism can be used as a serial printer (one letter at a time rather than a whole line at a time). Solenoids (electromagnets) under each key mechanism would pull down on the key or push on the key from above [Figure 3-11(a)]. The average typewriter keyboard has about 52 keys, including control keys and space bars. Using 52 solenoids to push or pull on the keys sounds awkward, but there are interface units out there that do just that: in fact, we've seen some that just fit over the keyboard of the

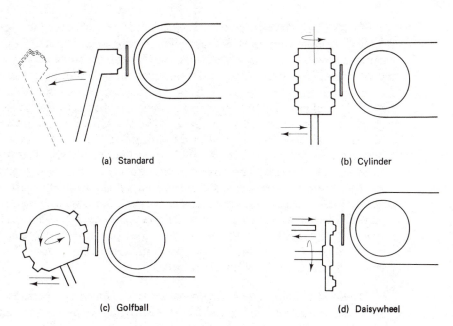

(a) Standard

(b) Cylinder

(c) Golfball

(d) Daisywheel

Figure 3-11   "Typewriter"-type mechanisms

typewriter like a hood. This sort of mechanism is simple, but not particularly fast. Manual typewriters can type about five characters a second without jamming; electric typewriters are slightly faster.

Figure 3-11 shows the mechanisms of the standard typewriter, cylinder, golfball, and daisywheel printers.

Cylinder (teletype).   This is similar to a standard typewriter, but instead of moving the entire carriage, platen, and paper every time another character is struck, the print head moves. The print head of the **cylinder** printer is shown in Figure 3-11(b). It has several rings of characters embossed around it. The head-carrier mechanism lines a particular character up with the ribbon and paper by rotating the print head until the correct column is aligned with the paper, then lifting or dropping the cylinder until the right row is aligned with the paper. Once it has been aligned, the head is driven toward the ribbon and paper, strikes the ribbon, and presses it against the paper, making an impression of the character.

The basic mechanism described here is used in Teletype machines, and is called a Teletype printer by everyone except companies competing with Teletype Corp. It is faster than a manual typewriter, printing about 10 characters per second—still pretty slow by lineprinter standards. The teletype printer is an old work horse that's been around for many decades. The mechanism is noisy but rugged, and used/reconditioned teletypes, costing a few hundred dollars, are very popular with small-computer enthusiasts.

Golfball (IBM selectric). This type of mechanism [shown in Figure 3-11(c)] is called an IBM Selectric by everyone except IBM's competition (sound familiar?). It is a variation on the cylinder (Teletype) printer that permits faster printing. The characters are embossed in rings around a sphere, and are aligned with the paper by a combination of a tilt and a rotate motion. This aligns the proper latitude and longitude on the sphere with the paper, and then the head is driven toward the paper, striking the inked ribbon and then the paper. The combination of tilt and rotate accomplishes the same type of positioning as the rotate and lift of the Teletype without having to lift and drop the entire printhead. This makes the golfball faster than the cylinder, because it's easier to swivel the head than lift it. Golfball printers print up to 15 characters per second, but cost more than Teletypes. There are fewer used or surplus units available, since the Selectric is a more recent development than the Teletype. Over the next few years, as used and surplus Selectric teleprinters become available, prices should come down from a thousand to a few hundred dollars.

Daisywheel/thimble (Diablo/spinterm). In these designs [Figure 3-11(d)] a windmill-shaped wheel (**daisywheel**) carries petals with an embossed character on each petal. A hammer strikes a petal on the fly, driving it against the inked ribbon and paper, to print each character. Timing of the hammer-firing determines which character is printed. As with the chain printer, horizontal misregistration is possible if hammer timing is off, but vertical misregistration cannot happen.

Since only two motions—continuous rotation and hammer firing—are needed to print, the daisywheel is faster than either the golfball or cylinder printer. It prints at speeds up to 60 characters per second.

Daisywheel printers provide the highest speed and print quality available for printers in the under-$10,000 range. They are more expensive than golfball or cylinder printers—over a thousand dollars—but their high speed and inexpensive print element (daisywheels can be replaced at lower cost than golfballs or cylinders) are attractive features. Daisywheel/thimble printers seem to be capturing a large part of the golfball/cylinder market despite their higher initial cost.

Matrix printers: 5 × 7 matrix wire printer. Matrix printers eliminate the need to rotate or swivel the embossed characters on a print head by eliminating the print head. Instead of a separate embossed character for each letter, the **matrix wire printer** uses seven wires driven by electromagnets to print dots by striking an inked ribbon against the paper. As the seven-wire print head is moved across the paper, letters are formed in the same character set used for an LED matrix.

In this design (Figure 3-12), the print head is also its own print hammer. As it moves across the paper, it prints part of a character on each

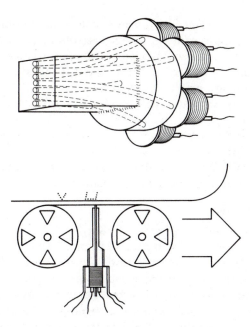

Figure 3-12 Matrix or "needle" printer mechanism

stroke. For a 5 × 7 head, five strokes are used for each character with a sixth "dead" stroke between characters (an "undot"). The limiting factor on speed is how long it takes a wire to strike the ribbon/paper, bounce back, and reposition to be fired again. Top speed is about 200 characters per second. (Florida Data Corp. has one that runs at 900 cps!)

Designs that use overlapping dots can produce dot matrix characters that look almost as good as formed-character print. These use more dots vertically (11 or 13 as opposed to 7 or 9) and more strokes horizontally, so they are slower than 5 × 7 printers, but still faster than daisywheel/thimble machines. As print quality and speed improve, matrix printers may replace formed-character printers. At the present time, fast matrix printers produce characters of such low quality (compared to "letter quality" formed-characters printers) that they are not acceptable for word-processing (office) applications. For data-logging and calculational applications, even low-quality print is good enough, so the 5 × 7 matrix has already replaced formed-character heads in such applications as cash-register-tape printers and printing calculators.

3.6.2 Nonimpact Printers

In the foregoing sections we have discussed printers that have multi-copy capability—that is, they can be used to make carbon copies at the same time the original is being printed. In this section we'll see printers that are faster or cheaper, but do not have multicopy capacity.

Formed-character printers.   The only formed-character nonimpact printer we've seen is the **oscillographic printer,** which uses photosensitized paper to make a copy of an image on an oscilloscope. If the scope is used as a vector display, the characters on the paper are formed, but if raster display is used, the characters on the paper are matrix characters.

A variation on this is a printer that uses a row of LEDs or a moving LED to scan a picture on photosensitive paper.

Photosensitive paper has a tendency to fade with time, especially if it's left out exposed to sunlight.

Both of these are used more as plotters than as printers and do not represent an important fraction of any market as printers.

Matrix printers (Non-impact)

Thermal.   Thermal printers [Figure 3-13(a)] use a print head made of small electric heating elements with a small thermal lag (they heat up and cool down quickly). A head with seven elements can print 5 × 7 dot-matrix characters by moving across a sheet of thermal paper and printing one stroke at a time, like the wire matrix printer. Thermal paper is coated with a chemical that changes from light to dark when it is heated. The printer is inexpensive. It has the same transport mechanism (to move it across the paper) as a wire-matrix printer, but doesn't have the expensive electromagnets in the print head. The paper is more expensive than plain paper, but not outrageously so. The only quibbles we have with thermal printouts are the lack of ability to make carbon copies as the original is being printed, and the thermal paper's tendency to go gray over long periods of time. There is one other problem with thermal paper that makes it "soft" hardcopy. One of our friends discovered this when he left a five-page printout from a thermal printer lying on the radiator for a couple of hours. He came back to find a beautiful thermal photograph of the radiator top, with *some* of his printout still visible in the spaces.

Ink-jet.   Ink-jet printers [Figure 3-13(b)] have no print head at all. A *nozzle* squirts tiny drops of ink at the paper. The drops of ink are charged electrically, then deflected on their way to the paper like the electron beam in a CRT. The dots (actually small splatters) formed as each drop hits the paper are formed into matrix characters. With overlapping dots, the print quality approaches that of formed-character printers.

Since there are no moving parts in an ink-jet printer except the ink, these printers should be faster than anything we've seen so far. Their speed should be limited only by the time it takes the ink to dry. If the ink isn't dry when the paper starts to fold up on the floor, you end up with a Rorschach inkblot instead of a printout.

We can't think of any reason why this type of printer hasn't caught on a lot better than it has. It seems to have great promise, but hasn't made an impact on the market.

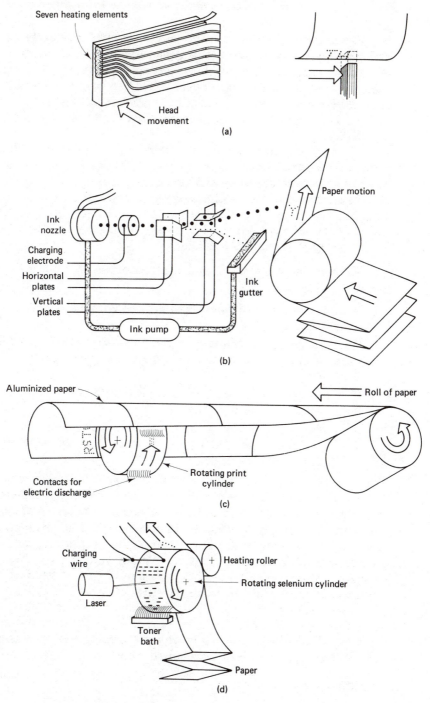

Figure 3-13 Non-impact printing mechanisms: (a) Thermal; (b) Ink jet; (c) Electrostatic; (d) Xerographic

Electrographic printer.   The **electrographic printer** [Figure 3-13(c)] writes on aluminum-coated paper by vaporizing the aluminum covering with an electric current.   Two steel needles trail along the paper making marks whenever current is passed between them.   A group of seven pairs of styli can produce reasonable 5 X 7 matrix characters.   Underneath the aluminum coating, the paper has a black layer, so that the print has a black-on-silver appearance.

Advantages: Although this is a serial matrix printer, we've seen an experimental model cranking out paper at 4000 characters per second.   That's faster than some lineprinters with drums and chains.

Disadvantages: No multiple-copy capability; the paper looks like aluminum foil and crinkles like aluminum foil.   Fingerprints and black creases where the paper has been wrinkled make it unreadable after it has been subjected to a large amount of handling.

Xerographic printer.   This is a xerox copier without a sheet of paper. It works in four steps:

1. A laser beam scans (raster) the image of letters onto a charged selenium drum [Figure 3-13(d)].
2. The charges are dissipated by the photoelectric effect where the laser beam strikes the drum, so that a charge image of the dark spaces on the drum remains.
3. The charged areas on the drum pick up black powder toner, which sticks where the drum is charged.
4. A heated roller transfers the toner to a sheet of paper by melting it from the drum onto the paper.   It soaks into the paper and bonds to the fibers when it cools off.

Since this type of printer prints a whole page at a time from a raster scan, it's faster than any other type of printer.   Like electrostatic copiers in general, this printer is expensive, and not for the microcomputer.   Although it doesn't have carbon-copy capability, this printer is useful in high-volume business applications because it can run off five copies by printing them in the time it takes an impact printer to print one five-ply carbon copy.   This is a modest estimate.   Speeds of 10,000 lines per minute can be handled easily by an electrostatic printer.   Prices are in the range of tens to hundreds of thousands of dollars.   Service calls and repairs/adjustments to machines of this type are quite frequent compared to other printer types.   The main application of this type of printer is in very high volume printing applications, where thousands of pages per hour may be required.

3.6.3 Graphic Plotters; X-Y Drives

We split the world of human-readable documents into two parts, printouts and graphic plotting.   Devices that produce pictorial rather than alphanumeric output are called **plotters**. Some types of printers (especially matrix types) can be used as plotters, but in this case we'll confine our discussion to devices that move a pen around on a sheet of paper.

An **X-Y drive** (Figure 3-14) is the mechanism that moves the pen around on the surface of the paper. It's basically a digital-to-analog (motion) converter whose output is a position specified by a binary number input. There are several methods for using a binary-code number to select a position; the simplest is to use the same kind of feedback we used with the printers to "see" what letter was being printed (Figure 3-14). An input device detects the position of the pen, the computer (or the plotter, if it's a smart plotter) compares it with the desired position, and activates an actuator to

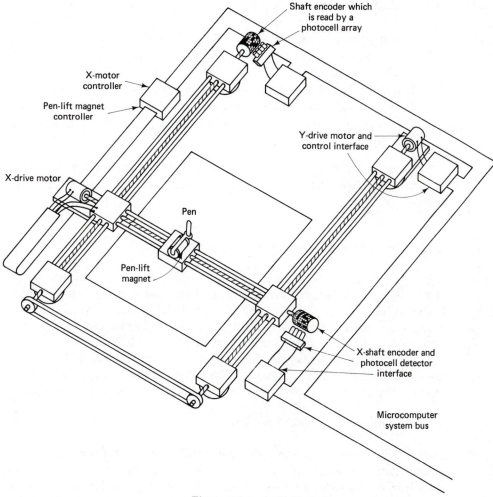

Figure 3-14   An X-Y plotter

move the pen. The pen's moved forward (if it's too far back) backward (if it's too far forward) or stays where it is (if it's already where it belongs).

What's an actuator? Actuator is the word for something that moves things in response to a digital signal. A good candidate for the job is a *stepper motor*, a device that moves in equal-size steps when its controller gets pulses of digital code. Since steppers can be directly controlled digitally, they need no feedback to determine if they are positioned correctly.

DC motors are more inexpensive than steppers, and can move either forward or reverse depending on the (+) or (−) polarity of the voltage. A rotation counter or shaft encoder is needed to feed the pen's position back to the computer so that it can properly control the motor.

The X and Y positioning motors are used by the plotter to draw pictures in the following way:

1. Two numbers (X, Y) are sent to the controller.
2. The controller moves the pen to a position where (X, Y) matches the desired position.
3. The controller lowers the pen point to make a dot on the paper—or it's been drawing a line on the paper all the time.
4. The next numbers (X, Y) are sent to the controller. (The next step is step 2.)

Using the plotter, all pictures are just a list of points described by pairs of binary numbers (X, Y) and joined by lines connected to the last and next point.

3.7 HARDCOPY (MACHINE-READABLE DOCUMENTS)

Some people-readable documents are machine-readable documents (see OCR, Section 2.6) and some people can read the documents intended for machines (if they know Hollerith or BCDIC code). What we mean by "machine-readable" in this section is "documents generated by a machine that are uniquely intended for machine reading." For the most part, we've discussed the documents and their use in the input chapter (2). Details that are discussed here will concern only the output devices that generate the documents; the details of those documents themselves will not be repeated here.

3.7.1 Hollerith/Punched Paper Tape, etc.

Figure 3-15 shows a general-purpose **punch** mechanism for punching holes in cards, tape, or whatever. Its actuator is an electromagnet, as with many of the other output devices we've discussed (the interface for switching on and controlling electromagnets is discussed at the end of this chapter). Unlike

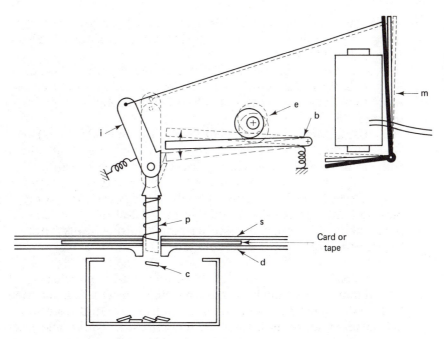

Figure 3-15   Punch mechanism for paper tape or punchcards

some of the other designs we've looked at, this punch derives its power mainly from a motor, and the magnets only control the action; they don't provide the driving force.

The *motor* (not shown) rotates the shaft of the *eccentric roller* e, which makes the *bail* b rock up and down. If the *punch magnet* m is energized, its armature pulls on *punch wire* w, and moves the *interposer* i so that it gets caught by the moving bail and pushed down. The *punch blade* p is attached to the interposer, and is pushed through the *stripper* s into the card, where it punches a hole. The rest of the card is held back by the *die* d as the blade cuts through the card, and the cardboard hole which is called *chad* c falls out the bottom of the die into the *chad bucket*. When the bail rocks back up, the spring withdraws the punch blade from the card, which is held down by the stripper. If the *magnet* de-engerizes, the interposer will return to a position where the bail does not touch it, and no hole will be punched on the next stroke of the bail unless the magnet is energized again.

Since the energy used to punch the cards comes from the motor and not the magnets, small magnets are used which can be interfaced directly with the outputs of an output port. The exact nature of this interface is discussed later in this chapter.

Hollerith cards. For Hollerith cards with 80 columns and 12 rows of punches, two card-punch designs are possible. A punch assembly with 80 punch blades, which completes a card in 12 punch cycles, gives maximum speed, with cards moving through the punch assembly 9-edge (bottom) or 12-edge (top) forward.

A punch assembly with 12 punch blades, which completes a card in 80 punch cycles, is slower but less expensive. It would be used to punch cards traveling through the punch assembly 1-edge (left) or 80-edge (right) forward.

IBM automatic card punches (such as the model 1402) are constructed along the "80-blade, 12-cycle" design. They punch 250 cards per minute, with cards fed into the machine with their 12-edge forward.

IBM keypunches (such as the model 29 and 129) are normally manual machines but can be interfaced as output devices for a computer, have 12 punches, and are constructed along the "12-blade, 80-cycle" design. They punch about 60 cards per minute running automatically, with cards fed into the machine with their 1-edge forward.

96-Column cards.   The IBM 96-column card is punched as three rows of 32 columns of six-punch holes. The punch mechanism for these cards still looks like Figure 3-15, but the punch blade is round instead of rectangular, and smaller than the hole for an 80-column card. The arrangement of punches could be either 18 punch blades operated in 32 punch cycles, or 32 punch blades operated in 18 punch cycles.

Punched paper tape.   The punch mechanism in Figure 3-15 can be used for paper tape. The holes will be round, but larger than those on the 96-column card. Only one arrangement of blades is possible since tape is a continuous form. The five-, seven-, or eight-track tapes require five, seven, or eight punch blades. These could be operated from a single 8-bit output port. A drive sprocket uses the sprocket holes down the middle of unpunched tape to synchronize punch cycles with tape motion.

3.8 MAGNETIC (I/O) STORAGE DEVICES

3.8.1 Tape

Figure 3-16 shows the basic construction of a magnetic r/p head. When it's used to record, current pulses run through the coil, producing a magnetic field in the iron magnet core. At the gap in the core, the magnetic field jumps to the ferrite recording surface—because it's a better conductor of magnetism than the air in the gap. The ferrite is magnetized by the field from the head. Some designs employ an erase head to clear the ferrite of magnetic fields before the record head magnetizes new data onto the surface.

In Chapter 2 we discussed two types of data recording, saturation and

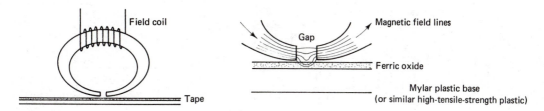

Figure 3-16   Writing on magnetic tape

audio. Although the TRS-80 standard and Kansas City standard methods of cassette recording were described, we said nothing about the multitrack and disk recording schemes (although we did mention that the TRS-80 recording scheme was similar to IBM disk recording).

Reel-to-reel seven-track and nine-track formats. Figure 3-17 shows five schemes used for saturation recording on tape and other magnetic media.

The first [Figure 3-17(a)] is called **RZ (return-to-zero) recording**, because the current in the head has a HIGH direction and a LOW direction, but returns to zero amperes of current (neither a HIGH nor a LOW pulse) between data pulses.

The second [Figure 3-17(b)] is called **RB (return-to-bias) recording**, and has current flowing in either a HIGH or LOW direction during data pulse times, and is in the LOW direction between data pulses. The name derives from the fact that the head is magnetized (it has a bias) at all times.

The third and fourth methods [Figure 3-17(c) and (d)] are called **NRZ (non-return-to-zero)** and **NRZI (modified non-return-to-zero) recording**. There is no space between data pulses. One data level follows immediately after the previous data level. In NRZ recording, current flows through the write head in the HIGH or LOW direction through the entire bit time. In the NRZI method, a toggle in the direction of write-head current during the middle of bit time identifies a 1, while a steady level identifies a 0.

The fifth method [Figure 3-17(e)] is called **phase-encoded recording** (also called the Manchester standard, or "biphase"). If the other methods of recording were level-triggered, this one is edge-triggered logic; a falling edge during the middle of bit time identifies a 1, while a rising edge during the middle of bit time identifies a 0.

Although this section is concerned primarily with output (i.e., how to put the recording onto the tape), we've included waveforms that show how the magnetic field looks on the tape and how the playback head will "see" the field when the tape moves past it. If you've had a course in the branch of mathematics called calculus, or if you've studied differentiator and integrator circuits in an electronics course, you'll recognize that the read-head waveform is a differentiated version of the write-head waveform.

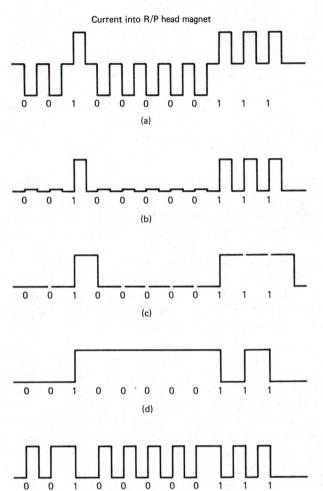

Current into R/P head magnet

0   0   1   0   0   0   0   0   1   1   1

(a)

0   0   1   0   0   0   0   0   1   1   1

(b)

0   0   1   0   0   0   0   0   1   1   1

(c)

0   0   1   0   0   0   0   0   1   1   1

(d)

0   0   1   0   0   0   0   0   1   1   1

(e)

Figure 3-17 Magnetic tape formats: (a) RZ; (b) RB; (c) NRZ (d) NRZI; (e) Manchester Standard or Biphase

Cassette: serial KC standard and TRS-80 tape. Both types of cassette, and most types of floppy disk and rigid disk as well, record on ferrite-coated surfaces with r/p heads the same as the one in Figure 3-16. Details of the recording formats were discussed in Chapter 2.

3.8.2 Disk

Both rigid disk and floppy disk recording methods have been discussed in Chapter 2. Some disk and drum recording schemes involve recording a timing pulse on a separate track alongside data. For the five recording methods

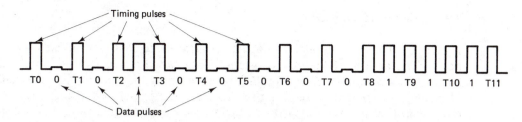

Figure 3-18   TRS-80 tape or IBM disk format

described for tape in the last section, a timing pulse would be essential to determining when bit time was for each new data bit. The self-clocking code used to record TRS-80 cassette tapes (Figure 3-18) simplifies this by putting the timing pulses on the same track with the data, between data pulses. This does, of course, reduce the density with which data can be recorded on the track by half, but simplifies the hardware requirements from a dual-track to a single-track head. For floppy diskette recording, where one-track data recording saves cost on the diskette drive, this same format is used.

3.8.3 Bubble Memory

As an output device, the bubble memory storage records data by distorting the domain structure of a ferromagnetic crystal. A bubble is created when current passing through a loop on the surface of the YIG (yttrium–iron garnet) crystal forms a strong local magnetic field in a direction opposite to the external bias on the crystal. A compact mobile *domain* is formed (a bubble) when current in this *generate loop* is strong enough to saturate the magnetic surface under it. The bubble is a 1. It can be destroyed by pulsing a reversed current through the generate loop as the bubble passes beneath it.

3.9 ELECTROMECHANICAL OUTPUT (CONTROLLERS)

In previous sections of this chapter, we've discussed output devices where the actual interface between the computer's output port and the final document (printers, etc.) was an electromagnet. Using the logic outputs of the latches in an output port to switch on magnets, relays, and motors is termed control, and the circuits that do the switching are termed *controllers*. The mechanisms (usually electromagnetic) that convert the control into actual work are called *actuators*. They produce motion from electricity, and do the work we want them to by producing controlled motion at the command of signals from an output port.

3.9.1 Relays/Electromagnets

Figure 3-19 shows an electromagnet interfaced to one bit of an output port. The action of the electromagnet (also called a *solenoid*) is binary in nature. It's magnetized, and pulling on something, or it's not. In the case of a *relay*, the magnetic field is used to close (or open) switch contacts. It may seem that a switch closed or opened by a digital signal should be solid-state, to eliminate moving parts and reduce switching time. For most purposes, this is true, but if you want to use a +5-V digital signal to switch on a 220-V (ac) motor that uses 10 A of current, the solid-state control gets complicated—especially if you don't want any of that motor's horrendous noise output to get back into the 5-V logic system. With a relay, the switch contacts closed by the magnet can be electrically isolated (not connected in any way) from the logic circuits. Those contacts can then carry any kind of electric energy—whether it's dc, ac, high-frequency RF, or whatever.

Since the relay's contacts are a metallic switch, they can connect things together with very low resistance, but like other switches, they bounce. In most control applications, this doesn't matter. Few loads attached to a relay are affected by bounce.

A more serious problem with all kinds of solenoids is the "back-EMF" problem. When the current in a magnet's coil is switched off, the collapsing field of the magnet generates a voltage that tries to keep the current going.

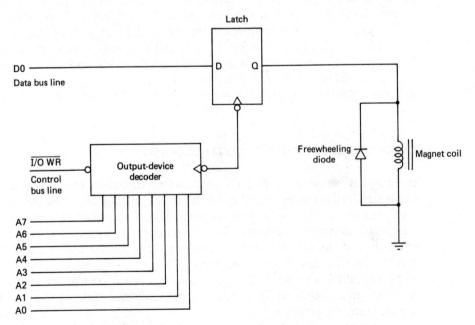

Figure 3-19   An actuator for electromagnets

This voltage is called a *back EMF*, and can be hundreds of times as large as the steady-state voltage on the coil. To protect the driver transistor and logic from these "EMF spikes," a diode called a *freewheeling diode* is added in parallel with the coil. In normal operation, the diode does not conduct, because it has the wrong polarity. When the back EMF develops, its polarity is backwards to the normal operation, and the diode conducts the back current. This clips off the high voltage of the diode and protects the rest of the circuit.

The punch magnets, print magnets, and so forth, that we saw in earlier parts of this chapter are all interfaced like the one in Figure 3-19, at one magnet per bit of output. For a gismo like the 80-column card punch, the 80 magnets would require 10 output ports, or 10 addresses of memory in a memory-mapped system.

3.9.2 SCR/Four-Layer Devices

A family of solid-state devices called thyristors has the control characteristics of a relay without moving parts. The SCR can be used to switch on power to dc devices and the Triac can be used to switch on (and off) AC devices. Although these devices don't provide as much isolation as a relay, they can switch faster, consume less power, and take up less space than relays. Figure 3-20 shows how an SCR and Triac could be switched on and off by a bit from an output port. Like the magnet interface, these four-layer devices are basically binary in nature, and operate off one bit of digital data. The SCR is, unlike the relay, a latching device, and will keep conducting once its gate has received a pulse. To turn off the SCR, the current in the load must be interrupted.

3.9.3 Solid-State Relay (Opto-coupler)

In Figure 3-21 a circuit called an **opto-coupler** provides the link between the digital control signal and the load. One bit of an output port is used to turn an LED on and off. The light from the LED controls the current flow through a *photodetector*, and the photodetector's current switches on a power-handling device like a power transistor or Triac. This type of circuit provides isolation as good as a relay's. It has better speed, doesn't bounce, and doesn't generate back-EMF voltage spikes when the driver shuts off. Its only disadvantage compared to relay control is slightly higher resistance in the circuit used to switch the load.

3.9.4 A Motor Drive with Directional Control

Figure 3-22 shows a circuit that uses SCRs and diodes to control a dc motor. The SCRs are the control devices and the motor is the actuator. The

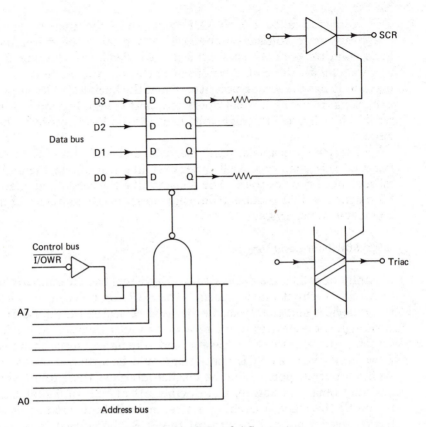

Figure 3-20   DC and AC actuators

final user of the mechanical power is whatever the motor's attached to. Two motors like this could be used to make an X-Y drive, provided that some sensor tells the controlling computer when the actuator has moved everything to the right place.

One bit of the output port is used to switch on an SCR that lets current flow around the circuit in the foward direction. The other SCR permits current in the reverse direction. There is ac voltage available at the transformer secondary, but the SCR permits current in only one direction. When the forward bit of the output port is HIGH, the current passing through the motor will make it rotate in one direction. When the reverse bit is HIGH, the current passing through the motor will make it rotate in the opposite direction. If both forward and reverse bits are LOW, there will be no current either way, and the motor will stand still. If both forward and reverse bits are HIGH, you're trying to do a silly thing—run the motor both ways at once. What actually happens is that an ac current flows in the dc motor, making it vibrate back and forth at 60 Hz. It's doing its level best at trying to go

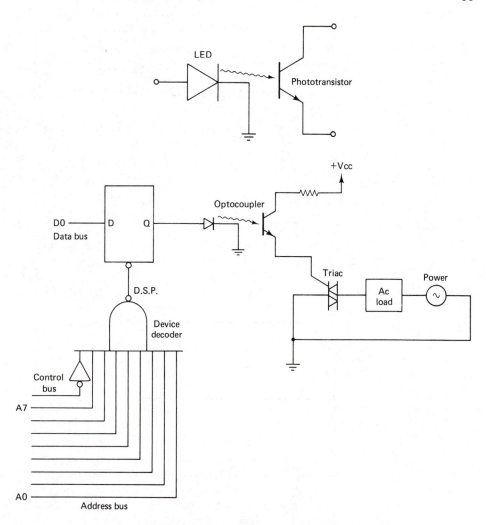

Figure 3-21   Optocouplers for output actuators

both ways. What will happen? Probably the motor will burn out, since the electrical energy is producing heat rather than motion.

All these conditions are shown on the diagram—with the last one (both forward and reverse HIGH) indicated as a constraint.

3.9.5 Computer Numerical Control (Discussion)

Motors controlled like the one in the preceding section are used in industrial settings for things like smart machine tools. Combined with disk or drum

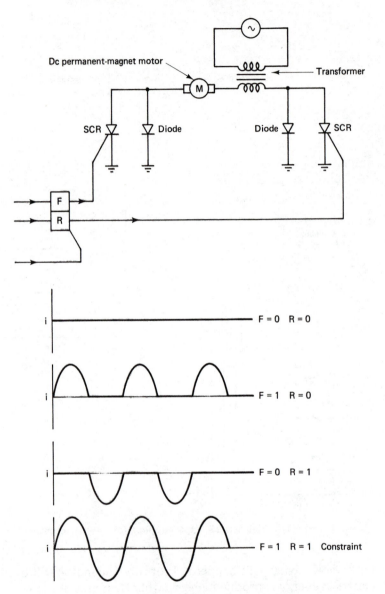

Figure 3-22   An SCR motor controller

encoders, motors like this can be controlled by computer programs to perform automatic drilling, milling, cutting . . . any industrial machining operation.   With enough sensors, actuators, and smart enough programming, the
smart machine tool becomes a robot machinist.   The operation of such machines changes hands from a skilled manual laborer to a skilled computer
programmer.

Such systems are called **numerical control systems,** because the motions of all parts of the mechanism are controlled by numbers from the output ports.   In the overall view of system operation, the system is a digital-to-analog converter that makes binary numbers into mechanical action.

3.9.6 Audio Output

By attaching a speaker [Figure 3-23(a)] to one bit of an output port, the computer can generate sounds of various frequencies ("beeps").   Using a D/A converter [Figure 3-23(b)], waveforms of more complexity can be formed by the computer up to, and including, human speech and music synthesis.   In the future, the computer that "talks back" may become more popular than the computer that "prints back."

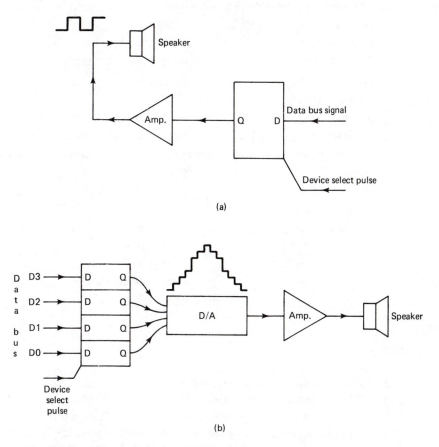

Figure 3-23 Audio output devices: (a) simple tone generator; (b) waveform synthesizer.

3.10 SUMMARY: INPUT AND OUTPUT DEVICES

In the last two chapters, we have divided I/O devices into three main categories:

1. The *human-computer* interface

Input:	Output:
Bit switches	Binary readouts
Keyboards	Segmented/matrix readouts
Light pens	CRT displays
Joysticks	
Tablets	
Audio (microphone)	Audio (speaker)

2. The *document-computer* interface

Input:	Output:
Card readers	Card punches
Papertape readers	Papertape punches
OCR readers	Printers
Video digitizers	Plotters
Magnetic tape (player)	Magnetic tape (recorder)
Magnetic disk (read)	Magnetic disk (write)

3. The *machine-computer* interface (instrumentation and control)

Input:	Output:
Sensors with:	Actuators with:
A/D converters	Controllers
Digital measuring instruments	Lights
	Heaters
Code wheels/shaft encoders	Motors
	Solenoids etc.

QUESTIONS

3.1. What is the task of an output device?

3.2. The $\overline{Q}$ outputs of Figure 3-1(b) drive the LEDs. Why?

3.3. Describe how a software lookup table replaces a 7446.

3.4. As more segments are added to a segmented display, the range of numeric and alphabetic characters it can display is extended. (True or False?)

3.5. What is the main advantage of LCD displays for calculator and wristwatch digital displays?

3.6. Describe how the electric field in a LCD digit darkens and lightens each segment.

3.7. What hazard is present in circuits with Nixie displays that is not generally found in circuits with LED displays?

3.8. Briefly describe each of the numeric/alphanumeric displays (described in Sections 3.1 through 3.4) in terms of brightness, readability, power consumption, life span, and versatility.

3.9. Name the two types of CRT deflection techniques.

3.10. Develop the waveforms for a letter T done with random scan and raster scan CRT displays. Show X, Y, and Z waveforms as in Figure 3-8.

3.11. Describe what a character-generator ROM does.

3.12. Name two different kinds of hardcopy.

3.13. In the following 10 parts, identify whether the type of printer listed is impact or nonimpact, formed character or matrix character, serial printing or parallel printing.
  (a) Drum printer
  (b) Chain printer
  (c) Cylinder printer
  (d) Golfball printer
  (e) Daisywheel printer
  (f) Wire matrix printer
  (g) Thermal printer
  (h) Ink-jet printer
  (i) Laser (xerographic) printer
  (j) Electrographic printer

3.14. Suppose that a graphic plotter is used to draw a giant letter A on a piece of paper. Would its action be more like a raster-scan display or a vector-scan display (random scan)?

3.15. The mechanism in Figure 3-15 derives all its "punch power" from the punch magnet. (True or False?)

3.16. Two different types of Hollerith card punches could be designed, one with 12 punch blades and another with 80 punch blades. What's different about the way each one feeds cards?

3.17. Describe briefly the following magtape recording schemes.
  (a) RZ   **(b)** RB   **(c)** NRZ   **(d)** NRZI
  (e) Manchester standard   **(f)** KC standard

3.18. The IBM disk recording format is used by Tandy for TRS-80 tape recording. (True or False?)

3.19. Define "actuator."

3.20. Why is a "freewheeling diode" used in a relay or electromagnet interfaced to an output port?

3.21. What solid-state switching device could take the place of the electromechanical relay for power switching?

3.22. What type of coupling is preferred between the output port and the actuator, if the load it controls is noisy?

3.23. CNC (computer numerical control) cannot be done as only output devices. Some feedback must be provided through input devices as well. (True or False?)

3.24. Describe how you would make a voice output device for a computer combining the circuit in Figure 3-23 with a ROM and a counter.

4

Introduction to Microprocessors

Even before the first integrated circuits were made, engineers engaged in a sort of wishful thinking that asked the question: "Someday, couldn't we put complicated circuits together in a single piece of semiconductor as nature has "built" the complicated circuits of the brain?" Always in their minds, as more and more complicated circuits were developed on single chips, the engineers imagined the ultimate digital circuit—perhaps the ultimate electronic circuit—being built in a single package as a single device. They were imagining the digital computer—the "thinking machine" of 1950s science fiction—as a single throwaway component like a resistor or a light bulb. Today, that wish is a reality. The **microprocessors**, "computers-on-a-chip," which first appeared in the early 1970s, contain all the essentials of a computer's central processing unit (thus the name "microprocessor").

In the realm of digital electronic circuits, the microprocessor falls into the same position the TV set does in the realm of analog electronics. To the analog electronics engineer, the TV is the one circuit that contains "a little of everything else." In the world of digital systems, the microprocessor is the one circuit that has almost everything digital in it.

Because the microprocessor is programmable, the many circuits inside it can be switched on in any sequence the programmer desires, and the numbers each circuit produces can be passed to another circuit for further processing. Since there's a circuit inside the micro for virtually any digital function, the microprocessor, suitably programmed, can imitate any other digital system—or combination of them— that you want. A clever and knowledgeable programmer can make the microprocessor do anything that another digital system does, replacing boards and boards of hardware (custom wiring between gates) with a microprocessor and suitable software.

In the beginning, microprocessors were CPUs for computers of very limited size. Early microprocessors handled numbers of 4 or 8 bits at a time. Later models have word sizes of 16 bits, and one-chip CPUs with 32-bit word size are envisioned for the near future. (As I write this, Intel and Hewlett-Packard have just announced that they have developed 32-bit processors.)

Most of the currently popular microprocessors are still 8-bit machines (byte machines), and it is to these that we will devote most of this chapter. A wide variety of types and plans exist—but they share certain features in common. We will look first at those features found in all 8-bit micros, and later at what makes each of the three main families unique. At the end of the chapter, we explore 16-bit machines and look at those features that make them similar to, and different from, the 8-bit micros.

4.1 HOW COMPUTERS DECODE INSTRUCTIONS

We'll begin our discussion of microprocessors by seeing how digital computers, in general, do what they do. It's easier to understand new ideas when they relate to something familiar, so we'll begin with an analogy. Let's imagine that we want to use a common pocket calculator to do the automatic computing of a number. Our starting point will be an "el cheapo" pocket calculator with 16 keys [Figure 4-1(a)]. The keypad in our picture permits you to key the 10 decimal digits; a decimal point; the add, subtract, multiply, and divide operations; and an "equals" key. A simple calculator like this is called a "four-function" or "four-banger" because it has only four math operations.

This calculator does only one thing at a time—the thing on the key you are pressing at the moment. To add 8 plus 6, you must perform four keystrokes, 8, +, 6, and =. This is a manual operation—it is not automatic. If, after you have struck the 8, +, and 6 keys, you do not strike the = key, you won't be able to see the answer—14—on its display. Even though 8 + 6 has been calculated, and we're pretty sure that there's a 14 hiding in the calculator, the answer isn't displayed because we haven't struck the =. Actually, we can't even be sure that there's a 14 inside the calculator. Suppose that your key sequence proceeds like this: 8, +, 6, 0. You're actually entering the calculation of 8 + 60 (68), and it won't do to have a 14 popping out at you before you finish keying in the 60. You're not ready for an answer, yet, and besides, the 6 belongs in the tens' place.

It seems that this pocket calculator business is more complicated than we thought. The order in which you strike the keys is as important as the actual keys you strike. If we strike the 8, +, and 6 keys in a different order (+ followed by 8, followed by 6, for instance) we get a different result (86).

In the sequence 8, +, 6, =, we see two different kinds of key strokes—

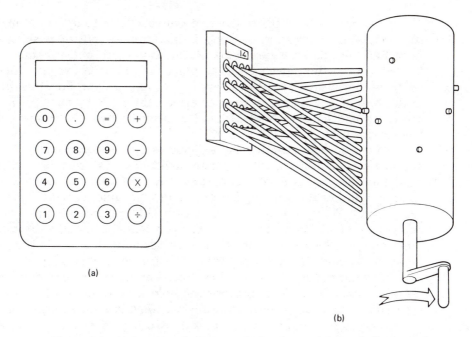

Figure 4-1   Automatic calculation—the hard way: (a) Simple "4-banger" calculator; (b) Program unit

the 8 and 6 are data. These are the numbers that are the victims of our mathematical operation (another name for these data we're operating on is operands). The + and = keys are the operations that will be performed on the data. The + key, we suspect, will send the 8 to the full-adder circuit in the calculator's innards. The = key has a more complex task—letting the calculator know that the second number (6) is finished (it's not part of a 60), and this number should be added to what's already waiting in the adder (the 8). Further, the = key directs the calculator to put the adder's result on the display.

Now, a series of operations that adds 8 to 6 and displays the 14 on a display is hardly worthy of a digital computer. Suppose that we are using our calculator for a more challenging task, such as computing sales tax on items in a store. If the sales tax on merchandise is 6%, every price must be multiplied by 1.06 (the whole value, plus 6% more) to determine the cost after taxes. This can be done on our calculator for any number. First we key in the number; we'll represent this keywork by N, even if the number has a lot of digits and a decimal point. Then we multiply it by 1.06. The whole key operation is N, ×, 1, ., 0, 6, =. That's seven keystrokes even if N is only a one-digit number. Wouldn't it be nice to make this 6% tax calculation an automatic operation? How do we go about doing it?

Since we push on the buttons of our calculator to operate it manually, the first thing that comes to mind is an automatic button-pushing mechanism like the one in Figure 4-1(b). The drum with pins sticking out of it is used in music-box mechanisms to plink the notes. We've just scaled it up to a size that pushes calculator keys. If we forget about how this thing gets in the way of our fingers, we can imagine entering N by hand, then turning the crank and having "N + 6% tax" displayed when it's all over. A great labor-saving device!

This is, in fact, exactly what a digital computer does when it carries out automatic computation. True, there aren't any push rods or a drum with pins, but the idea is what's important. An "automatic" job like 6% tax computation has the same operation, $\times$, and the same second operand, 1.06, every time. The number 1.06 is a constant that doesn't need to be reentered by hand every time, if we can just manage to make the calculator remember it. This is the function of the drum-with-pins. It is a memory device that remembers the sequence of keystrokes mechanically.

It would make a lot more sense to use an integrated circuit memory to do this, wouldn't it? The memory can hold a list of keystrokes in a lot less space than our drum, and retrieve them a lot faster than fingers can move. We can do away with the push rods, too, by using a decoder to close each set of key contacts in the following way.

Suppose that each key on the keyboard has a four-digit binary identification number associated with it, as shown in Figure 4-2. The numbers 0000 through 1001 are the codes for the keys with the decimal numbers 0 through 9. That makes sense, because these are the binary codes for these decimal numbers. The rest of the keys are identified by the remaining 4-bit codes (1010 = +; 1011 = –; 1100 = $\times$; 1101 = $\div$; 1110 = . and 1111 = =). The first 10 codes are data codes and the last six are opcodes (operation codes). Now, we want to push each key when its four-digit code appears at the memory device's outputs. What are we doing when we push a key? The key is just a switch connecting two wires beneath the keyboard. Instead of pushing on the key, we can get the same effect by switching a transistor ON, if the transistor is connected to the same two points as the key. A 4-line-to-16-line decoder can take any 4-bit code from the memory, and switch on a FET transistor wired across the key contacts (Figure 4-2). The 6% tax problem is now a string of opcodes and data codes. For our example, we need six machine codes to operate our "automatic machine" (1100, 0001, 1110, 0000, 0110, 1111).

We now have a *digital computer*. It's still very crude, and has a ridiculously small instruction set (+, –, $\times$, $\div$, ., and =), but it works the same way the "big guys" do. An *instruction decoder* in "real" computers identifies the current opcode or data from the memory and one of its outputs switches on circuit(s) that carry out the operation or transfer the data.

We have a name for the list of instructions to the keyboard (1100,

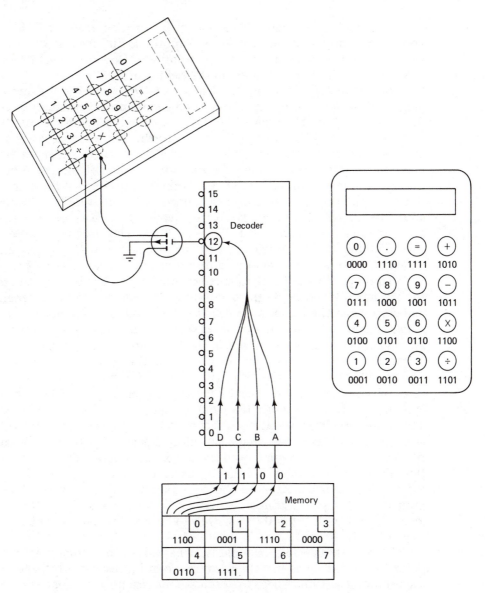

Figure 4-2 Automatic calculation using memory

0001, 1110, 0000, 0110, 1111). We call such a list a **program**. When the list works the way this one does, on a circuit wired to respond directly and uniquely to each code, the codes being used are called **machine codes** and the program is a *machine language program*. **Machine language** is the language the computer is wired for. For any real machine, the machine language it is wired for is the only language it knows.

Our pocket calculator "computer" is wired to recognize 16 machine codes. We know that the decoder is important, but the order in which the codes operate the circuits is equally important. How do we get the memory to send the codes to the decoder in the right order?

In Figure 4-3, our computer has a *counter* attached to the memory device. We assume that the memory already contains the program stored in its memory cells. In the figure, the 1100 is stored in address 0, the 0001 in address 1, the 1110 in address 2, and so forth. The instructions of our program are stored in the same address order as the time order we want the computer to see them. To get the items in the memory to come out in sequence, a binary counter is attached to the address lines of the memory. In our example, this is a very small memory with eight storage locations. The addresses are all 3-bit numbers, so we have a 3-bit binary counter (the **program counter**) that counts 0, 1, 2, 3, 4, 5, 6, 7. This program counter makes the computer do the instructions in our program in the right sequence, by "walking" through the memory addresses one at a time, in increasing order.

To do just one 6% tax calculation, we have to be able to start and stop the program. When we do the computing, we want to run the program once, and stop when the result is displayed (after the =). For this reason, we've added a connection to the output of the decoder that goes on when there's an = (1111) code. Since the = is the last step in most calculations, we've arranged it so that the counter stops counting when an = comes along. The = (1111) code makes the 15 output of the decoder become LOW. A LOW level switches on the FET transistor across the = key on the calculator, but it also disables the clock pulses going to the program counter. The counter then freezes at the last step and won't go any further (which is a good thing, because there aren't any more steps!). To get the computer to run another 6% tax program, we have to get the program back to the instruction in address 0. This is done by using the reset input of the counter. We've added a pushbutton to the counter that will reset it (to 000) when pushed. This reset button is our way of making the computer run the program starting with "step 0" after we've keyed in the data N, which we want to add tax to.

Clumsy though this example is, it has all the important parts of a computer. We'll see items like the program counter, reset control, and clock in the following sections where we discuss some real microprocessors.

4.2 8-BIT MICROPROCESSORS

Since the microprocessor was designed for, and is intended to be, the CPU of a digital computer—all circuits that use microprocessors are really *microcomputers*, even if the label on the package says "football" or "calculator." The architecture of any circuit with a microprocessor in it is the architecture

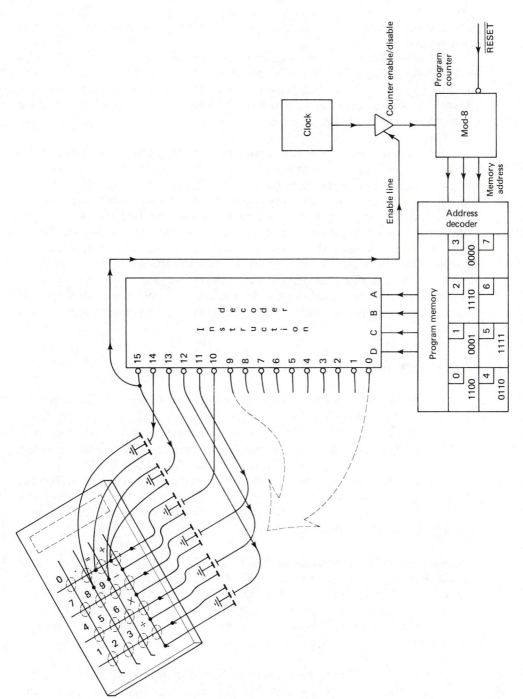

Figure 4-3 Addressing and the program counter

of a microcomputer. We'll begin by looking at what any 8-bit computer must contain.

All microcomputers are bus-oriented (rather than monolithic). This means that, for example, if you're adding an 8 to a 6 the 8 *or* the 6 can be on the bus at one time, but both are not simultaneously brought into the adder. Your computer has to fetch the 8, then store it somewhere, then get the 6, before the adder can be used.

Why is this necessary?

A *monolithic* computer has separate wiring for each of the numbers. A two-address machine, for instance, fetches the 8 and the 6 into the adder at the same time. The monolithic computer also has more circuits, more wiring, costs more, and takes up more space than the bus-oriented computer. It also runs faster, but the other factors make bus-oriented architecture the "only way to go" in one-chip computers. In IC chip design, where the designer is trying to push the greatest number of advanced features into the smallest space (smallest number of gates and interconnects), monolithic design would be nonsense. Bus-organized architecture also cuts down the number of external connections to the IC package, an important consideration where additional pins add cost to packaging. (For 20% more pins, you pay a lot more than 20% more money.)

4.2.1 Bus Organization in 8-Bit Systems

The address and data buses. Three buses are necessary for any microcomputer or minicomputer; these are the address, data, and control buses described in Chapter 1. The name "8-bit computer" comes from the size of the data being handled by the machine—8-bit words—and the data bus has eight wires. These are called D_0, D_1, D_2, D_3, D_4, D_5, D_6, and D_7.

The address bus (of most 8-bit microprocessors) has 16 wires called A_0, $A_1, \ldots, A_{15}$. They permit control of 2^{16} (65,536) locations. In some systems, all 65,536 addresses may be used for memory devices; in others, some of the locations are used for I/O devices.

The control bus: signals found on all micros. The control bus is the most variable part of the microprocessor. Each type of microprocessor has a different mix of signals used to control the parts of the microcomputer outside the CPU (output control signals) and to operate and control the CPU itself (input control signals). Some signals which all microprocessors share in common are:

Input   1) Clock (ϕ)—synchronizes and drives all actions in the synchronous logic of the microcomputer—which is practically all the logic of the microcomputer.

Input	2) Reset—resets all bits in the address contained in the program counter to zero (forces the computer to start running a program that begins with instruction 0).
Input	3) Interrupt request (INT)—asks the CPU to accept commands from a peripheral device and run a special subroutine directed by that peripheral device (details in Chapter 20).
Output	4) Interrupt granted—shows that the CPU has accepted the interrupt request and is used by the requesting peripheral as a "go-ahead" signal for it to proceed with its interrupt.
Input	5) DMA Request—asks the CPU to go "on hold" and float the data, address, and part of the control bus.
Output	6) DMA granted—shows that the CPU has floated the buses, and the DMA controller can take control of the memory. Data can be transferred directly from a peripheral to the memory.
Output	7) Read (RD)—says when CPU is using the data bus for incoming data (picking data up off the bus).
Output	8) Write (WR)—says CPU is using the data bus for outgoing data (placing data on the data bus).
Input	9) Wait—makes CPU freeze data, address, and control signals on the buses to wait for slow memory or peripheral devices.

The control bus: special design concepts.   The control bus of practically every microprocessor has the nine signals listed above. For this chapter we have chosen the Intel 8080, Zilog Z-80, Intel 8085, Motorola 6800, and MOS Technology 6502 as representative 8-bit microprocessors. Additional signals described below are found only on some of these micros, depending on how the designer wants to handle certain important concepts.

Multiplexing.   To limit the number of pins on the microprocessor's IC package, some designers use the same pins for multiple purposes.

The Intel 8080 uses the data bus to output eight control signals called a status byte. The rest of the time, the data bus pins carry instructions and data between the CPU and the memory or I/O systems, but during status time, the data are latched and decoded into control signals. A special signal called the status strobe identifies when it's status byte time on the data bus.

The Intel 8085 has separate pins for all its control signals, but its data bus is also the "low" half of its address bus. When the data on the A/D bus are really address, a signal called *Address Latch Enable* is used to catch the low half of the address in a latch, for later use by the memory.

These are basically things designers do when they run out of pins. Going from a 40-pin package to a 42- or 44-pin package costs a lot. The 40-pin package is so standard that designers will do some pretty extreme things to keep it.

True and Memory-Mapped I/O. Microprocessors in the 8080 family generate signals called I/O Read and I/O Write (input and output) as well as Memory Read and Memory Write signals for normal memory operations. With a 16-bit address bus, this allows the CPU to read and write at 65,536 memory locations, and to input and output from 65,536 I/O devices as well (the Intel machines use only half the address bus, allowing 256 I/O devices, but the Zilog Z-80 can actually address 64K of I/O ports).

Other microprocessors that have only the Read and Write signals cannot tell memory from I/O. There's no way they can use all 65,536 addresses. Some of the memory must be sacrificed to acquire I/O ports. Part of the I/O system must be mapped into memory locations.

Nonmaskable Interrupt (NMI). Interrupts normally break into a running program. If there is a command in the program to disable interrupts, it causes the CPU to ignore an interrupt request. The Disable Interrupts command has masked the INT pin (like masking tape is used to cover up the chrome and glass on a car before a spray-paint job). An NMI is an interrupt demand, not a request. The CPU, regardless of what software it is running, cannot ignore a nonmaskable interrupt. This input is used for some "can't-wait" routine, like one that kicks in the emergency battery pack when the power fails. Details of interrupt action are given in Chapter 6.

Polyphase and Single-Phase Clocks. Some microprocessors require two clock inputs. The phase 1 clock, $\phi(1)$, goes from LOW to HIGH, then LOW again. When the $\phi(1)$ is LOW again, the phase 2 clock, $\phi(2)$, goes HIGH. When $\phi(2)$ goes LOW again $\phi(1)$ can go through its cycle again. This is called a *two-phase, nonoverlapping clock* [Figure 4-4(a)].

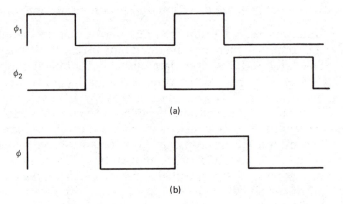

(a)

(b)

Figure 4-4   (a) Two-phase and (b) single-phase clocks

A microprocessor that only requires a single-phase square-wave input for its clock uses a *single-phase* clock [Figure 4-4(b)] .

4.2.2 8-Bit CPUs

Figure 4-5 shows the CPUs of the Intel 8080, Zilog Z-80, Intel 8085, Motorola 6800, and MOS Technology 6502. The 8080 and 8085 have multi-chip CPUs.

The 8080 has a three-chip CPU. In addition to the 8080, two other chips are necessary for complete CPU performance. The 8228 systems controller has two jobs. One is to "catch" the status byte when the STSTB (status strobe) is active and decode the control signals multiplexed onto the data bus. The other job is to buffer and boost the signal power of the data bus signals when authentic data are traveling in and out on the bus. In this function, it is a bidirectional buffer.

The 8080 also requires a clock-generator chip (the 8224) to generate the two-phase nonoverlapping clock it needs. There is also logic in the 8224 for decoding the status strobe signal and boosting the power of one of the of the clock phases.

The 8085 needs a latch to catch the low half of the address bus when the ALE signal is active. No elaborate clock generator is needed. To clock the 8085, a crystal is attached to two pins on the IC, or a single-phase square wave is input to pin 1 (pin 2 is left floating). For full implementation of the address bus, the 8085 is really a two-chip CPU.

The 6800, like the 8080, needs a two-phase, nonoverlapping clock. Unlike the 8080 system's 8224, the Motorola clock generator is simply an oscillator, and does not contain any logic-decoding functions. Although generation of this type of clock signal is a fairly complex function, we'll call the 6800 a one-chip CPU. Clock pulses, like voltage from the power supply, are essential to the operation of the CPU, but the circuits that provide them aren't usually considered a part of the CPU itself.

The Zilog Z-80, hardware-wise, is like the 8080, 8224, and 8228 rolled into one chip. A single-phase square-wave clock is still needed to keep it going. Like the 6800, we don't count the simple square-wave oscillator as a part of the CPU, so the Z-80 qualifies as a single-chip CPU.

The MOS Technology 6502 attempted to go the 8085 one step better, having its two-phase crystal oscillator built in and needing only an external crystal to operate, while functioning without the 8085's multiplexed-bus latches. Unfortunately, the internal clock design lacked reliability in early 6502 models and has been replaced by a model that has an external clock.

All of these devices, with the sole exception of the 8080, operate from a single 5-V power supply, already used for the TTL latches, buffers, or multiplexers normally attached to the buses in full-buffered designs. The 8080, being the earliest, was designed at a time when 12 V was still needed

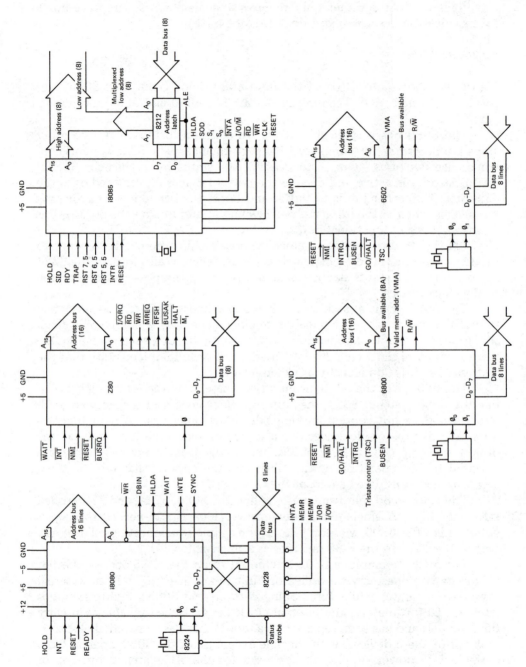

Figure 4-5 Popular 8-bit microprocessors (logic diagrams)

to obtain optimum operation of the MOS gates in its CPU. The 8080 has +5 V, –5 V, +12 V, and ground connections. With 10% of the pins on a 40-pin package tied up in power connections, it's no wonder some of the control bus signals had to be muliplexed onto the data bus.

4.2.3 Working Registers and Their Use

Within every microprocessor there are a limited number of memory locations called **registers**. Some of them are connected with the calculating circuitry in the processor, whereas others are not, but are used to hold numbers while the calculating registers are in use (*scratchpad* registers). There are registers that count addresses for use by the address bus, registers that hold instructions fetched in from the data bus, and registers made of **flags** (which indicate whether the results of arithmetic came out positive, negative, or zero, overflowed the available space, and so on).

Figure 4-6 shows what registers are available in each of the 8-bit processors we described in earlier sections of this chapter. Just because a processor has more registers, it is not automatically better than another processor with fewer registers. The number of registers in a processor is only one measure of how powerful it is—there are many others.

In each processor, the register called the **accumulator** is identified as register A. The accumulator is the one register that participates in all arithmetic operations. Some of the processors have more than one accumulator, but every micro has at least one. In micros with true I/O, the accumulator is also the recipient of all input and the source of all output data. It has a "privileged" relation to the data bus. When memory is read or written, the data are transferred between a memory cell and a register in the CPU. Some processors permit transfer between memory and a large number of registers—others, only one or two—but the accumulator is always one of the registers used for Memory Read and Write operations.

Registers in 8-bit computers are 8 bits in size. Most micros permit grouping of register pairs which are then treated like 16-bit registers—but not all micros allow this. Some 16-bit registers exist—especially for addressing—which can't be used 8-bits at a time. On the illustrations, registers that can be paired are shown as rectangles joined at the edge, single registers are shown as detached rectangles, and 16-bit registers are shown as double-wide rectangles without a line in the middle. Flags, which are really independent one-bit registers, are grouped together in a byte (8-bit register) called the *flag byte* or *CCR*. On the diagrams, the flags in the byte look like a register broken into eight smaller parts.

The *program counter* and *stack pointer* are used to keep track of addresses in two areas of the memory. The program counter contains a memory address which points at the next instruction in the program. The stack

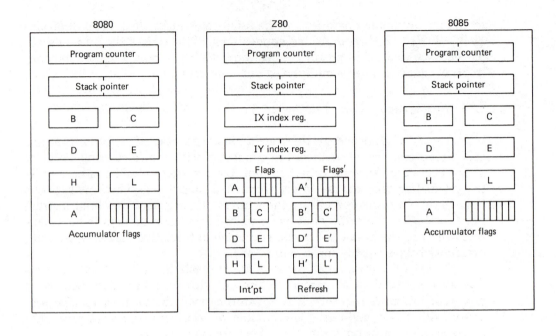

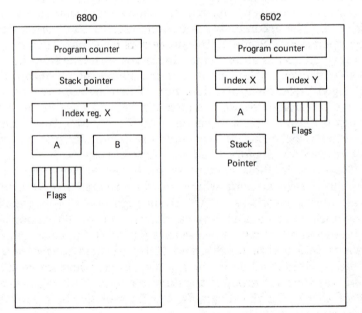

Figure 4-6 Popular 8-bit microprocessors (register architecture)

118

pointer also contains a memory address, which points at a part of memory called the *stack*. This is described in greater detail in Chapter 6.

All registers in microprocessors aren't available from outside to the programmer. Some of them are "for internal consumption only." We aren't including them on the diagrams, because they're of absolutely no use to the microcomputer technician—if you can't do anything about them . . . why worry about them?

4.2.4 The ALU

The **arithmetic-logic unit** (ALU) of a computer is the part that gives it its name. It is the section that computes or calculates with numbers. Most microprocessors have no arithmetic circuits beyond an *adder/subtracter*. The logic part of the ALU includes AND, OR, and NOT circuitry, as well as EXCLUSIVE-OR.

Register A is used by the ALU for all arithmetic operations. A limited number of operations may be done in other registers. In the Motorola 6800, register B is a second accumulator, and duplicates all the functions of A, while the 8080, Z-80, 8085, and 6502 have only one accumulator that performs all arithmetic and logic functions.

The *flag byte* contains independent 1-bit registers which show the state of numbers after the ALU has worked on them. In the 8-bit processors we've described, all five have a plus/minus *sign* flag, a *zero* flag (that tells if the result is all 0s in A), a *half carry* flag (used only for BCD arithmetic), and a *carry* flag (which acts as a sort of ninth bit on the accumulator when numbers get too big for 8 bits). (You may recall from Chapter 7 that the carry output of a multibit adder/subtracter is also its borrow bit when it's subtracting.) An odd-even parity flag is provided on the 8080/Z-80/8085, but not the 6800. The 6800 has an *overflow* flag, that tells if the number is in true positive or two's-complement negative form. In the 6502, a separate BCD mode of operation can be invoked by setting the *BCD/binary* flag—not found in any of the other processors.

All five processors contain, as part of their ALU, a "10-or-bigger" detector and "fudge factor" adder that convert binary to BCD when that conversion is desired. Binary-to-BCD conversion is not specifically used in the 6502, since it can operate in an all-BCD mode (if you skipped to this section without reading Appendix A, or if you've forgotten the details of BCD arithmetic, this is a good time to go back).

A limited amount of 16-bit arithmetic may be done within the register pairs of the 8080/Z-80/8085 family (addition and subtraction in the Z-80; addition only in the 8080).

For the technician, the ALU and registers of the CPU are a "black box." If everything doesn't work, there's not a thing you can do to replace just a piece of the CPU; the whole part has to be replaced with a new one.

That's the whole point to telling you what's inside the CPU. If you know it's one of the things locked inside the box, you know that there's nothing further to do but replace the box.

If, for instance, you find that something's wrong with register A, or that the ALU doesn't do a certain piece of arithmetic properly, but everything else works, you need to know that these parts are "locked in the box." and the only thing to do is replace the whole CPU (no matter how much of the rest of it stills works). On the other hand, if you see a problem involving an address or data, such as writing to memory, the problem can be inside or outside the box and exploring the buses first (looking for shorts and opens) is a good place to start.

4.3 16-BIT MICROPROCESSORS

The main difference between 8- and 16-bit micros is the word size of the data they handle. Of course, a 16-bit microprocessor handles 16-bit words of data, and has 16-bit arithmetic for all operations instead of just a few.

Our target processors are the Zilog Z-8000, Intel 8086, and Motorola 68000. Figure 4-7 shows the package layout of these three processors.

4.3.1 Zilog Z-8000

The Zilog Z-8000 processor is available in two packages called the 8001 and 8002.

The 8001 is a maximum system chip which can control more memory and has expanded capabilities compared to the 8002. It also has a 48-pin package.

The 8002 is a simplified, 40-pin version of the 8001. We will concentrate on it here, because it has all the essential features of a 16-bit machine.

The 8002 multiplexes its data bus and address bus on the same 16 pins (called A/D in the figure). Control signals AS and DS (Address Strobe and Data Strobe) identify whether the numbers on this bus are address or data bits.

Special signals called Mo and Mi are provided to permit the Z-8000's use in a network of processors. *Networking* or *multiprocessing* is an important concept (also called *distributed processing*) that lets a bunch of independent CPUs share a resource, such as a printer. The Mo and Mi are signals that allow the designer of such a network to daisy-chain the processors together so that they share the resource evenly, and take turns using it.

Three interrupts, VI (vectored interrupt), NVI (non-vectored interrupt), and NMI (non-maskable interrupt) are available on the Z-8000 (more than on a Z-80, but not as many as an 8085).

A S/N control signal identifies whether the processor is in system or

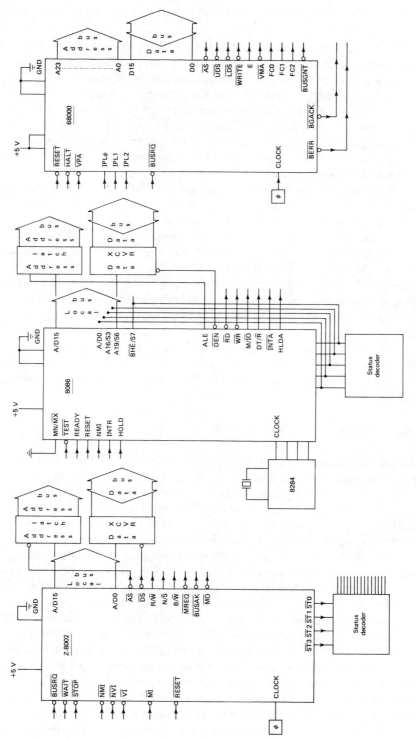

Figure 4-7 Some 16-bit microprocessors

121

normal mode. In the system mode the CPU can do special privileged instructions that it can't do in normal mode. If this sounds obscure, consider that you, as a technician, will probably not have to worry about it.

You will seek in vain for interrupt granted, I/O, or memory strobe signals. These and other conditions are encoded in a group of 4 bits called ST (*status*) signals. They can be decoded to identify any one of 16 conditions. The conditions chosen are mutually exclusive (only one of them at a time is ever active), so the designers decided that four pins (decoded externally) were more economical than 16.

The rest of the control signals on the Z-8000 are the standard ones you would expect on any microprocessor (see Section 4.3.1). It has a single-phase clock and a single 5-V power supply.

From the standpoint of external circuitry, the Z-8000 is fairly similar to 8-bit micros we've seen. It can handle a memory of 65,536 addresses through its bus (a 48-pin package called the 8001 can handle more). Although there's a 16-bit data bus, each byte (8-bits) of memory is separately addressable; thus 65,536 bytes of memory exist in a segment. The 8001 can have up to 128 segments of 65,536 bytes, while the 8002 stays within one segment.

The Z-8000 has a two-chip CPU, even in the minimum system (the 8002), because an address latch is needed to handle the multiplexed A/D bus. The maximum system (an 8001) needs a special memory-management chip as well.

4.3.2 Intel 8086

The Intel 8086 has features similar to the Z-8000. Like the Z-8000, it comes in a maximum version and a minimum version, with the minimum one requiring far simpler support hardware. Unlike the Z-8000, both versions are available in the one chip, selectable by wiring an input (MAX/MIN) to a HIGH or LOW logic state. In keeping with the Z-8000 description above, the 8086 description that follows is for the simple system.

The 8086's 16-bit data bus is multiplexed onto the same pins as the address bus. Two signals, ALE (Address Latch Enable) and DEN (Data ENable), identify what's on the A/D bus (they correspond to the Z-8000 signals AS and DS). An additional five address-expansion signals are provided for maximum system memory of 1,048,576, while minimum system operation uses only 15 bits of address for 32,768 addresses. These four address bits are also multiplexed as status bits, used like the Z-8000 ST signals.

Like the Z-8000, the 8086 addresses memory one byte at a time, but can address either the low, high, or both halves of the data bus, through a combination of the address-bus bits and a signal called BHE (Bus High Enable). BHE is multiplexed with a fifth status bit. The rest of the control signals are the same ones found on 8-bit microprocessors, although a special wait request input exists (called TEST), that can be software enabled and disabled.

Like the 8080, the 8086 requires a special clock chip (the 8284), and like the 8085, it needs a latch for the address. The maximum mode of operation requires additional decoding and buffers, but at a minimum, the 8086 is a processor with a three-chip CPU.

4.3.3 Motorola 68000

The Motorola 68000 is an upward enhancement of the 6800/6809 family of 8-bit processors. This 16-bit processor has a 24-bit address bus and 16-bit data bus, but unlike the '80 family, these two buses are not multiplexed on the same pins. This makes the 68000 a real centipede (it's in a-64 pin package). With a 24-bit program counter, the 68000 can address 16M bytes of memory. Like the other machines, this memory is byte addressable, and can be controlled 8 bits at a time rather than in 16-bit words only.

The control signals on the 68000 are pretty standard 6800-series stuff. One "exotic" feature of the 68000 is its ability to pull a software interrupt when certain illegal operations (called *bus errors*) are done. If, for instance, a word operation, which is supposed to take place at an even address (because words start at even addresses) is done at an odd address instead—that's a bus error. The 68000 will pull a *software interrupt* to an *interrupt service routine* (we'll see what that is later) when one of these errors occurs. The 6800 had software-interrupt capability, but the 68000 is vastly more powerful.

The 68000 has a number of long word operations, that use 32-bit words—much like the 8080 and Z80 have limited 16-bit operations although they are 8-bit machines.

If you have an understanding of the operation of 8-bit machines and their hardware, the 16-bit machines are just more complicated—not different. Troubleshooting 16-bit systems will be just like troubleshooting 8-bit systems, except everything's bigger (This reminds me of Tom Lehrer's statement that octal is just like decimal—if you're missing two fingers!)

QUESTIONS

4.1. Write a program for the calculator in Figure 4-2 that will calculate 10% sales-tax. Show all the machine codes in a memory like the one at the bottom of the figure.

4.2. Where is the data bus in Figure 4.3?

4.3. Describe briefly the difference between bus-oriented and monolithic computer design. Use anecdotes or examples to aid you in your description.

4.4. How many memory addresses can a microprocessor with a 24-wire address bus control?

4.5. Describe how Intel uses multiplexing to reduce the number of control bus pins on its 8080 microprocessor.

4.6. What's a polyphase clock?

4.7. Identify which of the microprocessors below have a one-chip, two-chip, or three-chip CPU.
(a) Intel 8080   (b) Zilog Z-80   (c) Motorola 6800   (d) Mos Technology 6502
(e) Intel 8085

4.8. Of the five 8-bit microprocessors discussed in this chapter, which has the largest number of registers?

4.9. Of the five 8-bit microprocessors discussed in this chapter, which has the largest number of addressing modes?

4.10. Part of the functions of a microprocessor's ALU do not work properly. What do you, as a technician, replace?

4.11. Every program run on a microprocessor "messes up" when the program counter reaches address 16 in the memory. Would you replace the CPU? If that didn't work, what would you replace?

4.12. The Motorola 68000 has 64 pins. What's the advantage of using a design like this that doesn't multiplex address and data (or address and control) onto the same pins?

5

Machine Language Programming for the 8080 and Z-80

The **machine language** of a computer was described in general terms in our calculator example in Chapter 4. We found out that opcodes and data were used—like keystrokes on the keyboard of a calculator—to activate circuits within the CPU. You may have heard the names of high-level languages like FORTRAN and COBOL and wondered how many languages a microprocessor, like an 8080 or Z-80, really knows. The answer may surprise you. Any computer you see knows just one language—its own machine code—and all the other languages are translators that "cook down" FORTRAN or COBOL (or whatever) into the machine's own machine code. If the system breaks down, all those other languages will be gone, and there will be only one language in which you can talk to the machine, really—the stuff that's wired into the machine.

We hope that this chapter can answer the question: What is a "typical" microprocessor like (in terms of the commands it is wired to do)?

As of this writing, the majority of microprocessors being used are still 8-bit machines. We chose the Z-80 as a model, because it has the best features of most 8-bit microprocessors.

In some places, a command for the Z-80 will have a different mnemonic on the 6800, 6502, or 8080. Too bad that they can't all agree on what to call a *move* command.

We're not going to attempt to describe the alternate mnemonics and commands of every processor, but we will use Z-80 and 8080 mnemonics side by side, and most manufacturers use either Intel's or Zilog's name for a mnemonic.

The Z-80 has more registers than any other 8-bit processor in this group. It also has at least as many addressing modes as any of the others. Seeing how programs are written for the Z-80 should provide good background for learning (and using) the language of any 8-bit processor, and a good headstart for learning 16-bit machine programming.

5.1 WHY A TECHNICIAN SHOULD KNOW ABOUT PROGRAMMING

Recently, we tested 61,440 flip-flops in packages of 1024 each. It took us about half an hour. How long would it take a technician with a breadboard, a meter, an oscilloscope, and a logic probe to test the same 60K flip-flops? Odds are, the poor soul would die of boredom or old age (or both!) before the job got done. This is a job for a computer!

Computers have an infinite capacity for boredom. The more boring, tedious, and repetitive a job is, the better a computer does it. In fact, repetition and sameness are the things computers do best. Consider testing RAM integrated circuits. You'd have gone nuts if you tried to test 60 (1K X 1) RAM chips by hand. Not only would it take too long to be worth it, by the time you got even one chip tested, you'd be so thoroughly bored that you'd be getting really sloppy about the last half of the testing.

Also, computers can do the boring, repetitive stuff faster than any human being can—or would want to. Our test takes less than a minute to set up, run, and interpret, and most of that's the human time delay. The computer program tests all 1024 locations on the chip in a fraction of a second.

We have no intention of attempting to teach you the complete art of programming in this book. Our purpose is to explain what operations a typical microprocessor can do on its own, and show how some of these can be put together to solve some small digital design problems. We expect that after reading the next few chapters, you should be able to pick up a manufacturer's documentation of any microprocessor and understand enough of it to pick up the details you need to read and understand a specific program.

There are two reasons why this is necessary. The first has to do with the "my computer doesn't work—fix it" problem. If the "doesn't work" is hardware, you can fix it with chips, wires, and so on—but if the problem is bad software, the computer itself isn't really broken. It is necessary for the technician to know the difference. Few technical experts can "debug" both hardware and software, but you need to know something about both to know if it is the computer or the program that needs fixing.

The technician who comes to fix a "sick" computer will often be equipped with a set of diagnostic programs in a package. If these programs work, then the hardware is OK. Occasionally, the technician will have to make up the software test procedure on the spot to look at a specific problem. Knowing how to use the machine's instruction set for this purpose is as important as knowing how to operate a hardware test instrument like a scope or meter.

The second reason concerns digital design. The engineer of the future will not design a unique random-logic board for each digital application. Instead, the design will use a standard microprocessor development board programmed to do the tasks of the random logic it replaces. This means that the technician who services the units will often see the same board doing vastly different tasks. You, as the technician, will have to know—or have some understanding of—the way the engineer used the program to solve each design problem, in order to troubleshoot the board.

It seems likely that the technician's job in the future will polarize into two categories. There will be the techs who mash the keys and watch the lights on a high-technology tester, and throw the boards into two piles—good and bad. And then there will be the techs who program that same high-technology tester with the test procedures for each model of the board being tested. The first group of techs will be doing "chimp work" and getting paid accordingly. All the "smarts" will be in the board tester. If you want to be in the second group of technicians, *be patient*. You'll have to put up with what's in this chapter, which is pretty dry, to get to the real technician stuff (troubleshooting with machine language programs) in the next chapter.

5.2 THE DATA TRANSFER GROUP OF INSTRUCTIONS

The simplest and most typical operation you can do within a computer system is to transfer data from one place to another and make copies of them. Inside the CPU, there is a local data bus that is connected to all the registers in the CPU. Each register is an 8-bit latch whose outputs and inputs are attached to this bus. The data on the bus can be clocked into the inputs or enabled onto the bus from the outputs. Suppose that you want to transfer a number from register A to register B. The outputs of register A are enabled to the bus and register B is clocked. This makes a clone of register A's contents in register B. Nothing happens to the contents of register A. The same is true for all transfers from anyplace in a computer to anyplace else. The closest analogy we can think of is copying a tape cassette. The "source" cassette is played back on one cassette deck; its output is recorded on another cassette deck onto a "destination" cassette. If there is already something recorded on this destination cassette, it is overwritten and replaced by the copy of the source cassette's contents.

5.2.1 Register to Register

In the 8080, there are eight 8-bit registers, called B, C, D, E, H, L, M, and A, that can be addressed. Data can be transferred from any one register to any of the others. The Z-80 has these eight registers, and eight more called the *primed registers* (B′, C′, D′, E′, H′, L′, M′, and A′). A single command in Z-80 code permits swapping the primed register set with the others, and the commands that transfer data between them are the same as the 8080 commands.

The Intel name for the instructions that transfer data from one register to another is MOV. The Zilog name for instructions that transfer data between anywhere and a register is LD (LoaD). An example would be:

(Intel) MOV B,A   (Zilog) LD B,A

It might look like this says, "Move B to A" but the MOV described here actually moves "A" to "B"! Why Intel chose to do it this way is a mystery somehow connected with an earlier 8-bit chip, we're told. Zilog chose to keep the destination before the source, but changed their mnemonic to read, "Load B with A". We load B with the contents of A when we do this LD.

The actual binary code for a MOV or LD instruction has 8 bits. Each register can be identified by a 3-bit identification number since there are eight 3-bit numbers and eight registers. The actual opcode for one of these MOV instructions contains a register code for the destination register, a register code for the source register, and two more bits. If these bits are 01, that identifies the instruction as a MOV.

The identification number for each register can be represented with an octal digit (0, 1, 2, 3, 4, 5, 6, 7). The octal system of numbering is a natural code to use for representing Intel and Zilog mnemonics, since each octal digit actually means something. In this system, B = 0, C = 1, D = 2, E = 3, H = 4, and L = 5.

In this case, the MOV A,B becomes 170 in octal (01,111,000 in binary). The 1 says that this is a MOV instruction, the 7 is the A, and the 0 is the B. The general form of the MOV instruction is 1 D S, where D is the number of the destination register and S is the number of the source register.

Register M is a special case. It appears to be another register, and in Intel code it is handled just like the other seven registers in the CPU. There is actually no register M in the CPU. It's a location in the external memory (hence the name M). Zilog doesn't even use the name M; they identify it as a memory location.

5.2.2 Register to/from Memory

The same instruction that transfers data from register to register within the 8080 can also transfer information from the registers (B, C, D, E, H, L, A) to a memory (M) location—provided that the address of the memory location is already in registers H and L. Since an address in the 8080/Z80 memory is 16 bits long, only half an address can fit in one register. The top half (most sig-

nificant 8 bits) or the address we want to use is held in the 8-bit register H
(the HIGH byte). The bottom half of the address is held in register L (the
LOW byte). Together, H and L hold the entire 16-bit address of memory
location M. Any 8080 instruction that comes along with an M in it will end
up using HL to find where M is.

Zilog uses the *infix notation* representation of the M register—(HL)—
when they represent their register-memory MOV instruction. We'll see how
infix represents numbers, registers, and addresses in a little while, but you'll
get some idea of how it works from Zilog's mnemonic in this example:

$$\text{(Intel) MOV A, M} \qquad \text{(Zilog) LD A, (HL)}$$

Suppose that you want to move the contents of the memory location at
address 5000 (decimal) to register A. The instruction you need is the one
above, but you must first prepare the memory pointer (register H and L) by
putting the number 5000 in it. This is done by finding the binary value of
5000 (Table 19-1). (If you haven't done this for a while, here's a good
chance to practice decimal-to-binary conversion.) We see that the binary
code for 5000 is 1001110001000, a 13-bit number. This is too large for one
byte. We expected that, and planned to put half the address in register H
and the other half in register L. First we'll pad our number out to 16 bits:
0001001110001000. The HIGH byte of this word is 00010011, and its
LOW byte is 10001000.

Before we can use the MOV A, M instruction, we need to load 00010011
(which is a decimal 19) into H and 10001000 (which is a decimal 136) into
L. We don't know how to do that yet.

TABLE 5-1 DECIMAL TO BINARY
CONVERSION

Numbers	Odd/even	Place value
1	1	4096
2	0	2048
4	0	1024
9	1	512
19	1	256
39	1	128
78	0	64
156	0	32
312	0	16
625	1	8
1250	0	4
2500	0	2
5000	0	1

5.2.3 Constant to/from Register

The Intel MOV commands (Zilog LD commands) can move a number from one register to another like this:

Mnemonic		Result
(Intel) MOV H, B	(Zilog) LD H, B	H←B

We would like to have a command that can move a 19 directly into H and a 136 into L without getting the numbers from another register. There is such an instruction for the 8080 and Z-80; to load a 19 into H, for example, the mnemonics are:

Mnemonic		Result
(Intel) MVI H, 19	(Zilog) LD H, 19	H←19

Since these instructions load H with a number that's *immediately* available (it's right in the code for the instruction itself!) they're called MoVe Immediate (MVI) instructions by the Intel people. Zilog just calls them LoaD (LD) like all other data-transfer instructions.

The difference between these load instructions and the ones in Section 5.1.1 is that B is a variable and 19 is a constant. With the instruction MOV H, B, the number put into H can vary. If the computer executes this instruction a number of times in a program, the value in B can be different every time, depending on the history of what has just happened to B (since it can vary, it's a variable).

The number 19 cannot change (it is constant). It will always be put into H when a MVI H, 19 instruction is done. The computer may execute this same instruction at different times in a program, and H will have a value of 19 afterward every time.

So, to summarize, instructions with the immediate addressing mode use a constant (which is usually found right in the body of the instruction itself). Instructions that use only register addressing use variable quantities whose value cannot be guessed just by looking at the instruction.

Now, in case you forgot, we needed the immediate instructions because we wanted to put the contents of memory location 5000 in register A using a MOV A, M instruction. The 5000 must be put into registers H and L as page 19 and line 136 (decimal) of memory. In the HL register pair (the memory pointer), these two numbers will address memory location 5000 as M whenever an 8080 instruction containing an M, or a Z-80 instruction containing (HL), is executed. Using the following program segment, we can get the number in memory location 5000 into the CPU's register A:

Mnemonic		Result
(Intel)	(Zilog)	
MVI H, 19	LD H, 19	H←—19
MVI L, 136	LD L, 136	L←—136

(the number 5000 is now in register pair HL)

MOV A, M	LD A, (HL)	A←—(5000)

where the infix notation A←—(5000) says: "Put the number found in memory location (address) 5000 into register A. This does not put a 5000 into A. 5000 *won't fit*! Register A is like any 8-bit microprocessor register; the largest 8-bit binary number it can hold is 11111111 (decimal 255).

If we choose to put a number into A from a different memory address, all that we need to change is the numbers in H and L. Address 5000 was at page 19 and line 136 in the memory. Another address, like 3000, would be at a different location (line 11 and page 184). We could get a number into A from address 3000 this way:

Mnemonic		Result
(Intel)	(Zilog)	
MVI H, 11	LD H, 11	H←—11
MVI L, 184	LD L, 184	L←—184

(the number 3000 is now in register-pair HL)

MOV A, M	LD A, (HL)	A←—(3000)

(since HL is 3000 now, there's a different result)

There's another way to get a number loaded into register A from memory location 3000. This one is more direct than the MOV command, and doesn't use the HL registers to point the way to the address:

Mnemonic		Result
(Intel)	(Zilog)	
LDA (3000)	LD A, (3000)	A←--(3000)

Goodness, that looks easy! If you want to load register A with the number stored at memory address 3000, you tell the computer the address 3000 right in the instruction. This is called **direct addressing**. The address is available to the CPU directly in the instruction. That's certainly simpler than looking for it in the register HL. Also, Intel and Zilog almost agreed on the mnemonic for this one.

Unfortunately, this instruction is quite limited. It's a great way to load something into register A, but it's only available for register A, and you can't load register B or C, or any other register with it. The MOV instruction with register M—the Zilog LD instruction with (HL)—could be used to load any register with the number stored at 3000 (or anyplace else, for that matter).

Another thing that makes LDA a bit awkward is its size. Although it appears there would be only two parts to this instruction—the opcode, which says that it's a LoaD, and the address 3000—there are really three bytes of code in the "final" machine language. The opcode is 58 in decimal and the address is made of the bytes 184 and 11. Notice that the line number (184) comes before the page number (11). This is always true of Intel machines. When a 16-bit number is broken into a page and a line, the line comes first, even though it's the LOW part of the address. The whole instruction LDA 3000 would be stored in consecutive memory addresses as 58, 184, 11.

Also, in Intel jargon, a LD instruction always transfers data out of memory to a register. If you want to transfer data into memory from a register, Intel calls everything a STore (see below):

Mnemonic		Result
(Intel)	(Zilog)	
STA (3000)	LD (3000), A	(3000)←—A

The number in register A is stored in memory location 3000 by this instruction.

The memory pointer—register pair HL—is not the only place where the CPU can go to find an address. The indirect mode of addressing allows BC and DE to be used as memory pointers too. Intel calls these instructions LDAX (LoaD A indirect—don't ask us where X comes from) and STAX (STore A indirect). Like other Intel LD and ST instructions, these only work between memory and register A:

Mnemonic		Result
(Intel)	(Zilog)	
LDAX B	LD A, (BC)	A←—(BC)
LDAX D	LD A, (DE)	A←-(DE)
STAX B	LD (BC), A	(BC)←—A
STAX D	LD (DE), A	(DE):—A

Let's use one of these instructions to solve the same problem we've solved with other instructions in this group—moving a number to register A from the memory:

Mnemonic		Result
(Intel)	(Zilog)	
MVI B, 19	LD B, 19	B←——19
MVI C, 136	LD C, 136	C←——136

(now the BC register pair contains the number 5000)

LDAX B	LD A, (BC)	A←——(5000)

The Zilog Z-80 has two additional 16-bit registers that may be used as a memory pointer. These are registers IX and IY. They can be used like BC, DE, or HL, but have an additional feature. In the instruction, you can tell the computer to find a memory location forward or backward from the number in the pointer. A one-byte signed binary number (this will be discussed in detail later) is added to the contents of the 16-bit register. If it is a positive number, the address formed by this addition points ahead of the address in the pointer. If the number (called a **displacement**) is negative, the address formed by this addition points behind the address in the pointer. This method of reaching a place in memory in the neighborhood of a specific address is called **indexed addressing**. We'll use the same example we've used in the rest of this section to illustrate this point:

Mnemonic	Result
LD IX, 5000	IX←——5000
LD A, (IX + 1)	A←——(5001)

Now this is something new! We loaded A with the number stored at address 5000 + 1. The number 1 could be replaced by any positive number up to 127, or any negative number down to (–128).

The same operation can be done in the reverse direction. A register can be put into memory using

$$LD \ (IX + 1), A \quad - \quad LD \ (IX + 2), B \quad - \quad LD \ (IX + 3), C$$

and so forth. Every register is usable, and all addresses can be reached up to half a page on either side of the address in IX or IY.

There are two other registers Zilog has that Intel does not. The R (refresh) register and I (interrupt) register can be loaded to or from register A (and only register A). The function of these registers is outside the scope of this chapter. For now, think of them as "just another" 8-bit place in the CPU where we can get or put numbers.

5.2.4 Extended Precision

Although the 8080 and Z-80 are 8-bit computers, they can do some 16-bit operations as well. Such operations are called **double precision** when they deal in double bytes. The number of 16-bit "things" we can do in the 8080 and Z-80 are more limited than the number of 8-bit things. This is partially due to the fact that 8-bit registers must be grouped together in **register pairs** to do double-precision operations. Since there's only one register pair for every two registers, there aren't as many 16-bit places to work in as there were 8-bit places.

We hinted at 16-bit load capability in the last section (did you spot it?). In the example of a LD A, (IX + 1) instruction, we showed the instruction LD IX, 5000. The IX register is a 16-bit register. You can load a 5000 into it, so it must be bigger than 8 bits! There are six 16-bit registers (four in the 8080) that can be used for double-precision work. They are:

AF	BC	DE	HL	SP	(8080 or Z-80)
	IX	IY			(Z-80 ONLY)

(the Z-80 also has a duplicate set of registers)

AF′	BC′	DE′	HL′	SP′	IX′	IY′

Four methods of addressing exist for these data transfers: register, immediate, direct, and indirect.

Register transfers let you move a 16-bit number from one register pair to another:

Mnemonic		Result
(Intel)	(Zilog)	
XCHG	EX DE, HL	HL swapped with DE
SPHL	LD SP, HL	SP←—HL
	LD SP, IX	SP←—IX
	LD SP, IY	SP←—IY
Z-80 only	EX AF, AF′	AF swapped with AF′
	EXX	BC←—→BC′
		DE←—→DE′
		HL←—→HL′

We used an **immediate** load instruction when we put the number 5000 into register IX. Other instructions of this kind are:

	Mnemonic		Result
(Intel)	(Zilog)		
LXI B, 5000	LD BC, 5000	BC←—5000
LXI D, 5000	LD DE, 5000	DE←—5000
LXI H, 5000	LD HL, 5000	HL←—5000
	LD IX, 5000	IX ←—5000
	LD IY, 5000	IY ←—5000

Of course, any 16-bit number could be used; it doesn't have to be 5000. Numbers loaded into one of the register pairs can have values from 0 to 65535 (unsigned arithmetic) or -32768 to $+32767$ (signed arithmetic).

Direct addressing permits you to load the register pairs from memory addresses. Each address can be either the source or the destination of a data transfer. In our examples below, we'll use the address 3000, but any 16-bit address will do equally well:

	Mnemonic		Result
(Intel)	(Zilog)		
LHLD 3000	LD HL, (3000)	HL←—(3000)
SHLD 3000	LD (3000), HL	(3000)←—HL
	LD BC, (3000)	BC←—(3000)
	LD (3000), BC	(3000)←—BC
	LD DE, (3000)	DE←—(3000)
	LD (3000), DE	(3000)←—DE
	LD SP, (3000)	SP←—(3000)
	LD (3000), SP	(3000)←—SP
	LD IX, (3000)	IX←—(3000)
	LD (3000), IX	(3000)←—IX
	LD IY, (3000)	IY←—(3000)
	LD (3000), IY	(3000)←—IY

When these are done, the bytes in two consecutive addresses (in this case, 3000 and 3001) are transferred between memory and the registers. You might expect that the bytes from 3000 and 3001 would be put into the registers (in a register pair) in alphabetic order. Not so. If we're using register pair HL, the 3000 byte goes in L, and the 3001 byte goes in H.

Since the transfer instructions that put HL back into memory work the same way, there's no reason to notice what order this happens, unless you want to use just one half of the 16-bit word that was transferred. In that case, you'll need to know this to find the register that has the half you want.

Indirect addressing permits you to load a register pair to/from an address in memory, but the memory address doesn't have to be a part of the instruction. Instead, the address is taken from another register pair. In the case of 16-bit numbers, the memory pointer is almost always "SP" (the stack pointer). The memory the stack pointer points to is called the stack. The data-transfer operations that transfer 16-bit numbers between the stack and the register pairs are called PUSH and POP instructions instead of LD (even by Zilog!).

A **PUSH** puts a number onto the stack and a **POP** takes it off the stack. Unlike the 8-bit instructions that use indirect addressing, stack instructions change the pointer after they've been done. The stack pointer is an up/down-counter. It will decrease by 2 every time a PUSH has been done. When a POP is done, it will increase by 2. This makes the stack a last-in, first-out (LIFO) shift-register. The most recent entry PUSHed on the stack will be the first one POPped back off the stack if a POP is done.

Here are the PUSH and POP instructions available in the 8080 and Z-80 instruction sets:

Mnemonic		Result
(Intel)	(Zilog)	
PUSH B	PUSH BC	(SP)◄——BC
PUSH D	PUSH DE	(SP)◄——DE
PUSH H	PUSH HL	(SP)◄——HL
PUSH PSW	PUSH AF	(SP)◄——AF
	PUSH IX	(SP)◄——IX
	PUSH IY	(SP)◄——IY
POP B	POP BC	BC◄——(SP)
POP D	POP DE	DE◄——(SP)
POP H	POP HL	HL◄——(SP)
POP PSW	POP AF	AF◄——(SP)
	POP IX	IX ◄——(SP)
	POP IY	IY ◄——(SP)

There are even some instructions that do both a PUSH and a POP at the same time. These are the **indirect exchange** instructions:

Mnemonic		Result
(Intel)	(Zilog)	
XTHL	EX (SP), HL	(SP)$\longleftrightarrow$HL
	EX (SP), IX	(SP)$\longleftrightarrow$IX
	EX (SP), IY	(SP)$\longleftrightarrow$IY

Each time an EX instruction is done, two 16-bit numbers change places. In this case, one of the numbers is stored on the stack, and the other is in the CPU. Afterward, they have changed places.

We can say that stack operations are like other memory operations that use a memory pointer, except that the numbers we are storing and retrieving are 16-bit numbers, and the pointer follows the numbers as they're stacked and unstacked.

5.2.5 Block Moves

In the Z-80, a group of **block transfer** instructions allow you to move a block of memory as large as you want from one place to another. This is a characteristic of *variable-word-length computers* found in no other microprocessor. To use these instructions, three numbers 16 bits long must be put into the BC, DE, and HL register pairs:

> HL$\longleftarrow$-starting address of the source memory block
>
> DE$\longleftarrow$--starting address of the destination
>
> BC$\longleftarrow$—byte counter for the length of the block

There are up-counting and down-counting versions of the block move instruction, and even ones that "bump" the counter but stop after one byte of data has been moved. Here they are:

Mnemonic		Result
LDI	(DE)$\longleftarrow$ (HL);	bump BC down and HL, DE up
(Single byte move)		just one time
LDIR	(DE)$\longleftarrow$(HL);	bump BC down and HL, DE up
(Block move)		and repeat until BC is 0
LDD	(DE)$\longleftarrow$(HL);	bump BC, DE, and HL down
(Single byte move)		just one time
LDDR	(DE)$\longleftarrow$ (HL);	bump BC, DE, and HL down
(Block move)		and repeat until BC is 0

These instructions may seem a bit mysterious to you. That's understandable, especially for the single-byte memory-to-memory transfers. Unless you've had the experience of programming an IBM 1400-series data processor or a Honeywell 200-series processor, it's unlikely that you'll see the usefulness of these instructions. We've had the experience of those machines. Take our word for it, an experienced programmer can find these very useful.

5.2.6 Register to/from I/O

There are three possible places for numbers to live in a microcomputer system, CPU registers, memory, and I/O devices. The 8080 has only one method of I/O operation. A number transferred between the I/O port and CPU of an 8080 must use register A. Each I/O port has a number called its **device code**. In the 8080, this code is included in the instruction directly. If data are being transferred in to the CPU, the instruction is "IN" and the port an input port. If data are being transferred out of the CPU, the instruction is "OUT" and the port an output port.

The Z-80 has a lot more ways of handling I/O. The device code can be direct or indirect. When indirect addressing is used, the pointer holding the device code is register C. Instead of A, an I/O port can transfer data to or from any one of the 8-bit registers. There are also single-byte and block moves between a port and a block of memory. In our examples, we'll use I/O port 7 and register B in the IN and OUT instructions, but others are certainly possible.

	Mnemonic	Result
(Intel)	(Zilog)	
IN 007	IN A, (7)	A←PORT 7
OUT 007	OUT (7), A	PORT 7←A
	IN B, (C)	B←Port (C)
	OUT (C), B	Port (C)←B
	INI	(HL)←PORT (BC)

(BC will count down and HL up, but only a single byte will be moved)
INIR   (HL)   PORT (BC)
(this instruction can be used to load data from 256 I/O devices to 256 memory locations by counting down at B and up at HL until B is 0)

Mnemonic		Result
(Intel)	(Zilog)	
	IND	(same as INI except HL counts down by 1)
	INDR	(same as INIR except HL counts down until B is 0)

5.3 ARITHMETIC-LOGIC INSTRUCTIONS

The 8080.   There are eight arithmetic/Boolean operations that the 8080 microprocessor can use to combine or compare two numbers. They are:

(ADD)   Add (A plus Register)

(ADC)   Add with Carry (A plus Register)

(SUB)   Subtract (A minus Register)

(SBB)   Subtract with Borrow (A minus Register minus the Borrow)

(ANA)   (logical) AND (Register) with A

(XRA)   (logical) XOR (Register) with A

(ORA)   (logical) OR (Register) with A

(CMP)   Compare (A minus Register) (look-ahead subtraction)

There are also a number of operations that the 8080 can do on single numbers. They are:

(INR)   Increase (by 1)

(DCR)   Decrease (by 1)

(CMA)   Complement (invert all bits)

(DAA)   Decimal Adjust

5.3.1 Register-to/from-Register Arithmetic

The eight operations that combine two numbers can be used to combine a number in register A with a number in any other register. A typical instruction of this type is:

Mnemonic		Result
(Intel)	(Zilog)	
ADD B	ADD A, B	A ←— A plus B

All the instructions in this group of 8 do something to the A register. In Intel mnemonics, this is implicit. The A register is not shown as a part of the instruction, but any time numbers in two registers are combined, one of the registers is always A. Zilog chooses to state register A explicitly (sometimes) in some of its mnemonics. We're not sure why the Boolean functions have an implicit A and the arithmetic ones have an explicit A in Zilog assembly language. Intel's code, although it doesn't show that register A is used, is at least consistent.

Add with Carry and Subtract with Borrow allow "chaining" together numbers in several registers to do multibyte arithmetic. Examples of this will be discussed in a subsequent chapter. For now, we'll just say that Add and Add with Carry are software that does the same thing as a half-adder and full-adder do in hardware. Subtract and Subtract with Borrow are the software equivalents of the half-subtracter and full-subtracter in hardware.

As with Intel's other register instructions, there is a register M that may be used in any of these instructions, but is really a memory location addressed by HL. This means that a number may be taken out of memory to be combined with A by the ALU. The results will be in A, of course, after the arithmetic/logic is completed—so if you want to store the results in memory, you'll still need a Data Transfer instruction to do the job (see the preceding section).

We should note at this point that the *Increase* (INR) and *Decrease* (DCR) instructions defy the general rule that arithmetic is only done in the accumulator (register A) and permit you to "bump up" or "bump down" a number in any of the 8-bit registers (including M).

The Complement, the Accumulator (CMA) and Decimal Adjust Accumulator (DAA) instructions, of course, only exist for register A.

The Z-80. The Z-80 has two additional memory pointers (IX and IY) that are used for indexed addressing. Arithmetic in the Z-80 has all the instructions of the 8080 but has slightly different mnemonics, and allows use of (IX + d) and (IY + d) as well as (HL) to do arithmetic with numbers in the memory.

Zilog's mnemonics for these instructions are:

(Dyadic Arithmetic Operations)

(ADD)　Add (A plus Register)

(ADC)　Add with Carry (A plus Register plus the Carry)

(SUB)   Subtract (A minus Register)

(SBC)   Subtract with Carry (A minus Register minus the Carry)

(Dyadic Logical Operations)

(AND)   (logical) AND (Register) with A

(XOR)   (logical) XOR (Register) with A

(OR)   (logical) OR (Register) with A

(CP)   Compare (A minus Register) (look-ahead subtraction)

(Unary Arithmetic Operations)

(INC)   Increase (Register) by 1

(DEC)   Decrease (Register) by 1

(Unary Logical Operations)

(CPL)   Complement (invert all bits)

(NEG)   Negate (form two's complement of A)

(DAA)   Decimal Adjust (register A)

5.3.2 Constant-to-Register Arithmetic

The 8080.   The same eight operations can be done with a register and a **constant.** In the 8080, the constant is always combined with register A. Instructions have slightly different mnemonics in Intel code when one of the numbers is a constant. Like the MVI instructions, these instructions are immediate (the constant is immediately available in the instruction itself). Because of the immediate mode of addressing, these mnemonics all contain an I:

(Arithmetic Operations)

(ADI)   Add Immediate (constant to A)

(ACI)   Add with Carry Immediate (constant to A)

(SUI)   Subtract Immediate (constant from A)

(SBI)   Subtract with Borrow Immediate (from A)

(Logical Operations)

(ANI)   AND Immediate (constant with A)

(XRI)   EXCLUSIVE OR Immediate (constant with A)

(ORI)   OR Immediate (constant with A)

(CMP)   Compare Immediate (constant with A)

We'll go into the uses of these instructions in a future chapter, especially the Boolean ones, since it may not be obvious what they're good for.

The Z-80.   The Z-80 permits the same immediate mode addressing operations as the 8080. The mnemonics used are the same ones Zilog uses for its register-to-register arithmetic. The only difference is the use of a constant in the operand—represented by a number—instead of a register (a variable)—represented by a letter.

5.3.3 Extended-Precision Arithmetic

The 8080.   When you plan to use numbers larger than 255 (decimal), you need more than 8-bit spaces to work in. We've already mentioned that a way exists to use the Carry and Borrow flags with the 8-bit arithmetic instructions to extend the results of a one-register ADD or SUB into another register. The 8080 has one 16-bit ADD instruction, Double Add (DAD). It uses the HL register pair as a 16-bit ACCUMULATOR. The remaining register pairs can be added to HL. The register pairs can also be increased and decreased. Extended-precision mnemonics for the 8080 always contain an X (except double add):

(DAD)   Double Add (register pair to HL)

(INX)   Increase (register pair) by 1

(DCX)   Decrease (register pair) by 1

These operations allow you to build up numbers as large as 65,535 in register pairs as easily as single-byte arithmetic allows you to build numbers up to 255.

The Z-80.   Zilog permits 16-bit subtraction as well as addition. There are ADD, ADC, and SBC mnemonics for these 16-bit operands (the numbers in the register pairs), but no SUB (subtract without using the Borrow from the last subtraction). Since two more register pairs, IX and IY, exist in the Z-80, some 16-bit operations exist which use them as accumulators, like the HL. There are ADD, INC, and DEC operations for these two registers. You'll recall that Zilog uses the same name for all ADD instructions—including DAD—whether they're 8-bit or 16-bit arithmetic.

5.3.4 Boolean Operations

You may have wondered how a register could be ANDed or XORed with another register or an 8-bit constant. All the AND and XOR gates you've seen combine 1-bit numbers, not 8-bit numbers. Actually, the AND, XOR, and OR instructions have eight parallel gates that combine the 1-bit of one operand with the 1-bit of A, the 2-bit of the operand with 2-bit of the A, the 4-bit of the operand with the 4-bit of A, and so forth, combining each of the operand's 8 bits with the corresponding bit of A.

For example, let's suppose that the number in A is 10101010, and we're going to AND it with 11110000. The operand and A are written like this:

$$10101010$$

$$\text{AND} \quad \underline{11110000}$$

as though we were going to ADD them. Then, starting at the right, we can AND each column of 2 bits (as though we were doing addition or subtraction). On the rightmost column 0 AND 0 equals 0. Moving to the left, we have 1 AND 0 equals 0. We continue this column by column, until we reach the leftmost column—1 AND 1 equals 1. The result looks like this:

$$10101010$$

$$\text{AND} \quad \underline{11110000}$$

$$10100000$$

If you know what the output of a two-input gate is for any kind of logic, you know the output for a combination of two 8-bit numbers (or any other size), by following the rule above. Since each Boolean gate has a single output, each column of two 1-bit numbers results in a 1-bit answer, and two 8-bit operands give an 8-bit answer without generating any Carry or Borrow output.

There is also one Boolean (sort of . . .) operation the Z-80 does that the 8080 does not. This is the Negate (NEG) operation, which forms the *two's complement* of the number in register A. It's a two-byte mnemonic. 8080 users could use two one-byte instructions CMA (invert all bits of A) and INR A (A + 1) to get the same results.

Retracted Precision(?).   There a few 1-bit arithmetic-logic operations in the 8080 and Z-80. They set, reset, complement, or test a single bit. Two operations affect the Carry flag:

(Intel)	(Zilog)	
STC	SCF	Set the Carry (flag)
CMC	CCF	Complement Carry flag

In the Z-80, any bit in any register can be set or reset using one of the following:

(SET)	Set a bit
(RES)	Reset a bit

These registers include any memory location that HL, IX + d, or IY + d points to.

A 1-bit Compare instruction, called a **bit test** (BIT), is available in the Z-80 instruction set to test whether any bit in a register (includes memory) is ON or OFF. The Z (zero) flag in the ALU is set or reset to indicate if the bit is 0 or not. For example, the instruction

BIT   7,A

tests whether bit 7 (the most significant bit) of A is a 0 or a 1. After the instruction, the Z flag is ON if the number is 0 and OFF otherwise.

5.4 CONTROL INSTRUCTIONS

There are three types of **control** operations, called **jump, call,** and **return.** These operations affect the program counter, which is the register that points at the next instruction. A jump puts a new number into the PC, so that the computer "jumps" to a new section of the memory to get its next instruction. Imagine that the program counter is "fetching" instructions from memory in this order: 23, 24, 25, 26, 27, ... If a jump occurs on line 26 of memory, the count could look like 23, 24, 25, 26, 12, ... The next address in the program counter, which would have been 27, has been overwritten by a 12. From here on, the program counter will count 13, 14, 15, . . . , until it reaches 26 again. At that point, it would go back to line 12 again, and continue to repeat the instructions between 12 and 26 over and over.

Why should anyone want to do that?

As an answer, think of how you would make the computer test 1024 memory locations by writing and reading data. You could write the same test routine 1024 times, or write it once and go back to the beginning of the routine 1024 times. The second procedure is much simpler than the first, if you can make the jump that goes to the beginning of the routine stop after 1024 times.

This requires a **conditional** type of instruction—in this case, one that checks a counter to "see" if the count is 1024 yet, and jumps as long as it is not. There are several conditions that can be tested that will enable or disable a conditional jump instruction. They are all related to the flags in the arithmetic/logic unit. We will begin by studying these instructions.

5.4.1 Unconditional/Conditional Jump

The term "unconditional" means "always, no matter what." There is an instruction, JMP (Zilog JP), that loads a number into the program counter every time. This number is gotten directly from the instruction itself, something like a MVI, except that when the program counter is loaded with a number (a 16-digit number) the number is an address, not a data. In the program counter, this number controls the program itself.

The form of JMP instructions is shown by an example:

	Mnemonic		Result
(Intel)	(Zilog)		
JMP 5000	JP 5000		PC◄——-5000

We used the address 5000 in an earlier example. When the number 5000 is stored in H and L, it is broken up into two bytes, the page number and line number. You might remember that address 5000 was the same as page 19, line 136 (decimal) in our example. We don't have to deal with two separate bytes of code in the JMP instruction, because the PC is large enough to hold 5000 as a single number. In reality, however, the 5000 is part of a three-byte instruction in machine code. The first byte has the decimal value 195. This is the opcode, and it tells the computer that the next two bytes will be "jammed" into the PC (and will clobber anything that's already there). The next two bytes of the code are 136 and 19, which are there because, despite the size of the PC, the program itself is stored in a memory with words of only 8 bits' length. The complete instruction for JMP 5000 is stored in three consecutive bytes of memory as 195, 136, 19, although it's unlikely they would be expressed as decimal numbers in any computer printout. The general standard is to use hexadecimal, which represents the same instruction as C3, 88, 13. You'll notice that the line number comes before the page number just as it did in the LDA instruction in Section 5.2.

The term "conditional" means "sometimes—when something else is true." There is a group of instructions for the 8080 and Z-80 that jump only if a condition is met in one of the flags. There are four flags that are tested by conditional jump instructions: the Zero, Carry, Parity, and Sign flags. These are flip-flops that are set or reset by the ALU when it does arithmetic or Boolean operations. 8080/Z80 conditional jump instructions are called "IF" statements or "conditional BRANCH" in other languages. They all have pattern "Jump IF (condition) TRUE." The four flags tested by the 8080/Z80 conditional jumps give rise to eight jumps:

	Mnemonic	Action
(Intel)	(Zilog)	
JNZ	JP NZ	Jump if Not Zero
JZ	JP Z	Jump if Zero
JNC	JP NC	Jump if No Carry

Mnemonic		Action
(Intel)	(Zilog)	
JC	JP C	Jump if Carry
JPE	JP PO*	Jump if Parity Reset*
JPO	JP PE*	Jump if Parity Set*
JP	JP P	Jump if Plus Sign
JM	JP M	Jump if Minus Sign

Each of these instructions is a three-byte code, an opcode followed by a two-byte address that's put into the PC if the condition is true. A typical instruction of this type is:

Mnemonic		Result
(Intel)	(Zilog)	
JM 5000	JP M, 5000	PC←5000 IF sign is (−)

When the Sign flag is set (the ALU has just calculated a number with a negative result) the address in the PC is replaced by 5000. What happens if the Sign flag is reset? If the number in the PC is not replaced, it's still there! When this happens, the CPU fetches its next instruction from the place it was going to, anyway. The program flows on from the last instruction to the next as though nothing has happened. (This action is sometimes called a "fall through" in programming.)

5.4.2 Relative Addressing versus Absolute Addressing

An address "points to" a place in the memory where the CPU wants to fetch or put a byte. In the case of the program counter, the address in a Jump instruction is fetched out of the second and third bytes of the instruction itself and put into the PC. The only difference between a Jump and a Load Immediate is the register where the number is put; there are no LXI instructions that load the PC. Just as the Load Immediate is not the only way to move a number into a 16-bit register, the Jump instructions we've seen are only one of several ways to move a new number into the PC.

The Jump instructions we've just seen load a 5000 into the PC. This is a type of immediate load is called *absolute* addressing; because the address is right there in the instruction, it's absolute and unvarying. It (the address) is just loaded directly into the PC. There are other ways of changing an address. You can increment, decrement, add to, or subtract from numbers in a register. Since the PC automatically increments as the CPU moves from one instruction to the next (which leads us to suspect that we can ADD to the PC), we might ask if numbers other than one can be added to the PC.

The answer is yes, and the numbers can be either positive or negative. A Jump Relative instruction is used to tell the CPU things like "Jump ahead five lines" or "Jump back three lines," instead of "Jump to 2351" or "Jump (if No Carry) to 6315." The relative addressing implied in the JR instructions (found on the Z-80, but not the 8080) is useful for two things:

1. Relocatable code. If you want to take the same instructions that work in the 5000 area of memory and transplant them to the 8000 area, there will be no need to rewrite the Jump instructions for the new addresses. The software will be perfectly transplantable if all the jumps are relative.

2. The instructions themselves will be shorter, since the "jump forward" and "jump backward" are done with only one byte of address. The one byte (in signed binary that can be positive or negative) permits the programmer to "jump" 127 bytes forward or 128 bytes backward.

Examples of the JR (Jump Relative) instructions include both unconditional and conditional types. An explanation of each one is given with the mnemonic:

Mnemonic	Result
JR FROG	PC←—PC + displacement
JR NC, FROG	PC←—PC + displacement, IF No Carry

(Carry flag OFF)

In both cases, "displacement" refers to the number you would have to add to the present address in the PC to get to the address called FROG. Only the Carry and Zero flags are used by JR instructions to do conditional, relative branching.

There are also instructions that a programmer can use to jump the computer somewhere indirectly. An address in HL, IX, or IY can be used as the address of a jump. In this case, the instruction itself doesn't even need to contain a part of the address. The PC is simply loaded from the HL, IX, or IY (16-bit) registers. The 8080, of course, has no IX and IY registers, and can only load the PC with HL.

Mnemonic		Result
(Intel)	(Zilog)	
PCHL	JP (HL)	PC←—HL
	JP (IX)	PC←—IX
	JP (IY)	PC←—IY

5.4.3 Subroutine Calls and Returns

You use the Jump instructions to tell the computer where to go (to fetch its next instruction). Usually, when you tell someone where to go, you don't bother telling them how to get back. In this case, there's a polite instruction for the jump that tells the CPU how to get back.

This instruction is called a CALL. When a CALL takes place, the computer doesn't just transfer a new number into the PC, it also saves the old PC. The old PC is saved by being written into the memory. A special memory pointer is used to keep track of where the return address is.

Later, another instruction—Return (RET)—is used to get back to the place where the PC was at the time of the CALL.

At the place where the CALL jumps to, we do a number of instructions terminated by a RET. This group of instructions is called a **subroutine**. The program that contains the CALL is referred to as the **main program**. Any time a CALL to a subroutine takes place, the RET at the end of the sub-routine brings the computer back to the main program. The difference be-tween a subroutine and any other routine a computer might jump to is the reusability of the subroutine from any place in the program. If you want to do the same thing seven or eight times in a program, for instance, there are two ways to do it; either write the same identical group of instructions in the program seven or eight times, once for each place where it's wanted, or make the group of instructions into a subroutine.

Writing the same identical routine eight times is wasteful. Writing it once is elegant. Subroutines are the only way to go in cases like this. Now, you might ask: "Why would you want to use the same routine eight times in a single program?" One example we can think of is *division*. None of the popular 8-bit microprocessors used in home computers have built-in circuits that can divide. To do a division, a small program (an *algorithm*) must be written that can divide two numbers using the *add*, *subtract*, and *move* cir-cuitry. While the algorithm isn't terribly complicated, if you divide some-thing at eight different points in the program, the code for the algorithm will have to be written eight times in the program. If you use a division subrou-tine, it's only necessary to write the algorithm one time. It can then be used by a CALL from any point in the program, or any other program that needs it. With the CALL instruction, a single command can take the place of the whole algorithm every time it's needed.

Like the Jump instructions, CALL and RETurns can be found in unconditional and conditional forms. Here are some examples:

	Mnemonic		Result
(Intel)	(Zilog)		
CALL MULT	CALL MULT		STACK←PC
			PC←MULT

Mnemonic		Result
(Intel)	(Zilog)	
CNZ DIVIDE	CALL NZ, DIVIDE	STACK←—PC
		PC←—DIVIDE IF Not Zero
		(Zero Flag OFF)
CALL 5000	CALL 5000	STACK←—PC
		PC←—5000
RET	RET	PC←—STACK
RNZ	RET NZ	PC←—STACK IF Not Zero
		(Zero Flag OFF)

In the third example, we really did the same thing as the first example—an unconditional CALL to a place in the memory. In the first example, there's a label (MULT) that identifies a place in the memory that the assembler keeps track of, but which we don't know. In the third example, the CALL uses a "real" address (5000) which isn't represented by a label. Instead, it is shown as an absolute address. The machine code that the assembler turns these mnemonics into has a number in either case; it's just easier to remember what the CALL does when the address of the subroutine is represented by a suitable label with some mnemonic value.

The RET instructions take back the number stored in the stack by the last CALL that was done. This number was the old PC that was pointed at the next instruction the main program was going to do after the CALL.

5.4.4 Restart (Trap) Instructions

There is a one-byte CALL instruction called a **Restart (RST)** in the 8080 and Z-80 instruction sets. An ordinary CALL instruction contains three bytes, an opcode, and two bytes of address. This address allows the subroutine being CALLed to be at any one of 65,536 places in the memory. Since the RST instruction is only one byte long, there isn't enough room in the instruction for a 16-bit address. Instead, there are eight different opcodes for the RST instruction, each of which CALLs a subroutine at a different place. The "destination" of each RST subroutine call is contained inside the opcode itself, as shown below:

Mnemonic	Action
RST 1	Same as CALL to address 010 (octal)
RST 2	Same as CALL to address 020 (octal)

Mnemonic	Action
RST 3	Same as CALL to address 030 (octal)
⋮	⋮ ⋮ ⋮ ⋮ ⋮
RST 7	Same as CALL to address 070 (octal)

All the addresses are on page 0 of the memory. There isn't enough room between each of these subroutines and the next for a decent subroutine. The instruction that's usually found at the destination of a RST is a Jump to a place where the rest of the subroutine is written. The rest of the subroutine is then located where there's plenty of room for all the instructions that are needed. When a Jump instruction is used this way, it's called a **vector**. Restart instructions are usually used in a hardware-driven subroutine call known as an *interrupt*. When the interrupt uses a vector as we just described, it's called a *vectored interrupt*. We'll study interrupts in more detail later.

Unlike subroutine CALL and RETurn instructions, the RST instruction has no conditional form. There isn't any such instruction as "RESTART, IF . . . " in the 8080 or Z-80.

5.5 MISCELLANEOUS OPERATIONS

These are operations which don't necessarily have much in common with each other, but differ in special ways from most of the instructions in the other groups.

5.5.1 Stack Operations

We discussed the stack for the first time in Section 5.2.4, in conjunction with 16-bit data-transfer operations. The stack is a special part of the memory, not because other memory operations can't reach it, but because it has its own special memory pointer—the stack pointer (SP)—which works differently from the index registers or program counters in the way it operates. The PUSH and POP instructions, described in Section 5.2.4, are 16-bit operations that permit the user to save or recover 16-bit operations that permit the user to save or recover 16-bit words one at a time between memory and register pairs in the CPU. These are used in much the same way that Move, Store, and Load instructions are used for 8-bit bytes. The stack pointer, however, differs from the (HL, IX, or IY) memory pointer by being a counter. Unlike the program counter, which marches forward through memory as it picks up instructions, the stack pointer marches backward in double steps after each word is pushed onto the stack. When a word is taken off the stack (POPped), the SP marches forward. The *stack* thus operates like a shift register that can reverse directions. Such a register is called a LIFO (Last In, First Out).

The CALL, RST, and RET instructions, described in Sections 5.4.3 and 5.4.4, use the stack in the same way as PUSH and POP, except that the words being stored and recovered are addresses used by the program counter.

5.5.2 Rotates and Shifts

The 8080 has a large number of *rotate* instructions, and the Z-80 has even more. *Shift* instructions use a register (usually register A—the accumulator) as a shift register for the bits it contains. The instructions called *rotates* use the register as a ring counter in which the Carry flag is part of the ring. In either case, these shifts and rotates include the ability to operate as a *left-shift register* or a *right-shift register*. In the Z-80, most registers can be rotated or shifted, while the 8080 allows these operations only on register A. The Z-80 also allows BCD shifts between the accumulator and memory. Whenever a register is used in ring counter mode, the Carry flag is added onto the front (most significant bit) of the register and its contents are rotated along with the bits in the register, or else it copies some bit inside the register. Here are examples of the rotate instructions for both processors:

Mnemonics		Action
(Intel)	(Zilog)	
RAL	RLA	Use the Carry flag and A as a ring counter, rotating to the *left*.
RAR	RRA	Use the Carry flag and A as a ring counter, rotating to the *right*.
RRC	RRCA	Use register A (only) as a ring counter, rotating to the *left*. The Carry flag "copies" bit 7 of A.
None	RL*	Same as RAL, but can use "*."
None	RR*	Same as RAR, but can use "*."
None	RLC*	Same as RLCA, but can use "*."
None	RRC*	Same as RRCA, but can use "*."
None	SLA* (Shift Left Arithmetic)	Acts like a left-shift register which uses the Carry as an MSB.
None	SRL* (Shift Right Logical)	Acts like a right-shift register which uses the Carry as an LSB.

Mnemonics		Action
(Intel)	(Zilog)	
None	SRA* (Shift Right Arithmetic)	Acts like a right-shift register which uses the Carry as an LSB and copies the MSB into the next lower bit as the shift happens.
None	RLD (Rotate Left Decimal)	Rotates a BCD digit from memory into the accumulator.
None	RRD (Rotate Right Decimal)	Rotates a BCD digit into memory from the accumulator.

*any register or memory location M that (HL), (IX + d), or (IY + d) points to

Rotate and Shift instructions are used for various mathematical purposes which we will not attempt to explain here. The usefulness of these instructions will become clear later.

5.5.3 NOP (Dummy) Instruction

This is an instruction that does nothing. It's as though there is no circuit connected to the instruction decoder that this instruction can turn on. The CPU fetches this instruction, puts it into the instruction decoder, and . . . nothing happens. The code for a NOP (No OPeration) is reasonable, considering it does nothing—its binary code is 00000000 (nothing!). NOP instructions are one byte long, and are often used to fill unused memory space, or to cover up an instruction with nonactive bytes during software writing and de-bugging. NOP is also a useful instruction when a short time delay—that does nothing else—is desired.

5.5.4 Halt Instruction

This is just what you would expect it to be. At the end of a program, when you want to stop the computer from going further in the memory, the Halt instruction stops the PC from counting ahead and fetching the next instruction. This is important because there will always be "something" in the memory locations that follow the program—even if the programmer didn't write anything there—and in most cases, the "something" is "garbage." If the computer should go on and fetch these bytes after the last instruction in the program, it will attempt to do what the garbage says it should do. The computerese expression "garbage in, garbage out" is all too true in this case; the instructions in the garbage that follows the program will probably destroy part, or all, of the data, program, and output, if the program isn't stopped. The Halt instruction also waits for an interrupt when the computer is stopped. The computer can be restarted if the interrupt input is activated. We'll see more about this later, but in this case, we'll just say that in certain microprocessor instruction sets (Motorola) the Halt instruction is called a WAI (WAit for Interrupt) instead of a HLT. It's really the same instruction with another name.

5.6 ASSEMBLERS AND ASSEMBLY LANGUAGE

In this chapter we've represented each code for the 8080 and Z-80 with a mnemonic. The actual binary number stored in the memory for each of the instructions we've discussed is shown in Appendix B. To simplify the numbers, we've used octal as "shorthand" for the binary value of each opcode. An assembly language program for the 8080 or Z-80 is a combination of the mnemonics and labels the programmer has used to solve a problem. If the computer is programmed directly in binary, the programmer will probably use a lookup table (like in the Appendix to this book) and write a program in assembly language first. It is easier to keep track of loops and variables in assembly language, and easier for someone else to look at an assembly language program when they're trying to see how it works. Ultimately, however, the programmer must code the program into the computer in binary. This means the assembly language program will have to be translated into binary before it can be entered. This can be done by hand, laboriously writing down, line by line, the translation of each mnemonic and label, and then entering the completed translation into the memory. An alternative is to have a program that takes lines of assembly language as its input and does the translation into binary for the programmer. Such a program is called an **assembler,** because it puts together the actual opcodes and addresses that take the place of the mnemonics and labels. When it's done, the assembler has assembled a twin of the assembly language program in the absolute machine language of the microprocessor. This program can then be entered by the programmer manually, but is usually used directly by the computer, since it's in the computer's memory already when the translation is completed.

QUESTIONS

5.1. We have stated that computers are best at doing very repetitive, boring tasks. Describe one such use for the computer (do not use the one WE used!).

5.2. How does the technician usually distinguish software from hardware "bugs" when a computer goes down during a program?

5.3. Describe the source and destination of the following Intel and Zilog mnemonics.

(a) LD A, B   (b) MOV M,A   (c) LXI H, 5000

(d) MVI H, 19   (e) LD A, (3000)   (f) STA (3000)

(g) LD A, (BC)   (h) LD A, (IX + 4) (i) SPHL

(j) LD DE, 5000   (k) EXX   (l) LHLD 3000

5.4. The 16-bit instructions in the 8080 and Z-80 transfer only 8 bits at a time, and do transfers to external memory in two steps. (True or False?)

5.5. What is meant by the terms "fixed word length" and "variable word length?"

5.6. In the 8080, I/O data transfers are limited to communication with only one register in the CPU. Which register?

5.7. Arithmetic and logic operations in both Z-80 and 8080 are mostly limited to one register. Which one?

5.8. Describe the difference between ADD and Add with Carry, and state where each is used.

5.9. Describe how the Compare instruction uses the ALU and flags in the 8080 or Z-80.

5.10. In the examples below, draw a diagram that shows what's in the registers and flags *after* the instruction is completed.

(a) Instruction: ADD A, E (Zilog)

Before	Register A	Register E
	10110100	01010111

(b) Instruction: SUB A, E (Zilog)

Before	Register A	Register E
	00110110	01100101

(c) Instruction: XRA E (Intel)

Before	Register A	Register E
	01110001	01000110

(d) Instruction: CMP E (Intel)

Before	Register A	Register E
	11110100	11110111

5.11. What do the instructions Jump, Call, and Return all have in common? What register do they affect?

5.12. What is the difference between a conditional and an unconditional Jump instruction?

5.13. Besides the opcode, each Jump instruction (JP—Zilog, or JMP—Intel) requires two bytes of data. Why two bytes?

5.14. Why doesn't a relative jump (JR—Zilog only) opcode require two bytes of data?

5.15. Describe what happens to the program counter if a conditional jump instruction *doesn't* jump.

5.16. What instruction is a RST (restart) most similar to in the group of Jump, Call, and Return instructions?

5.17. Are there Conditional Restart instructions in the 8080 and Z-80?

5.18. Describe what happens in a POP and a PUSH instruction. Is the POP or PUSH of single-precision or extended-precision type?

5.19. The Rotate and Shift instructions match the actions of two hardware circuits. What are these two circuits?

5.20. Where would you use NOP in programming?

5.21. What does an assembler program do?

6

Software Structures/Flowcharting

In this chapter we look at simple computer programs for the Z-80/8080 family of microprocessors. The purpose of these programs will be twofold:

1. The programs will show how some of the instructions in the instruction set are used, and how they are put together into larger structures (such as loops and subroutines) from which the entire program is constructed.
2. The programs will show how software may be used to check out the hardware to see if it is working properly, and how software may be used to aid in troubleshooting it when it isn't working properly.

In most cases, each program will be listed in 8080 and Z-80 assembly language and in absolute machine code (written in octal for compactness) as it would appear if you translated the instructions using the Appendix.

Flowcharts which indicate the action of the program will be shown alongside the assembly/machine listings. New flowchart symbols will be introduced as programs that use them appear.

6.1 BRANCHING AND LOOPING

In our first example of **software**, we'd like you to imagine that you've built the binary output device described in Section 3.1. Figure 6-1 shows this device attached to an output port (port 0), similar to the ones we first showed you in Section 1.6.6. The instruction we use to control this output

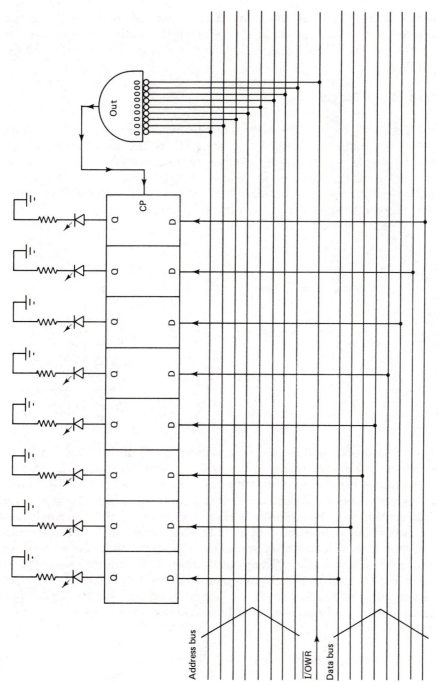

Figure 6-1 Output port 0

Address bus

$\overline{I/OWR}$

Data bus

157

device is OUT 000. It takes any number that's in register A and places it on the data bus; at the same time, it puts address 000 on the lowest eight lines of the address bus and makes the $\overline{\text{I/O WR}}$ (output) signal active on the control bus.

6.1.1 How to Get Lost

We are going to test the output device by sending it an 8-bit number and seeing if the number lights up on the LEDs of the device. Our first attempt will be simple, but incorrect. We have overlooked one major point in writing our test program—can you see what it is? Did you see the flaw in our reasoning? First the number octal 252 (binary value: 10101010) is put in register A, then the number in A is output to port 0, then . . . ?

"Aha!" you say. "Then what?"

Output to Port 0: Program 1

8080	Z-80	Octal	Flowchart
MVI A, 252	LD A, 252	076, 252	A ← 252
OUT 000	OUT 000, A	323, 000	Port 0 ← A

The answer is unpredictable. The next thing that the computer does depends on the instruction in the next memory location. The two instructions shown occupy four addresses of memory apiece. The 076 is, let's say, at memory location 0, and the 252 is at location 1. The 323 is at location 2 and the 000 is at location 3. What's at location 4? Will the computer fetch an instruction at location 4 after it finished what's at 3? To answer the last question first, the answer is yes. The computer will go ahead to 4 when it finishes 3. The question "What's at location 4? is a tougher one. The answer must be: "Whatever the computer had left over in the location before you put in *your* instructions." This could be anything. We don't want the computer doing "garbage," but we didn't do anything to make the computer stop.

6.1.2 Staying Out of the "Garbage"

Here's an improved version of program 1: Now, the program counter stops at address 4 of memory (if we started loading the program at 0). The HLT

Output to Port 0: Program 2

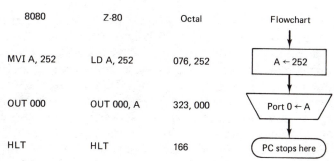

8080	Z-80	Octal	Flowchart
MVI A, 252	LD A, 252	076, 252	A ← 252
OUT 000	OUT 000, A	323, 000	Port 0 ← A
HLT	HLT	166	PC stops here

(halt) instruction makes sure that the PC won't "go ahead" to future lines of code we didn't write. This ensures that the computer won't be doing things we didn't plan just because it has finished what we wanted and kept going to parts of the memory that contain garbage.

6.1.3 Looping

There is another way to avoid the garbage past the end of our little program. Instead of stopping, we'll Jump away from the garbage in program 3.

This program goes back to the top line every time it reaches the bottom line. The computer keeps running instead of being stopped, but still never reaches the garbage part of the memory (where you didn't write any instructions). In this case, our program avoids the garbage area by using an Unconditional jump to form a loop. The name loop is obvious when we look at the flowchart at the right of the program. Whenever the computer reaches the bottom of the diagram, it finds its next step at the top of the same diagram. Thus it loops around, recycling the same instructions over and over, forever. In this case, what we have is called an **endless loop.** If we wait for this program to get finished (to halt), it will never happen. This may be a bad thing to do later on, but in this example, we see it as just another way to avoid "hitting the garbage" after we do the last instruction in the program.

Output to Port 0: Program 3

8080	Z-80	Octal	Flowchart
TOP: MVI A, 252	TOP: LD A, 252	076, 252	A ← 252
OUT 000	OUT 000, A	323, 000	Port 0 ← A
JMP TOP	JP TOP	303, 000, 000	

6.1.4 About Flowchart Symbols

A word about flowcharts. You have seen a flowchart at the right of each of the three example programs. The "shapes" in the flowchart each have a specific meaning. In program 1 we have a rectangle and a trapezoid. The rectangle is the shape for a process, which is something that goes on in the central processor or main memory. Data-transfer and arithmetic/logic instructions are represented with a process block. The *trapezoid* is the shape used with any input/output operation (either input or output). In program 2, we add an *oblong* shape that represents an *end-of-routine*. In this case, the routine ends when we HALT, but there are other ways to end a routine. Connecting all the blocks in the flowchart are *flow arrows*. You have probably already guessed that these show what comes next. In each case, the computer must finish the instruction it is currently doing before it can move ahead to the next one. The flow arrows show where this next instruction is found. In program 3 we see the flow arrows change direction for the first time. This has a special meaning. When the arrows keep flowing downhill from one instruction to the next, that means that the program counter is counting normally 0, 1, 2, 3, 4, . . . and when the arrows change direction, and go back to the top of the program in this case, the program counter has "broken the rules." Where the flow arrow loops back to the beginning of the program the PC counts 0, 1, 2, 3, 4, 0, 1, 2, . . . and keeps going back to 0, instead of counting from 6 to 7. This is how a Jump looks on the flowchart, and in this case, we used an unconditional jump to close the program into a loop. As we said before, the program keeps running and doesn't HALT, but once it's in a loop like program 3, it can't escape from that loop and must repeat the same instructions forever.

6.1.5 All Good Things Must End

Program 4 is almost the same as Programs 1, 2, and 3. It has two major differences; the number that is in A comes from a counting process—it has a different value every time the program loops—and the loop doesn't go indefinitely, because the JUMP is a CONDITIONAL BRANCH. When the number in A has counted high enough, it will carry a one into the carry flag. This will bring an end to the loop, because the loop only loops while the carry flag contains a 0 (the No Carry condition). After the Carry flag is turned on, the program counter isn't JUMPed. What it does instead is to keep counting in its normal fashion, as shown below the program.

Notice the use of the Boolean XOR operation. This XOR combines A with itself. Since A always matches itself, the XOR gate's output is always LOW. This ends up zeroing the contents of the A register. It's a fairly standard thing to do this (zeroing the value in A) with the XOR instruction, so we thought we'd better show it to you in an early part of the chapter.

Output to Port 0: Program 4

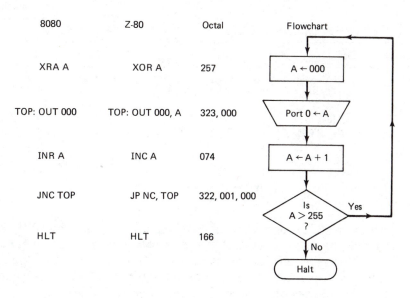

8080	Z-80	Octal	Flowchart
XRA A	XOR A	257	A ← 000
TOP: OUT 000	TOP: OUT 000, A	323, 000	Port 0 ← A
INR A	INC A	074	A ← A + 1
JNC TOP	JP NC, TOP	322, 001, 000	Is A > 255 ?
HLT	HLT	166	Halt

PC = 0, 1, 2, 3, 4, 5, 6, 0, 1, 2 . . . (255 times) . . . 5, 6, 7 (end)

Notice also the new flowchart block. The diamond is the symbol for a decision operation where a CONDITIONAL BRANCH is used to direct the program onto one of two different paths at a "fork in the road." The decision flowchart symbol always has one flow arrow entering into it and two (or more) coming out. In our flowchart, the two outcomes (yes or no) determine which arrow the program will "follow."

Since the A register of an 8080 or Z-80 is an 8-bit register, it will count like an 8-bit counter when it is incremented by the INC or INR instruction on the third line of the program. An 8-bit counter has a modulus of 256. This means that after the loop has run 256 times, the counter will count around to 00000000 and carry a one to the Carry flag. That is the condition that lets the computer "escape" from the loop.

Table 6-1 shows another way to look at the machine code which is produced by translating program 4.

The lines marked "line" in the machine language program are one memory address each. The "address" is a combination of the line number and the page number. In this example, all the lines are located on page 000 (the first 256 locations in memory). The line called "top" is really line 001. On lines 004, 005, and 006, the Jump if No Carry instruction jumps to line 001 on page 000. This is the same place as "top." The opcode of the jump in-

TABLE 6-1   OUTPUT TO PORT 0 PROGRAM 4

		Absolute machine code		
Assembly language		Address		
8080	Z-80	Line	Page	Instruction
XRA A	XOR A	000	000	257
Top: OUT 000	Top: OUT 000, A	001	000	323
		002	000	000
INR A	INC A	000	000	074
JNC TOP	JP NC, TOP	004	000	322
		005	000	001
		006	000	000
HLT	HLT	007	000	166

struction (322) says what kind of a jump it is, and the (001) and (000) are the line and page number of the place called "top" in assembly language.

Normally, all the bytes of an instruction (like the Jump, which is a three-byte instruction) are put on the same line, and at the beginning of each line, the address of the opcode byte is shown (Table 6-2).

After line 001, the next line is 003 because the instruction on line 001 takes up two bytes, stored at address 001 and 002. The next available space for an instruction is line 003. In another place, the address skips from 004 to 007 because the instruction on line 004 takes up lines 004, 005, and 006. The next available space for an instruction is on line 007.

Notice that there are never any gaps between instructions. In machine language, if you skip over a space between one instruction and the next, there will be something in that space. The program counter will not skip over that space. It will do whatever is in that space, whether it's something you want or not.

TABLE 6-2   OUTPUT TO PORT 0 PROGRAM 4

		Absolute machine code		
Assembly language		Address		Instruction
8080	Z-80	Line	Page	Opcode data
XRA A	XOR A	000	000	257
Top: OUT 000	Top: OUT 000, A	001	000	323,000
INR A	INC A	003	000	074
JNC TOP	JP NC, TOP	004	000	322,001,000
HLT	HLT	007	000	166

6.2 SUBROUTINES

We discussed subroutines and stack operations briefly in Chapter 5, but the only way to see how they really work is to see a subroutine in a program, and see how the program uses the subroutine.

To write a machine language program, ask yourself the following five questions:

1. Is this a problem that a computer can solve faster or with less work than if I solved the same problem "by hand"?
2. How do I want the output and input to look?
3. What steps will the computer have to do when it solves this problem?
4. How will I use this computer's instruction set to do the steps I worked out in question 3?
5. What are the actual codes and addresses that I will enter into the computer for this program?

The answer to the first question forces you to define the problem and decide if it is feasible for the computer to solve it. The answer must be yes, or there's no point going on to step 2.

The answer to the second question forces you to lay out a chart (an I/O chart) that shows exactly how you want the input to appear before it is put into the computer, and how you want the output to appear after the program is done.

To complete the remaining steps, you have to develop a flowchart (step 3), an assembly language program (step 4), and a machine language program (step 5).

6.2.1 RAM Tester Program without Subroutines

We'd like to build a RAM tester to test RAM boards as they come off the assembly line. The available hardware includes a working CPU and a working RAM TEST program written on a ROM located at page 000 of memory. The board we want to test is plugged into a socket that maps it into page 001 of memory. It is this program that we're going to develop. Before we do, we ask question 1: "Is it worth it?"

Since the memory boards contain thousands of flip-flops, and the CPU can address them to write and read them all in a fraction of a second, we decide that it's worthwhile to test these flip-flops with a microprocessor. Testing each flip-flop by hand would be time consuming (and boring) beyond description.

Since the answer to question 1 is yes, we go ahead to an I/O chart for this system (Figure 6-2).

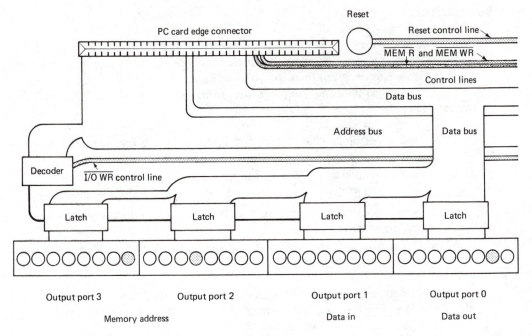

Figure 6-2 An I/O chart for a RAM troubleshooter board

In this I/O chart, we see that the input (plugging a board into the slot and pressing reset) is very simple. The output shows what would happen if a bad bit were encountered on line 020 of page 001. The page and line of the bad memory byte are shown on output ports 3 and 2. In addition to knowing where something is wrong, the numbers at output port 1 and 0 show what went wrong, by showing what we (attempted to) write into the memory, and what we read back from the same memory location. This display should only be activated when the number written does not match what we read back from the same location. The output displays information the technician should find helpful in troubleshooting the board that has failed.

What should the technician look for, and what types of tests will find these things? We'll look at a very simple group of tests that only look for two things: a short on the data bus and an open on the data bus. These are typical of the type of problems that might appear on boards that have just left the flow-soldering machine at the end of a production line. Sometimes the solder doesn't hit all the points it's supposed to, and this results in an *open;* at other times, too much solder flows, connecting points that are not supposed to be connected, a *short.*

Here's a flowchart for the program we're talking about (all numbers shown are octal):

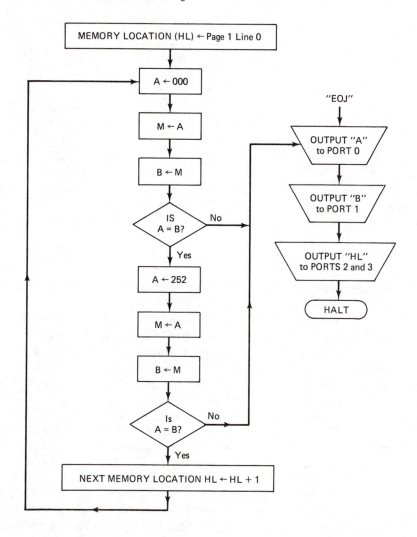

We could go ahead from this flowchart to steps 3, 4, and 5, but before we do, there's a reason not to. If you look at the flowchart above, you'll see this sequence of instructions repeated twice. The only thing that's different in the first and second versions of this sequence is the value of the number we called (SOMETHING) (see the flowchart on page 166). This is the number we've chosen to write and read in the memory.

Is there a way to write this routine just once and use it twice, with a different value of (SOMETHING) each time? We do this by changing the routine into a subroutine:

To test the memory, we'll write a number into the memory, then read

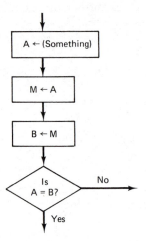

it back and compare what's written with what's read. The number we write depends on the type of test we want to carry out.

To detect an open, we'll write 00000000 into the RAM. If an unexpected 1 appears in the number that returns, it probably indicates an open. TTL and other TTL-compatible memory devices—most MOS memories are designed to be TTL compatible—behave as though a disconnected lead is a logic 1. We say that the inputs "float HIGH" when they're open, instead of being connected to something.

To detect a short, we'll write 10101010 at the RAM location being tested. This is based on the assumption that the traces on the PC board are next to each other in the same order as shown above. We expect that there's a 1 next to a 0 on adjacent traces of the data bus when the number 10101010 is being written or read. TTL-compatible outputs will have strong pull-downs and weak pull-ups, so a 0 that's shorted to a trace carrying a 1 will "fight" with the 1, and the 0 will always win. This will result in unexpected 0s in the number, as a 1 is grounded out by an adjacent 0 wherever there's a short.

The instruction CALL TEST asks the computer to use the subroutine "Test" at the bottom of the diagram. In the first instance, the value of A is 000 when Test is called. In the second, A is "252" (10101010) when the Test subroutine is called. Each time the same test is done on the memory; we write the number into the memory location from A, then read it out again into B, then compare A with B to see if they match. If they don't, we go to the EOJ routine. The name EOJ stands for "End of Job". It's a fairly standard computerese name for the end of a program. In this case, the program halts if an error is found so that the operator has time to read the displays and correct the defect in the RAM board. If the program continued to

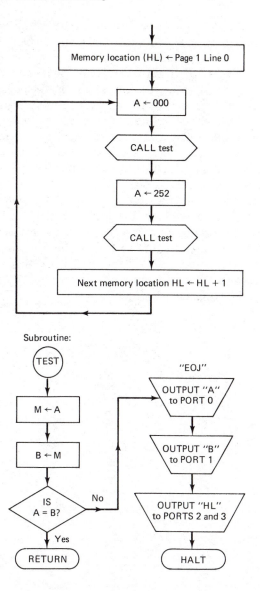

run full speed with the errors being displayed as each one is found, the average error message would flash on the displays for a microsecond (a millionth of a second) or two. Even with a super speed-reading course, nobody could keep up with that data rate.

What if all the As and Bs match everywhere? Will the program ever stop? If you look at the flowchart, there doesn't seem to be any elegant way to get out of this program—something has to go wrong for it to end.

This program does have an end. It isn't elegant, but there is always an end—when the program runs off the end of the memory board being tested. We can assume that the PC board we plug into the slot on our tester isn't a full 65,536 bytes of RAM (if it were, we'd have no place to put the ROM with our tester program on it). If the RAM board we're testing is 32K or less, there will be a gap in the memory map of the computer which has no memory circuits in it. When the computer tries to write and read in this area, it will fail. The first test—which looks for unexpected 1s—will fail when the computer attempts to read an area where there's a nonchip (which is open everywhere) since every line on the data bus will be floating, and all the floating lines will look like 1s.

Now let's finish the translation of this program into assembly language and machine language from the flowchart. Each block in the flowchart becomes a group of one or more instructions in assembly language. Each line of assembly language becomes a line of machine language (octal) code.

To answer question 4 ("How will I use this computer's instruction set to do the steps I worked out in the flowchart?"), we convert the flowchart into assembly language as shown below:

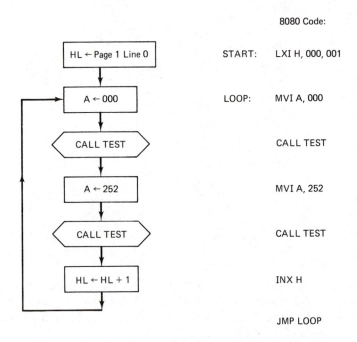

8080 Code:

START: LXI H, 000, 001

LOOP: MVI A, 000

          CALL TEST

          MVI A, 252

          CALL TEST

          INX H

          JMP LOOP

Two things need explaining here. First is the use of the CMP (compare) instruction. CMP B does a "look-ahead subtract" that finds out if "A minus

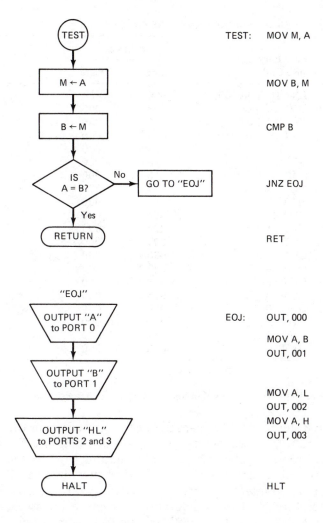

TEST: MOV M, A

         MOV B, M

         CMP B

         JNZ EOJ

         RET

EOJ: OUT, 000

         MOV A, B
         OUT, 001

         MOV A, L
         OUT, 002
         MOV A, H
         OUT, 003

         HLT

B" would be negative, zero, or positive. After the CMP B instruction, a JNZ (Jump if Not Zero) instruction does a test that's really "Jump if Not Equal." This is so because if A and B are equal, the look-ahead subtraction (CMP) says "A minus B" would be 0.

The second thing that needs explaining is the use of MOV instructions in the last three outputs. In the 8080, only register A may source a number to the output device. If the number we want to see is in another register, we must MOV it to register A.

To go ahead to the final step of writing this machine language program, we ask question 5 ("What are the actual codes and addresses that I will enter into the computer for this program?"). This is shown in Table 6-3.

TABLE 6-3 FINAL MACHINE LANGUAGE PROGRAM

Assembly language (8080 Code)	Address		Octal instruction
	Line	Page	Opcode data
START: LXI H, 000, 001	000	000	041,000,001
LOOP: MVI A, 000	003	000	076,000
CALL TEST	005	000	315,021,000
MVI A, 252	010	000	076,252
CALL TEST	012	000	315,021,000
INX H	015	000	043
JMP LOOP	016	000	303,003,000
TEST: MOV M, A	021	000	167
MOV B, M	022	000	106
CMP B	02{	000	270
JNZ EOJ	024	000	302,030,000
RET	027	000	311
EOJ: OUT, 000	030	000	323,000
MOV A, B	032	000	170
OUT, 001	033	000	323,001
MOV A, H	035	000	174
OUT, 003	036	000	323,003
MOV A, L	040	000	175
OUT, 002	041	000	323,002
HLT	043	000	166

6.2.2 What Happens during a Call and How Returns Are Possible

Figure 6-3 shows what happens in our tester program as the program counter "walks" through the memory picking up instructions. Each time the CALL TEST instruction takes place, the computer goes to the same place, but returns to a different return address. The first time the CALL takes place, the program counter is pointed at line 010 (octal), which is the next instruction after the CALL. This number is saved on the stack, and when a RETURN takes place, it RETURNs to line 010 of memory. The second time the CALL takes place, the program counter is pointed at line 015 (octal), where the instruction after the CALL is located. This time, a 015 is saved on the stack, and although the same TEST subroutine is being done at the same place as before, when it RETURNs, this time it RETURNs to 015.

Using a subroutine in this program didn't save much space over just writing the routine twice, but it did save some space. In programs where a subroutine is called at three or four or more places in a program, the more times the routine is called, the more space is saved by subroutining. Programs written to take advantage of "subroutinability" are called **structured programming**. Such programs run a little more slowly than programs written straight through, but they have advantages in taking up less memory space

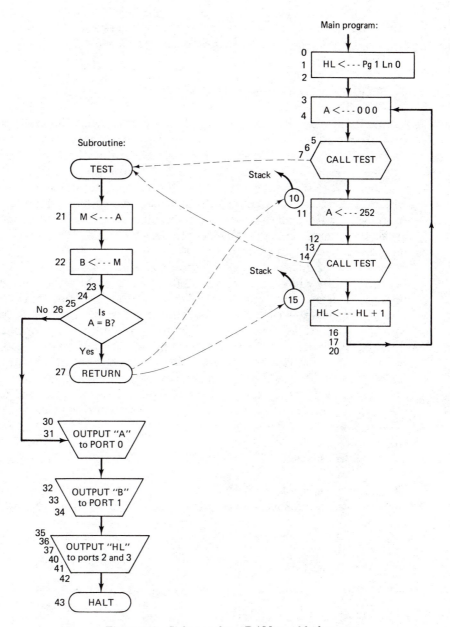

Figure 6-3 Software for a RAM troubleshooter

and being easier to reorganize if a rewrite is necessary. Structured programming is sometimes also called *modular programming*.

6.3 STACK OPERATIONS WITH SUBROUTINES

In our RAM test program, information is passed from the main program to the subroutine in register A. The first time the memory location M is tested, the number used is 000, and the second time, it's 252. In both cases, the number to be tested is placed in register A before the CALL goes to the subroutine. When the subroutine does the test, it doesn't care what's in A; whatever it is, it gets written into and read out of the memory. After the subroutine is finished and the program counter RETURNs to the main program, the number in A is replaced with another value. If an error occurs, the number in A is displayed on output device 0.

It's important, in case of an error, that nothing happens to A. We must be able to see what number we tried to write at M after the test fails, in order to identify the type of trouble. Another number that must be untouched during the time the subroutine runs is the number in HL (which points at the address being tested). In this program, the subroutine does not do anything to HL, so it's the same number both before and after the subroutine is called. The only register that's different before and after the subroutine runs is B, which receives the number that comes back from memory M. If we need the number at B to remain untouched after the subroutine (we don't need it, in this case), our TEST subroutine can't be used. Look at what it does:

6.3.1 PUSHes and POPs

To protect the number in B, if it's an important number, the subroutine should save and recover the original value of B as shown in the following example:

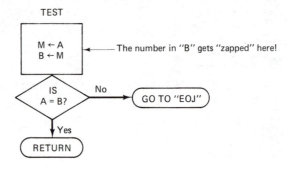

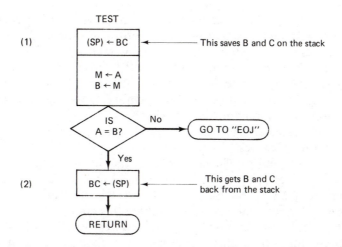

The operation on line (1) is called a PUSH (Zilog name: PUSH BC; Intel name: PUSH B), which is a 16-bit save-to-memory operation we discussed earlier. On line (2), we recover the number we pushed with a POP (Zilog name: POP BC; Intel name: POP B). With PUSH and POP operations, we can preserve any register or register pair that we don't want to clobber by temporarily storing it in the memory.

Which brings us to the question: "Where, in fact, is the stack in the memory?" We know that if we're running a program, the current instruction is where the program counter points. In doing stack operations, the current location of the top of the stack is the place in memory where the stack pointer (SP) points.

So where in the memory of our program is the stack pointer pointing? If there's no instruction that specifically puts a value into the SP (a LD SP, ***, *** instruction), it will be pointed wherever the laws of chance happened to leave it when the power was turned on. This will not be "zero." The SP could be literally anywhere, and if the "anywhere" turns out to be ROM, or a section of memory without any memory chips in it, too bad. Even if the section of memory where the SP points is populated by real RAM memory devices, it's possible that they could be defective—since the only RAM memory in the tester is the board being tested. We'll have to revise our RAM tester to provide a safe piece of RAM memory for the stack to be in. After we make sure that the hardware (some bytes of RAM memory) is there, we also need to provide the right type of software to position the stack in this piece of RAM.

But . . . wait a minute! Isn't all this worry based on the idea that we've got to save register B with PUSHes and POPs? What if we don't have to save register B? (We don't!) Is there any need to worry about the stack in this case?

Yes! The stack is used every time a subroutine CALL and RETurn is done. It's the stack that holds the return address while the subroutine is running, and from which the address is recovered into the program counter when a Return is done. To save and recover a return address, we must use RAM memory that can record and play back. The RAM test program itself is in a ROM, the rest of the memory is empty, except the board we're testing—which may not be working.

Does that mean that the RAM tester program we looked at in the last section won't work?

It sure does! The chances that the SP would be pointed at a usable section of RAM are very small. Imagine that our RAM tester is testing boards that hold 1K of memory, that the ROM with the test program in it is one page ($\frac{1}{4}$K), and the rest of the memory is empty. That comes out to 63K of NON-RAM and only 1K of (maybe defective) RAM in the memory map. If the SP could be pointed anywhere, the chances are 1 in 63 that the stack is in the RAM, and less than that for the stack to be in a working RAM.

We need to revise our hardware to include a small amount of RAM along with the ROM program and the test slot. This new hardware design is shown in Figure 6-4.

We also need a revised software design. The RAM (stack) added to our hardware has been wired in at the top of memory. We designed the hardware so that the RAM (which is actually made from a couple of 7489 16 × 4 RAM chips) is located in the last 16 bytes of page 377. The SP counts backwards as numbers are PUSHed into the stack. It's fairly common practice in complete systems, to put the stack at the top of memory and the program at the bottom, to give both areas the largest range of expansion before they overlap. In this case, it's not necessary, but we've decided to do it the same way, even for this simple microprocessor-based board tester.

The stack pointer has been placed at line 377 of page 377, which is the very top of the top of memory. As 16-bit words are PUSHed into the stack, the SP will back up in steps of two addresses apiece, to line 375, line 373, and so forth. This is shown in Table 6-4.

You can see that all we've done is to add one line at the beginning of the program. The line LXI SP, 377, 377 ensures that the stack is in the RAM we added, located in a place where it can use the maximum amount of memory cells available in the RAM. You'll also notice if you inspect the machine language program carefully that all the addresses associated with labels (except START) are new numbers. All the Jump and Call instructions have to be rewritten for addresses that are the "old addresses plus three," because we added a three-byte instruction to the beginning of the program. You can see that modifying machine language programs, even by a single instruction, is clumsy. If we had already "burned" a ROM with the old program on it, the ROM would have to be thrown out (or completely repro-

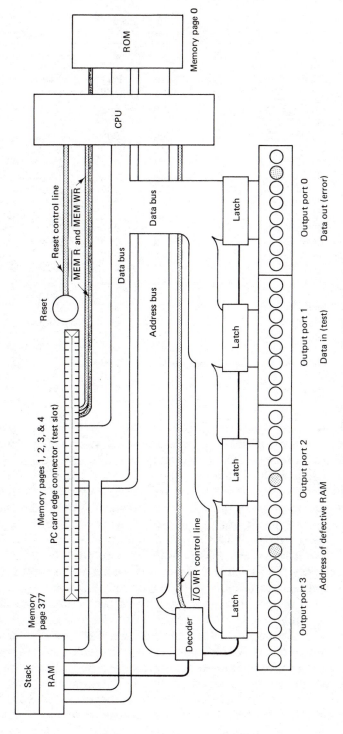

Figure 6-4 Hardware for a RAM troubleshooter

TABLE 6-4 REVISED MACHINE LANGUAGE PROGRAM

Assembly language (8080 code)	Address Line	Page	Octal instruction Opcode data	
START: LXI SP, 377, 377	000	000	061,377,377	added instruction
LXI H, 000, 001	003	000	041,000,001	
LOOP: MVI A, 000	006	000	076,000	
CALL TEST	010	000	315,024,000	
MVI A, 252	013	000	076,252	
CALL TEST	015	000	315,024,000	
INX H	020	000	043	
JMP LOOP	021	000	303,006,000	
TEST: MOV M, A	024	000	167	
MOV B, M	025	000	106	
CMP B	026	000	270	
JNZ EOJ	027	000	302,033,000	
RET	032	000	311	
EOJ: OUT, 000	033	000	323,000	
MOV A, B	035	000	170	
OUT, 001	036	000	323,001	
MOV A, H	040	000	174	
OUT, 003	041	000	323,003	
MOV A, L	043	000	175	
OUT, 002	044	000	323,002	
HLT	046	000	166	

grammed if it is an EROM). There is no way we could use the old instructions, because the addresses they contain are no longer valid.

You can also see that we did not add a PUSH or POP to the subroutine; we know that register B is not used anywhere else in the program, and it's not necessary to preserve the value of B between the Call and the Return.

A last word on the problem we solved when we wrote this program. We designed the hardware and the ROM software to do a specific, inflexible task—to test RAM boards for opens and shorts. That is all the complete system does, once it's finished. We're not taking full advantage of the computer capabilities of the Z-80 or 8080 chip in this system.

In fact, the system isn't a general-purpose computer at all—it's a one-program computer. We call machines like this dedicated machines. The same job could have been done by a network of counters and logic gates, using all hardware. A RAM board tester unit could be made of gates to do exactly what our programmed microprocessor does, but it would be many times bigger and more expensive to build. If the layout of the RAM boards it was designed for is changed, the all-hardware tester would become instantly obsolete. It can't be adapted to a new design of the RAM board without being totally rebuilt, and if we choose to change it to an I/O board tester—forget it!

With the microprocessor-based tester (it's not really a computer!), we can adapt the tester to a new RAM board design by pulling the ROM out of its socket, and replacing it with one that has a program for the new board design. Ultimately, the program written can test another, completely different type of board, such as an I/O board, provided that it plugs into the same socket and has its bus connections in the right places.

We can see that the microprocessor-plus-ROM combination called a dedicated machine is a much more powerful and flexible design than the random-logic board devised for only one kind of test. We can also see one other important thing: In this design, we've replaced hardware with software. Programming for logic design—using software to replace hardware—is the way to go in the design of "smart" test equipment, or anything else where logic circuits are needed. We'll come back to this concept of replacing hardware with a program in later chapters.

6.4 INTERRUPTS

An **interrupt** is hardware-driven software. When hardware outside the computer can control what's happening inside (the software), we call it an interrupt. When the hardware signal becomes active and the special software that services the hardware signal begins to run, we say that the computer is doing an interrupt or servicing an interrupt. The name of the software that runs during the interrupt is the *interrupt service routine* (ISR).

There are three types of interrupt that we will discuss in this section of the chapter. An interrupt that uses the full hardware "handshaking" capabilities of the microprocessor is called a *vectored interrupt*. A shorthand version of this called a non-maskable interrupt is available on the Z-80 and some other microprocessors (6800, 6809, 6502). It does not require as much hardware as the vectored interrupt, but does not have as much flexibility either (it's also not available on the 8080). The third type of interrupt is called a *polled interrupt*. It doesn't require any special hardware at all; it just uses the available I/O ports and is really more software than hardware. We'll begin our discussion of interrupts with the hardware used by each type of interrupt. After that, we'll discuss the ISRs and how they work hand-in-hand with the hardware to provide interrupt control of the computer.

6.4.1 Hardware

Vectored Interrupts. There are two signals found on the 8080 (or Z-80) CPU called the *interrupt request* and the *interrupt acknowledge* (these signals are found on the control bus). Each manufacturer seems to have slightly different names for these signals, but in any case, they are an input that asks the computer CPU to begin an interrupt, and an output that the CPU uses to tell the outside world that it has accepted the request, and is beginning the interrupt procedure. When a pair of signals like this (a "request" and a "reply") are used in a digital system to indicate when a special state is being used, the two signals are called a *handshake*. We have already seen some other handshake signals in our discussion of microprocessor CPUs (Chapter 4).

When an interrupt request appears on the INT input of the CPU, five things happen:

1. The INT input becomes "active." If it is accepted, then . . .
2. The CPU completes the cycle it is in.
3. The CPU "replies" by making the INTA (interrupt acknowledged) output "active."
4. The CPU fetches any instruction it finds on the data bus and executes it (the instruction should be a RST).
5. After it completes the RST instruction, the CPU finds itself in the ISR. At the end of the ISR, it returns to the next step in the program that was running at the time of the interrupt.

Everything will "work" if the hardware attached to INT, INTA, and the data bus are designed to cooperate with the five steps above. For instance, when the INTA signal becomes active, some logic circuitry must be activated that will "gate" a RST opcode onto the data bus. When the INTA signal is active on the control bus, the memory and I/O control signals will be inactive, so the data bus will be floating. Whatever circuitry is used to gate the RST instruction onto the data bus will have no interference from anywhere else. Now, when the CPU does the RST instruction (executes it) there must be a subroutine, or at least a Jump to a subroutine (a **vector**), at the address the RST makes the program counter go to. Remember that the RST instruction is just like a CALL to a subroutine.

It is possible for the interrupt request (INT) signal to be *denied*. This is done by disabling interrupts. A flag in the CPU can be set or reset by software commands that will permit or block the INT input. The software command that enables the INT input to "get in" is called *enable interrupts* (EI). When this instruction is "run" during a program, it sets the interrupt flip-flop. From that moment on, the software can be interrupted.

The software command that disables the INT input is called *disable interrupts* (DI). When this instruction is run in a program, it resets the interrupt flip-flop, making the INT input go away. This is done when the program that is running is sensitive and cannot afford to be interrupted for unimportant reasons. For instance, suppose that a program is running that is calling the Fire Department because a fire alarm has been detected in the input network. We don't want a trivial interrupt, like the digital clock driver, to interrupt this program every time the clock ticks. The fire alarm program has priority. It outranks the clock driver program.

Figure 6-5 shows a circuit for an interrupt-driven input from a keyboard. The keyboard, represented by a block, is attached to an 8-bit input port. The D7 data bit is an active-LOW keypressed signal ($\overline{KP}$) and the remaining 7 bits are ASCII code from the key being pressed. The port to which the keyboard is attached is input port 6; the decoder only enables the buffer when the address on the address bus is a 6 and there is an active input signal on the control bus.

When any key on the keyboard is pressed, the $\overline{KP}$ signal becomes LOW.

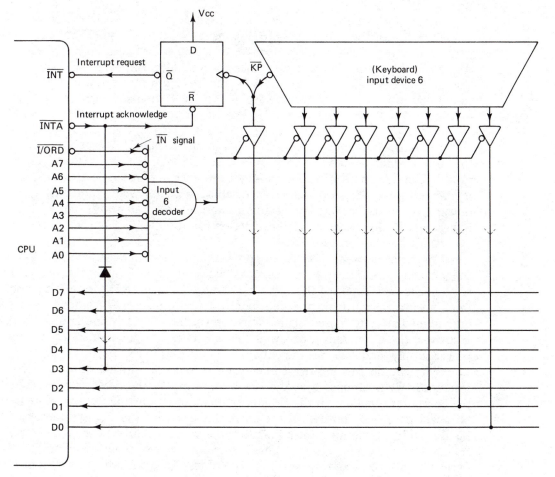

Figure 6-5   Vectored interrupt hardware

Its falling edge triggers the keypressed flip-flop, which sets. The output of the flip-flop makes the INT signal on the control bus become "active." For the Intel 8080, it is an active-HIGH signal; for the Zilog Z-80, it is active LOW (Figure 6-5 represents a Z-80).

As soon as the INTA becomes active (it is active LOW for both Intel and Zilog CPUs) it resets the flip-flop, and the INT request is turned off—since the CPU is already handling this interrupt, the request isn't needed anymore.

At the same time that it resets the flip-flop, the INTA signal also pulls down on data bus line D3. The rest of the data bus lines float, and their terminating resistors pull up the unconnected lines to a logic 1 level. The diode is used to connect INTA to D3 so that it doesn't conduct 1s to the D3 line when INTA is inactive. That would fight with authentic data, and we don't want to do that.

Why do we want to pull down on the D3 data line when INTA becomes active? With all the other lines HIGH, this makes the number 11110111 appear on the data bus. This is the code for a RST 6 instruction. It will cause the same results as a call to a subroutine at line 060. Hopefully, the subroutine at line 060 will "pick up" a data number from input device 6 and do something with it, then return. We will look at this software in Section 6.4.2.

Nonmaskable Interrupts. The Z-80 has an input called NMI (non-maskable interrupt) which is like the INT (interrupt request), but is really an "interrupt demand." The NMI takes priority over any software that's running, even if the interrupt flip-flop has been disabled. That's what "nonmaskable" means. A "mask" covers something up and makes it go away. The INT input is "maskable" because a DI instruction can disable it. The NMI outranks everything else in the system.

An example of an NMI is the power failure indicator shown in Figure 6.6. If the power-supply voltage falls below a critical value, the detector triggers the NMI input of the CPU. Unlike the INT, the NMI doesn't have to fetch an instruction from the data bus to figure out where it's going. It just goes immediately to a predesigned location (in the Z-80, it's line 146). When it arrives, the CPU finds a program that switches off the connection to the power supply, and attaches the emergency batteries (we hope).

Why should this interrupt have priority over the fire alarm routine, for instance? Well, suppose that the fire burns through the power cables while the computer is calling up the fire department and reporting the fire. The report will never get finished, if the power fails, so the interrupt is interrupted by the NMI. Switching into the alternate voltage source probably takes a fraction of a second, and the small "hiccup" in the report will probably never be noticed at the fire station. The power failure interrupt should have a higher priority than the fire alarm interrupt, just as the fire alarm interrupt

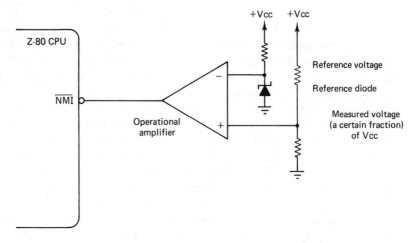

Figure 6-6 Non-maskable interrupt if power fails

has priority over the digital clock interrupt that adds ticks to the clock every second.

Polled Interrupts.   The **polled interrupt** is a program. It uses conventional input port hardware instead of special signals on the control bus. In a polled interrupt, the computer program kills time until one bit of the input becomes active.

Since there's no special hardware, we didn't include a circuit here.

Reset.   A **Reset** isn't an interrupt, but it is a hardware signal that can interrupt any software that's running. When the Reset is active, the program counter is automatically at memory line 0. Unlike the real interrupt, a Reset doesn't deposit the old value of the program counter in the stack. It's a case of "no deposit, no return." You can think of a Reset as a Jump to line 0, but not a Call to line 0.

Reset is usually not used to get to a special program as much as it's used to get away from one. It's used when you want to get the computer back if it's lost in an endless loop or stuck at a Halt.

Since there's no way to get back to the program that was running at the time of the Reset (and you usually don't want to, anyway!), the normal thing that's put at the Reset's destination is the main operating system program for the computer. In our RAM troubleshooter earlier in this chapter, we used Reset to begin the RAM test. Since every test ended in a Halt, the Reset was used to restart the program when there was a new board to be tested. Of course, the program had to start at line 0.

6.4.2 Software (and ISRs)

Vectored Interrupts. The software needed to support the hardware in Figure 6-5 must be located at line 060 (octal) on page 0 of memory. If the data from the keyboard have to be stored in memory and displayed on a video screen, and the memory pointer for the keyboard's memory space incremented, and so forth, the program to get a byte from keyboard 6 could be quite complicated. If there is a keyboard 7 which uses the RST 7 instruction, there won't be enough room for a complicated procedure like this between RST 6's destination and RST 7's destination. What's usually done to handle this is to put the ISR (in this case, the program that handles data from keyboard 6) in another part of the memory where there's lots of space. Let's call this routine KSR6 for Keyboard Service Routine 6), and suppose that our system's programmer has written it on line 000 of page 003. In this example, then, we won't find KSR6 at line 060. What we'll find there instead is:

$$\text{JP KSR6} \qquad \begin{array}{lll} 060 & 000 & 303 \\ 061 & 000 & 000 \\ 062 & 000 & 003 \end{array}$$

This Jump is called a *vector*. It's where the vectored interrupt gets its name.

We also have to remember that the INT is a maskable interrupt. The INT input is a "request" that can be denied if the program that's running at the time has higher priority. For instance, the fire alarm routine and the power failure routine we mentioned earlier would both contain a DI command at the beginning of their code. The keyboard in our example would be unable to get the computer's attention during these emergencies. At the end, there would be an EI command, to restore the system to interruptible status once the emergency has been handled.

Nonmaskable Interrupts. The software for a nonmaskable interrupt would be exactly like that of the standard interrupt, except that the NMI, since it is reserved for emergency use, would always disable other interrupts when it is running. This is not done by hardware, so the ISR must change a little. Suppose that we want to vector to a place called ESR (Emergency Service Routine) on line 005 of page 007. Here are two ways we could do it:

$$\begin{array}{lll} \text{DI} & \qquad 146 & 000 & 363 \\ \text{CALL ESR} & \qquad 147 & 000 & 315 \\ & \qquad 150 & 000 & 005 \\ & \qquad 151 & 000 & 007 \end{array}$$

	EI	152 000	373
	RET	153 000	311

or

	JP ESR	146 000	303
		147 000	005
		150 000	007
		. . .
ESR:	DI	005 007	363
.		. . .

rest of routine ESR

		. . .
.		
	EI	005 300	373
	RET	005 301	311

In these cases, the DI and EI commands could either be a part of the ESR or of the vector.

Polled Interrupts.   Since a polled interrupt is all software, we present an example using hardware similar in purpose to the vectored interrupt hardware.   Suppose that there is a keyboard attached to input port 6 in the standard I/O of our computer, and that its D7 data bit is its KP (active LOW) sig-

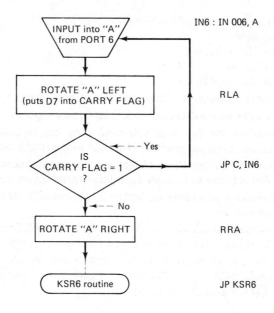

nal, while the remaining 7 bits are ASCII code for the key being pressed. Instead of using the KP signal to trigger the INT input, we use the software shown here to "wait" for the key to be pressed. Notice the use of a rotate instruction to see if the D8 bit is HIGH or LOW by testing the Carry flag. Sneaky, huh? Well, we told you those Rotate instructions were good for something.

In this program, the computer spins around in an input loop as long as the D7 bit is HIGH. As soon as D7 becomes LOW, which is the active condition for the KP signal, the computer proceeds to KSR6. Of course, when nobody's pressing on a key, the computer's just killing time—it can't do anything useful.

6.4.3 Summary

What are the advantages and disadvantages of various types of interrupts? The preceding paragraph should give you a hint: "Standard" (vectored) interrupts use the computer most efficiently, since the computer can run "useful" software between interrupts.

Polled interrupts use simpler hardware than vectored interrupts, but in between interrupts, they can't run "just any" software; the only software that they can run is the loop that keeps looking for an input bit to change.

QUESTIONS

6.1. Draw the symbol (flowchart block) for a:
   (a) Process
   (b) I/O operation
   (c) Decision
   (d) End-of-Routine

6.2. Sketch a flowchart with several blocks, using flow arrows to show what a loop is.

6.3. Describe how a decision block is used in a program to terminate a loop.

6.4. What are the five steps you must carry out to develop a computer program in machine language from the idea stage to the final program? (See Section 6.2.)

6.5. How can a subroutine call reduce the amount of code written to solve a problem? (You may use an example from this chapter if you wish to.)

6.6. Describe a procedure for testing a location of RAM to see if it does what it's supposed to do.

6.7. Describe a procedure for testing a 7400 Quad-NAND gate chip instead of RAM. The chip will have to be connected to input ports and output ports.

6.8. Why is it necessary to worry about where the stack pointer is pointing in the RAM troubleshooter diagnostic program used in this chapter?

6.9. What is a dedicated machine?

6.10. Describe the differences among the following:
   (a) Vectored interrupt
   (b) Polled interrupt
   (c) Nonmaskable interrupt

6.11. What is "handshaking"?

6.12. Describe what happens during a maskable interrupt that is masked (disabled).

6.13. Is the hardware in Figure 6-5 used for a vectored, nonmaskable, or polled interrupt?

6.14. Describe what a RESET does, and how it can be used as a "super-high-priority" interrupt.

6.15. Draw a schematic showing how the keyboard in Figure 6-5 could be interfaced for use with a polled interrupt.

7

High-Level Language Programming

Although every microcomputer works internally in the machine language of its microprocessor, few interact with their users in this language. Machine language programming is awkward and slow, and errors are easy to make. In this chapter, we will find out what a high-level language is, and, through examples in the language called BASIC, we'll see how certain problems that are "messy" in machine language may be very easy in a high-level language.

BASIC (Beginner's All-purpose Symbolic Instruction Code) was chosen for this chapter's examples because more microcomputers "talk" to their users in BASIC than any other high-level language.

Many microcomputers are **turnkey** systems. This means that when the power is turned on (when you "turn the key") the computer "wakes up" communicating in BASIC. "How is this possible?", you ask; "Isn't the 'native' language of the computer the machine language of its microprocessor?" Yes and no; the internal language of the microprocessor is still "doing the work," but the external communications between the user's keyboard and the computer's video display are controlled by a program called the **operating system**. This program, on most microcomputers, is mapped into the memory permanently in ROM. As soon as power comes ON (a power-on reset circuit is usually used) this program is running. In most microcomputers, this operating system is a BASIC **interpreter**.

"What's an interpreter?", you wonder. A program that translates lines of alphanumeric code into commands of machine language may be called an *assembler*, an *interpreter*, or a *compiler*. The assembler, we saw in Chapter 6, is the program that carries out the fifth step in our five steps to machine language programming (Section 6.2). Assembly is a little like using a dictionary to translate from one language to another. There are as many instructions in machine language at the end as there were mnemonics in assembly language at the beginning. The assembly language program is a little like a skeleton. We fill out the program as we translate to machine language by replacing the mnemonics with suitable binary opcodes, and by replacing labels with real addresses that refer to places in the memory. When the procedure described above is done by a program, the program is called an assembler. The final result is a clone of the assembly language program, duplicated in machine language. It is this clone which the computer runs, because its instruction decoder doesn't understand the alphanumeric mnemonics and labels of assembly language. The clone of the assembly language program is stored in the memory and then executed by the computer. This machine language program is called the *object program* or *object code*. The original assembly language program is called the *source program* or *source code*.

The higher-level languages of this chapter are written in alphanumeric codes also. They are even further from the final machine language program level than the assembly language is. We might describe the compiler of a large mainframe computer like an assembler that translates programs written at (or near) the flowchart level directly down to machine language. Both interpreters and compilers do this, but there is one major difference between them.

The compiler constructs an object program from the original alphameric program, as the assembler does. Until the object program is completely compiled, the computer cannot execute it. The interpreter does not make its source program into an object program. It works with the source code in blocks called *statements*. Each statement in the BASIC language is identified; then the interpreter finds, and runs, a machine language subroutine that does the same thing.

This means that an **interpreted language** (BASIC is almost always interpreted, rather than compiled) must reidentify every line it runs, no matter how many times it has been run before. If a BASIC statement is repeated in a loop 50 times, it is interpreted over again as though it's a new statement every time.

A **compiled language** (FORTRAN, for instance, is similar to BASIC, but is almost always compiled) is completely transcribed into machine language before any statements ever run. There's no need to reidentify the statement when it's repeated in the loop, because the computer runs the program in machine language form.

Because of this, high-level languages that use a compiler run fast and high-level languages that are interpreted run slow.

There is one important advantage of interpreted languages for microcomputers that gives them the edge over compiled languages. The object program of the compiled program is many times larger than the source code.

When it's finished, a FORTRAN compiler, for instance, has its source code (the program in FORTRAN) and its object code (the final translation into machine code) both "living" in the computer's memory. The object code takes up a lot of memory space, even for a simple FORTRAN program . . . often more space than a microcomputer has!

The program being run by the interpreter, however, has only taken up enough memory space for its source code, and the program in object code never gets written. Although it is slow, the BASIC program to do a specific task will occupy far less memory space than its FORTRAN counterpart. In a microcomputer of limited capabilities, this is an important consideration. If a program exceeds available memory space, it must be stored on an auxiliary memory device, such as a tape or disk file, and the computer must run the program in blocks, taking each block from the tape or disk as it's needed. This slows down the execution of the compiled program to the speed of the tape or disk device, and the FORTRAN may actually be slower than the BASIC if a really large program is run on *virtual storage* (using the tape or disk to supplement RAM memory).

Now that we've established that BASIC is an interpreter language run on micros to conserve memory space, and that it's slow compared to compiled or assembled languages, what difference does that make to you? None whatever! (unless it turns up on an employer's aptitiude test!!) If you can get to the computer in BASIC, you can troubleshoot it using that language as nicely as in machine code. Writing a diagnostic program will be easier, too.

There is a multitude of languages other than BASIC, and within the world of microcomputers, there are many dialects of BASIC. A program written in one dialect won't work on a computer that uses another. The interpreter will do what it can understand, then, when it finds a statement that's not part of its dictionary, it comes back with a "What's that?" called a syntax error message. At that moment, it goes on a sit-down strike, and refuses to go any further until you correct the statement it thinks is an error.

We'd like to show you how to program in BASIC in this chapter, but the question is: "Whose BASIC?" We can't show you, for example, how to program in "BASIC that works on everybody's computer" because no such BASIC exists. Instead, our goal in this chapter is to show you a few things about BASIC, which may vary from machine to machine. One goal will be to show you how the same operations done in machine language look in BASIC. This will be useful because, for the most part, assembly language and machine language are not as easily reached as BASIC on most microprocessors. A simple test can be programmed in BASIC very quickly and directly. A second goal of this chapter will be to see how the BASIC language does things more complicated than machine language allows; for instance, multiplication, which doesn't exist in the machine language of a Z-80, is part of BASIC on all Z-80 machines. A third point in seeing how BASIC (or any high-level language) works is to see how changes in a program are made. It's much easier to change your mind or insert an additional operation into the middle of a program in BASIC than in machine language.

7.1 THE BASIC LANGUAGE

The BASIC language is a machine-independent language. As far as possible, programs written in BASIC do not depend on how many registers are available in the microprocessor, what addressing modes the microprocessor permits, or what operations are possible in the ALU of the microprocessor. Any microprocessor equipped with a suitable BASIC interpreter should be able to execute the same source code by interpreting it in object code that uses the processor's capabilities. In fact, it shouldn't matter whether the program's running on a micro, mini, or mainframe.

That's not the way it works in reality. There are almost as many dialects of BASIC as there are manufacturers of micros. There is a small ray of hope, though. Microsoft BASIC (which is available for a large number of micros) has become the de facto standard version of BASIC in the microcomputer industry. The examples we use in the following sections of this chapter are developed from this version of BASIC.

The 8080 and Z-80 processors formed the basis of our understanding of machine language and microprocessor operation in previous chapters. Since Microsoft BASICs exist for machines that use the 8080 and Z-80 processors (the Interact and the TRS-80, for example), we'll use these dialects of BASIC in our examples, and later, we'll use the features of these BASICs to get to the machine language level of operation inside the virtual machine that we see through the eyes of BASIC.

7.1.1 BASIC Statements That Work like Machine Language Instructions

Data-transfer instructions. We'll begin by looking at the Z-80 data-transfer instructions that we found at the beginning of Chapter 19. Each of these has a comparable operation in BASIC. To see how BASIC statements are used to do operations similar to the ones that micros do, we'll show a Z-80 operation, the infix description of what the operation does in the Z-80, and a BASIC instruction that does essentially the same thing. From this we'll see how some of our programs written in machine language could be written in BASIC, but more to the point, we'll get an appreciation of how BASIC works for some operations we're already familiar with. Here are some examples from Chapter 5:

Zilog code	Infix description	BASIC statement
LD H,B	H ⟵ B	H = B
LD H,19	H ⟵ 19	H = 19

Zilog code	Infix description	BASIC statement
LD L,136	L ←— 136	L = 136
LD HL,5000	HL ←— 5000	HL = 5000
LD A,(HL)	A ←— (HL)	A = PEEK (HL)
LD (HL),A	(HL) ←— A	POKE HL,A
LD A,(3000)	A ←— (3000)	A = PEEK (3000)
LD (3000),A	(3000) ←— A	POKE 3000,A

The Z-80 instructions use registers, like A, B, H, and L; register pairs (HL); constants, like 19, 136, and 5000; indirect addresses, like (HL); and absolute addresses, like (3000). The BASIC instructions look almost exactly like the infix notation, except for two major differences. One difference is cosmetic—the ←— turns into a =. The other is more important. H, L, B, and HL are not registers or register pairs in the BASIC statements. They are variables, which are actually places in the memory used by the BASIC interpreter the same way the microprocessor uses registers. There are a great many more variables than the number of registers in the real microprocessor. You can name them after any letter of the alphabet (and on some BASICS, after any work of two, three, or more letters). There's no need to confine yourself to names that are acceptable Z-80 register names when you're writing in BASIC. The constants and addresses are exactly what they appear to be, although not all BASICS allow you access to the absolute memory with PEEK and POKE Instructions.

There's a reason for the use of the = sign instead of the ←— sign. It's historical, rather than logical; at the time BASIC was developed, keypunch machines didn't exist that had a ←— sign. BASIC's predecessor, FORTRAN, used the = sign instead of a ←—, so Dr. Kemeny (the developer of BASIC) decided to do the same.

It's important to remember that sometimes in BASIC, the = means the same thing as a ←—. In ordinary algebra, for instance, A = 25 is the same as 25 = A. This is not true of BASIC or FORTRAN. In BASIC, 25 = A means nothing, since 25 means the value of a number, not a memory address. The expression (25) ←— A, although it's not legitimate in BASIC, means "put the value in A into memory location 25." The expression 25 ←— A doesn't mean anything, even in infix notation.

Sometimes, the = means "is equal to" (as you would expect) when the = sign is used for comparisons. We'll see more about this when we see the BASIC instructions that do the same things as conditional JUMPs.

In 8080/Z-80 machine language, numbers were transferred between the CPU and PORTS. I/O ports send data in to the CPU (input ports) or out from the CPU (output ports). There are BASIC statements that are exactly the same as in the IN and OUT machine commands; here are some examples:

Zilog code	Infix description	BASIC statement
IN A,(7)	A ⟵ port 30	A = INP (7)
OUT (7),A	port 7 ⟵ A	OUT 7,A
IN B,(C)	B ⟵ port (C)	B = INP (C)
OUT (C),B	port (C) ⟵ B	OUT C,A

Of course, in the BASIC statements, A, B, and C are not really registers, they're variable names that "look" like registers. What the BASIC instructions *do* is the same as the action of the machine instructions. There are also instructions that do things similar to the Block Move and Block I/O instructions:

Zilog code	Infix description	BASIC statement
LDIR	memory ⟵ memory block block	D$ = H$
INIR	memory ⟵ block of block I/O ports	INPUT H$
OTIR	block of ⟵ memory I/O ports block	PRINT H$

INPUT and PRINT aren't exactly the same as INIR and OTIR instructions; the input device is the computer keyboard (which is usually memory-mapped or treated as a single port rather than a block of I/O ports) and the PRINT output device is the video display (which is often memory-mapped instead of being true I/O).

Arithmetic instructions.   In BASIC, the interpreter constructs a model of a virtual machine that works internally in BASIC and uses alphameric variables instead of registers and addresses. The ALU of this virtual machine is not limited by the arithmetic-logic capabilities in the microprocessor. The reverse is sometimes true; all the Boolean and arithmetic operations of a microprocessor may not be found in every version of BASIC (no BASIC we know of has an XOR operator, although it's standard in microprocessors).

In the examples below, we'll look at the Boolean and arithmetic operations normally found in microprocessors, and at the BASIC way of expressing the same idea. In some of these examples, we'll see a combination of operations in the BASIC version of a Boolean operation:

Zilog code	Infix description	BASIC statement
Arithmetic Operations:		
ADD A,D	A ⟵ A + D	A = A + D
SUB A,E	A ⟵ A - E	A = A - E
ADD A,5	A ⟵ A + 5	A = A + 5
SUB A,6	A ⟵ A - 6	A = A - 6

Boolean operations:

AND L   A ⟵ A AND L   A = A AND L

(Bits of A are ANDed with corresponding bits of L.)

AND 1   A ⟵ A AND 1   A = A AND 1

[A is ANDed with a binary 1. Only the 1 bit of the original number in A is left (D0). Bits D1 to D7 are 0. This is called **masking** bits D1-D7.]

OR H   A ⟵ A OR H   A = A OR H

(Bits of A are ORed with corresponding bits of H.)

OR 7   A ⟵ A OR 7   A = A OR 7

(A is ORed with 00000111. Bits D2-D0 are all 1s.)

The AND and OR operations are useful in machines like the 8080 which don't have Bit Test, Reset, and Set instructions. The AND instruction in the example above, for instance, can be used to test if D0 is on or off. If D0 is 0, the whole number will be zero. The condition (being zero) can be tested for using ordinary "test if zero" techniques. ANDing A with a number that contains only one 0 will reset the corresponding bit in A, while ORing A with a number that has only one 1 will set the corresponding bit in A.

Other Boolean examples:

Zilog code	Infix description	BASIC statement
XOR B	A ⟵- A XOR B	A = (A OR (NOT B)) AND ((NOT A) OR B)

(Bits of A are XORed with corresponding bits of B.)

XOR A   A ⟵ A XOR A   A = 0

(Used to zero the accumulator in machine language)

CP C   (Look-ahead subtraction)   T = A - C
CP 5   A - 5   T = A - 5

(T stands for "temporary" register. T is +, -, or 0.)

Compare and XOR instructions are useful in finding whether two bytes match, or if not, which one is larger. The XOR instruction is useful for "equality/inequality" testing—and also is used as the standard way of "zeroing" the accumulator. (No one would use XOR this way in BASIC, however; A = 0 is much easier.) Note that BASIC does not have an XOR primitive (built-in function). The XOR must be implemented by its Boolean equivalent expression in AND, OR, and NOT.

The CP (compare) is used for testing whether two bytes match (the result sets the Zero flag) or if not, which is the larger byte. If the Sign flag indicates +, A is larger; if the sign flag indicates –, A is smaller than the other byte. Since there are no flags in BASIC, a temporary register T is set up in the BASIC instructions; T can then be tested to see if it is +, –, or 0.

There are also some unary operations in the 8080/Z-80 set. These are operations that have only one operand instead of two. (ADD and SUB are examples of dyadic operations—they have two operands, the addend and augend or subtrahend and minuend.) Examples of unary operations are:

Zilog code	Infix description	BASIC statement
Arithmetic:		
INC B	B $\longleftarrow$ B + 1	B = B + 1
DEC D	D $\longleftarrow$ D – 1	D = D – 1
DAA	(Binary BCD conversion)	*

(*BASIC is automatically displayed in decimal.)

Zilog code	Infix description	BASIC statement
Boolean:		
CPL	A $\longleftarrow$ $\overline{A}$	A = NOT (A)
NEG	A $\longleftarrow$ (–A)	A = –(A)

Notice that the INC and DEC operations use the standard ADD and SUB form in BASIC. (In BASIC, there is no difference.)

Look at the last two BASIC examples. We said that the = sign in BASIC didn't mean "is equal to" in these cases; the CPL and NEG should remove all doubt.

Control instructions.   In machine language, the Jump, Call and Return instructions transfer control of the computer from one area in "program space" to another. In the actual microprocessor, this takes place by altering the numbers in the program counter. The *virtual machine* created by the BASIC interpreter also has a program counter of sorts. Although the line numbers in a BASIC program are not really the same thing as addresses in a machine language program, they are used in a similar way by instructions called GOTO, GOSUB, and RETURN. If we accept, for a moment, the fiction that a line number in BASIC is the same as a line number in absolute address space, the following instructions match:

Zilog code	Infix description	BASIC statement
JMP 10	PC $\longleftarrow$ 10	GOTO 10
CALL 50	a) (SP) $\longleftarrow$ PC	GOSUB 50
	b) PC $\longleftarrow$ 50	
RET	PC $\longleftarrow$ (SP)	RETURN

Actually, the line numbers depicted in the GOTO and GOSUB statements do not work exactly like memory addresses, nor do they represent absolute memory locations. An example illustrates this point:

Absolute machine language	Z-80 Assembly	BASIC
000, 000 257	START: XOR A	10 A = 0
000, 001 074	LOOP: INC A	20 A = A + 1
000, 002 323, 007	OUT (7),A	30 OUT 7, A
000, 004 303, 001, 000	JMP LOOP	40 GOTO 20
	END	50 END

(The lines called END in both the assembly and BASIC programs are "noisewords" that identify the previous line as the last one in the program, but don't actually do anything themselves.)

Both of the examples above are programs that will count upwards from 0 and output each number counted to output port 7.

The machine language program (represented in octal) has one byte in each address. Where two-byte and three-byte instructions occur, they take up two and three memory locations, respectively. There are no gaps between numbers, for in the absolute memory of a computer there is something in every space. If we don't put an instruction into a space, leaving a gap, there'll be some code there anyway.

Contrast that with the BASIC program. The line numbers that identify places in the program (like line 20, so that the GOTO instruction can form a loop) start at 10, and jump to 20, 30, and 40 with total disregard for the numbers in between. Remember that these line numbers have meaning only in the virtual machine. They can follow any rules that the interpreter's designer wants them to. Why the gaps? Suppose that, as an afterthought, you realize you'd like the output to appear at port 3 as well as 7. In machine language, there's no space to "sneak" a line into following the output to port 7. In BASIC, you would just type the line you wanted to add like this:

```
10   A = 0
20   A = A + 1
30   OUT 7,A
40   GOTO 20
50   END

35   OUT 3,A
```

and the virtual machine would slip it in between the other lines, so that if you made a LIST of the existing program in BASIC, you'd see:

```
LIST

10   A = 0
20   A = A + 1
30   OUT 7,A
35   OUT 3,A
40   GOTO 20
50   END
```

Notice that the line has been automatically spliced into the program in numerical order by the virtual machine. This is not a feature of the Z-80 hardware. It is only a part of the virtual machine defined by the BASIC interpreter, but it works the same way whether the BASIC is running on a TRS-80, an Apple, or a mainframe.

Conditional branch instructions. The conditional forms of Jump, Call, and Return have analogous instructions in BASIC. They all start with the word IF, and work like this:

Zilog code	Description	BASIC statement
JP NZ,5	Jump if Not Zero	IF A $<>$ 0 THEN GOTO 5
JP Z,100	Jump if Zero	IF A $=$ 0 THEN GOTO 100
JP NC,8	Jump if No Carry	IF A $<$ 256 THEN GOTO 8
JP C,45	Jump if Carry	IF A $>$ 255 THEN GOTO 45
JP P,30	Jump if Plus sign	IF A $>$ 0 THEN GOTO 30
JP M,12	Jump if Minus sign	IF A $<$ 0 THEN GOTO 12

(In case you aren't familiar with the $>$, $<$, and $<>$ signs as they're used in BASIC, $>$ means "is more than," $<$ means "is less than," and $<>$ means "is more or less than" (literally, "it is not equal to").) These comparative statements come from the "arithmetical" nature of BASIC. All relationships are expressed in terms of greater than ($>$), less than ($<$), or equal to ($=$), or some combination of them. Flags are not a part of the virtual machine of BASIC. Parity checking is not accessible to the BASIC user either, since BASIC was designed as a high-level language for the user who does not want to bother with individual bits in each number. There could be a BASIC statement for "jump if parity odd" or "jump if parity even," but such statements would be highly complex, mathematical, and awkward.

Subroutines. The GOSUB (GOto SUBroutine) and Return instructions in BASIC are transparently obvious to machine language users. There's very little to say about how they work that you couldn't already infer from the way the Z-80 works. The only significant fact worth mentioning is that the stack used to save return addresses in BASIC is not as easy to get at as the stack in machine language. Few versions of BASIC contain POP and PUSH instructions, for instance, but without these, you can't "mess up" the stack as easily during a subroutine as in machine language (mainly, it's harder to make fatal mistakes this way!).

Addressing modes. All that fancy stuff about direct, indirect, absolute, and relative addresses for jumps, calls, and returns can be pretty much forgotten in BASIC. This way there are fewer things to confuse the programmer (at least, that's probably what the designer of the virtual machine had in mind). The only possible exception might be the BASIC command

$$ON \quad N \quad GOTO \quad 5,10,15$$

which will go to different places when N equals 1, 2, and 3 (it will go to 5, 10, and 15, respectively). It's not exactly like a Z-80 indirect jump [JMP (HL), for instance], but it's something like it.

7.1.2 BASIC Statements That Do Things Machine Language Never Heard of

The virtual machine created by the BASIC interpreter is capable of a great many mathematical (and other) operations that are not part of the Z-80 instruction set. Examples are

W = X * 25	(multiplication)	W ⟵	X times 25
Y = Z / 12	(division)	Y ⟵	Z divided by 12

Note the use of the * for "multiply," instead of x. Most microcomputers whose working language is BASIC don't display uppercase and lowercase letters, like the "x" in "X x 25." They only display uppercase, which gives "X X 25." You can see that it's impossible to tell which "X" is an "X" and which means "times." On early keypunch machines, it was the same way. This led the designers of FORTRAN to adopt an alternate character found on the keyboard of a keypunch machine (a "*" is born!). BASIC followed FORTRAN, and maintained use of the same symbol, because in its early days, BASIC, too, was a punchcard-oriented language.

The BASIC virtual machine makes the use of multiplication and division possible, although they don't exist in the hardware of the Z-80 microprocessor, by the use of software modules called *algorithms*. Algorithms compute products (for multiplication) or quotients (for division) using nothing but ADD, SUB, and shift operations found in the Z-80. Each algorithm is a small subprogram in its own right, and the subject is sufficiently important that it deserves a few words of discussion.

Both *dyadic* and *unary* operations exist in BASIC that have no counterparts in Z-80 machine code. One example is:

$$C = SQR \ (A)$$

where SQR (A) means "the square root of A." This is a unary operation of sufficient magnitude that its pencil-and-paper calculation is beyond most people. Even so, an algorithm exists that can do this computation using nothing but basic Z-80 ALU operations. In fact, there are several different algorithms that exist for doing a square root, each of which has different advantages. The smallest (in terms of number of machine language steps) that we've seen (although not the fastest in working time) is the one shown below. (Assume that the *radicand*—the number to be square-rooted—is already in register A when this subroutine is called.)

SQUARE ROOT ALGORITHM in 12 bytes

Z-80 Assembly		BASIC	
SQR:	LD B,1	1000	B = 1
	LD C,0	1010	C = 0
LOOP:	SUB A,B	1020	A = A - B
	RET M	1030	IF A < 0 THEN RETURN
	INC B	1040	B = B + 2
	INC B		
	INC C	1050	C = C + 1
	JMP LOOP	1060	GOTO 1020

This algorithm can be written in terms of BASIC instructions, shown at the right. It is often easier to try out an algorithm or test procedure in BASIC than in machine language. If you make a mistake, or think of something you want to add, it's much easier to slip in a BASIC line (or overwrite one if it's wrong) than to rewrite and reenter an entire machine language routine when one byte has to be added to the middle and all the addresses change.

You can use BASIC as a sort of testing ground for machine language diagnostic routines in this way. That's why we showed you, first, the instructions in BASIC that could be used to imitate the actions of a Z-80 running machine language.

Since most microcomputers "power up in BASIC," it's easiest to try out test routines in BASIC; then, when it's confirmed that they work, the routines can be rewritten in machine language.

What about BASIC statements that don't have matching machine language instructions? Should you use them?

If you're developing a BASIC program and you've got no plans to make it into machine language, the answer is "yes." You should go ahead and use all the power of a high-level language for mathematical, graphics, or string-handling operations.

On the other hand, if you're using the computer to perform simple control operations, as you would in a diagnostic program, you should use BASIC commands that are easily converted into machine language. Use the flashy stuff only if you know the machine language algorithms for each BASIC statement, and don't mind writing all the lines of machine code needed to convert the high-level statements into low-level code.

7.2 EXAMPLE BASIC PROGRAM

Now that we've gone and scared you off using high-level BASIC operations for developing machine language diagnostics, what's left? There's a whole world of interesting things that can be easily written using high-level statements. It's beyond the scope of this book, but if you pick up any one of a number of "using and programming BASIC" manuals on the shelves of your local computer store, you'll find many hours of interesting things to do while learning to use the language. Be prepared, though, to find things in these BASIC manuals that don't work in the dialect your computer uses. You'll need the programming manual for your own computer (with a description of how it handles its own "unique" commands) as well as the "how to program in BASIC" manuals. With a little practice, you'll get the knack of interpreting other people's BASIC into statements that work on your computer.

Some examples of BASIC statements that may be found in the virtual machine of a BASIC computer are given in Table 7-1.

There are a great many more functions possible in BASIC, and there are several in the table that will not be found in all BASICs. These are shown to

TABLE 7-1 COMMON BASIC STATEMENTS

Basic statement	Mathematical function
Unary Operations	
C = SQR (A)	Computes the square root of A and puts it into C
Y = SIN (O)	Computes the trigonometric sine of O and puts it into Y
B = ABS (R)	Puts the absolute value of R into B (makes R positive)
D = LOG (N)	Computes the natural log of N and puts its value in D
T = INT (F)	Puts the integer part of F (the whole number part of the value in F) in T
P = EXP (Q)	Raises e to the Q power (e = 2.1828)
Dyadic Operations	
C = A ↑ B	Raises A to the B power (called exponentiation) and puts the result into C
W = X * Y	Multiplies X times Y and puts the product into W
U = T / V	Divides T over V and puts the quotient into U
SET (X, Y)[a]	Set (turn ON) a graphics point at X and Y on the video display
RESET (X, Y)[a]	Reset (turn OFF) a graphics point at X and Y on the video display
POINT (X, Y)[a]	Tests the state of a point at X and Y on the video display

[a]These are a combination of point-plotting and Boolean operations which combine the Cartesian coordinate system with a Boolean set, reset, or bit test function in the video RAM part of the memory.

give a feeling for what might be done in a fairly comprehensive BASIC program. As a final example of what a high-level language is like, we include a sample BASIC program (Table 7-2) to do a calculation of some values in an ac circuit. We'll "tear apart" the program to see how it works.

The first thing you'll probably notice is the large number of REM lines. These are lines with comments on them that are intended to explain what's

TABLE 7-2 SAMPLE BASIC PROGRAM

```
  10   REM PROGRAM TO FIND IMPEDANCE IN A
  20   REM PARALLEL R, L, C AC CIRCUIT
  30   INPUT "R="; R
  40   INPUT "L="; L
  50   INPUT "C="; C
  60   INPUT "F="; F
  70   I = 0 : J = 0
  80   I$ = " INFINITE "
  90   PI = 3.14159
 100   W = 2 * PI * F
 110   REM "W" IS OMEGA--THE ANGULAR VELOCITY OF
 120   REM THE ROTATION OF THE AC GENERATOR
 130   IF R=0 THEN J = 1 : GOTO 150
 140   G = 1 / R
 150   REM "G" IS CONDUCTANCE OF THE RESISTOR
 160   XL = W * L
 170   IF XL = 0 THEN J = 2 : GOTO 190
 180   BL = 1 / XL
 190   REM "BL" IS SUSCEPTANCE OF THE INDUCTOR (1/X)
 200   BC = W * C
 210   IF BC = 0 THEN I = 1 : GOTO 240
 220   REM "BC" IS THE SUSCEPTANCE OF THE CAPACITOR
 230   XC = 1 / BC
 240   REM "XC" IS THE REACTANCE OF THE CAPACITOR
 250   B = ABS ( BL - BC )
 260   REM "B" IS TOTAL SUSCEPTANCE OF THE CIRCUIT
 270   IF B = 0 THEN GOTO 290
 280   X = 1 / B
 290   REM "X" IS THE TOTAL SUSCEPTANCE OF THE CIRCUIT
 300   Y = SQR ( G * G + B * B )
 310   REM "Y" IS THE TOTAL ADMITTANCE OF THE CIRCUIT
 320   IF J = 1 OR J = 2 THEN Z = 0 ELSE Z = 1 / Y
 330   IF J = 2 THEN X = 0
 340   REM "Z" IS THE TOTAL IMPEDANCE OF THE CIRCUIT
1000   PRINT "XL =";XL;"OHMS"
1010   PRINT "XC ="; : IF I = 1 PRINT I$; ELSE PRINT XC;
1020   PRINT "OHMS"
1030   PRINT "X =";X;"OHMS"
1040   PRINT "Z (PARALLEL) =";Z;"OHMS"
1050   PRINT "INPUT NEXT SET OF PARAMETERS"
1060   GOTO 10
1070   END
```

happening to another programmer. REMarks are also useful to you if you want to look back at a program you wrote a long time ago, and need something to jog your memory to help you recall what you were doing at each part of the program. Putting REM statements in programs like this is called *documenting your code.* If the documentation accomplishes its task (makes the program easier to understand and the steps easier to identify), we say that it is a *well-documented program.*

The input statements on lines 30 to 60 contain output as well as input operations. Normally, when an input is done in BASIC, the virtual machine puts a ? on the video display and waits for you to enter a string of characters (usually a number). This ? is called a *prompt.* It is the machine's way of letting you know it's waiting for an input. In the inputs on lines 30 to 60, though, there are literals like R = and L =. These are strings of symbols that are actually printed on the screen in front of the ? sign. These add extra information to the prompt, letting you know which kind of number you should be entering at each input. In this program, several inputs are required. Instead of making you remember which one comes first, second, third, and fourth, the computer remembers for you. Remembering is one of the things that computers do better than people.

Literals are also used in the PRINT statements on lines 1000 to 1050. They are used for the same reason literals were used in the inputs; the program computes several different numbers and displays them. Without some sort of identification, it would be hard to remember which result was supposed to print first, second, and so forth. With the prompt, we let the computer "remember" for us.

Notice line 70. There is not just one statement on this line, there are two. The : symbol at the end of a statement lets the virtual machine know that there's another statement following it. Generally, only one statement is needed on a line, but occasionally, simple statements may be grouped on a single line. In this case, the variables I and J must be initialized at the beginning of the program (set to a starting value). Each initialization is a simple procedure, so we did all the initializing on a single line.

Line 80 is a *string variable.* Under certain circumstances (for example, if C = 0) the value of a certain number becomes uncomputably large. Our program must recognize when these circumstances occur and avoid the computation. In this case, we'd like to indicate that the results of calculating the number would be too large to express. The literal in line 80 is called a *string* when it's given a name of its own and isn't part of a PRINT or an INPUT. In this program, "I$" is used by a print statement later (on line 1010) and we could have written 'PRINT " INFINITE " ' instead of 'PRINT I$'. Operations that use string variables like I$ can connect them together, swap them, do internal manipulations within a string, or compare them. These sorts of operations are called *string manipulation* or *string handling.* Special programs called *word processors* use *string handling* routines to make writing, editing, business, and office typing easier and more convenient. (We are using one right now to write this book, although it's not a BASIC program.)

Line 90 defines a constant called PI (you can see that variables with names two letters long are permitted in this version of BASIC). Notice that this constant has a decimal point in it. It's not an integer, like many of the other numbers in this program. Such numbers are called *floating-point variables*. The input numbers may be floating-point variables also. All the numbers in this program are computed as floating-point numbers, whether they contain a decimal point or not. Integer calculation has to be specially marked by using a special type of variable name or defining the variable as an integer (DEFINT statement).

Line 100 is a *chain multiplication*. *Chain computation* is the placement of several mathematical operations in a single statement. Although it's impossible to do this in machine language, it's routinely done in BASIC.

Notice the IF statement on line 130. There are two statements on the line following the IF. Both of these statements will be done if the IF is TRUE, and neither will be done if the IF is FALSE. In an IF statement like this, all the statements that follow the condition in the IF are treated like a single routine to be done if the IF is TRUE and not done otherwise. Lines 170 and 210 are similar to 130 in this regard. The IF statements in lines 270 and 330 are simple IF statements that just do one thing. You'll notice that, unlike CONDITIONAL JUMP statements, these IF statements don't just do GOTOs when they're TRUE.

Line 320 is an "IF . . . THEN . . . ELSE" statement. It defines what to do if the IF is TRUE and also what to do if it is FALSE. This is even further from a machine language CONDITIONAL JUMP than the regular IF is, but it's a very powerful statement that can be used to handle a wide variety of conditional tests. Line 320 tests the possibility that Z is uncomputable by conventional methods. If this happens, the correct value is assigned to Z (Z = 0); otherwise, Z is computed by ordinary means.

Line 1060 is necessary to make this program a loop that repeats when new inputs are provided.

A PRINT statement like line 1000 can contain a mixture of literals and variables. In this line, both the words XL = and the value of XL are printed. The ; suppresses spacing between one field of characters and another (if a literal and a variable are separated by a ; in a PRINT statement, they will be printed together).

Lines 1010 and 1020 can PRINT either of two ways. When I is equal to 1, the literal INFINITY is printed after XC = (line 1010) and before OHMS (line 1020). When I is not equal to 1, a variable value (XC) is printed according to what was calculated by line 230. You can see the use of the IF . . . THEN . . . ELSE statement in this example. You can also see how a "flag" (the variable called I) is passed from line 210 to this routine to handle the "uncomputable" case we described earlier. The flag is set when the number (XC) will be uncomputably large. It is reset at the beginning of the program, and will arrive at line 1010 as a 0 if the number (XC) is computable.

There are other flags in this program, used to pass information about the ultimate value of Z down to lines 320 and 330, where Z is computed. They also relate to whether Z is computable by normal means. We'll let you investigate how they work for yourself.

7.3 ACCESSING MACHINE LANGUAGE THROUGH BASIC

One application of BASIC, we said, was to write small BASIC programs to test out whether an anticipated machine language program would work. Once you're certain that the idea of the program works, you rewrite it into machine language. Now what do you do?

If the computer you're using has the POKE instruction, you'll POKE the program into memory addresses. Loading the program could be accomplished by a routine something like this:

```
 10 N=65000                        10 RESTORE
 20 RESTORE                        20 FOR N=65000 TO 65011 STEP 1
 30 READ B                         30 READ B
 40 POKE N,B                       40 POKE N,B
 50 N=N+1                          50 NEXT N
 60 IF N<=65011 THEN GOTO 30       60 END
 70 END                           100 DATA 33,0,60,1,232,3,175
100 DATA 33,0,60,1,232,3,175      110 DATA 119,35,16,251,201
110 DATA 119,35,16,251,201
```

Notice the two versions of this routine. They both POKE the same bytes of code into the same area of memory, but the one on the right uses a shortcut called a FOR . . . NEXT loop. The FOR and NEXT statements are used wherever a routine must be repeated a specific number of times. The number is included in the FOR as its index. The index is a counter that can be counted either up or down from an initial value to a limit. In the program on the left, the initial value is set by N = 65000, the counter is incremented by the step N = N + 1, and the limit is set by IF N <= 65011 GOTO 30. The FOR loop on the right uses the statement FOR N = 65000 TO 65011 STEP 1 to count from 65000 to 65011. The NEXT N statement at the bottom of the routine does the same thing as the IF in the routine on the left. It says to loop back until the counter reaches (or overshoots) the limit. The FOR . . . NEXT loop is used in BASIC as a shorter way to do the same thing as the INITIALIZATION, INCREMENT, and IF statements in the "longer" BASIC routine. You can see in both program segments that the index (N) is used for more than just counting. In this POKE operation, N is the destination address of each byte of code taken from the data file by the READ statement. The numbers separated by commas in the data file are taken, one by one, in order, until all the data have been POKEd into memory addresses. Notice that there are 12 data numbers and 12 values of N when N is counted from 65000 to 65011. The loop will POKE 12 bytes of data into the memory—this is a 12-byte program to erase 1000 bytes of RAM, replacing the digits in the memory locations with zeros (ASCII nulls). By the way, we said the FOR loop could count either up or down, but the STEP size of 1 seems to count up only. How do we count DOWN? Use a step size of -1, of course! A negative step size will make the count become smaller as the counter is incremented (incidentally, in this case, the step size of 1 is optional; if no step size is included in the FOR loop, N will count up by ones anyway).

How do you RUN the program once it's poked into the memory? Some microcomputers have an instruction called CALL, others have a command called a USER CALL (USR). See the documentation for the particular BASIC on your computer to see how the machine code you POKE into the memory may be CALLed. Some machines do not permit a call to a machine language routine at all. Each one that does permit it seems to work in a different way. In the example above, the program segment is called by:

$$\vdots$$

```
5000 POKE 16525,232:POKE 16526,253
5010 REM THIS IS THE STARTING ADDRESS OF THE
5020 REM MACHINE LANGUAGE ROUTINE (65000)
5030 X = USR (0)
5040 REM THIS STATEMENT WILL MAKE THE COMPUTER
5050 REM CALL THE MACHINE LANGUAGE ROUTINE THAT
5060 REM BEGINS AT MEMORY ADDRESS 65000
```

$$\vdots$$

Of course, if the program is intended to do something that can be done directly in BASIC, there's no need to go to all this trouble, is there? If the BASIC interpreter is working, operations like RAM testing can be done just as easily using POKE and PEEK as the LD commands of machine language. After all that exposure to machine language in previous chapters, if this chapter has encouraged you to consider BASIC as an alternative option, then it's been a success.

QUESTIONS

7.1. What is the main advantage of programming in a high-level language (like BASIC) that is interpreted?

7.2. What is the main advantage of programs written in a computer's assembly language?

7.3. What is the main advantage of programming in a high-level language (like FORTRAN) that is compiled?

7.4. Which executes in the least time, a compiled program or an interpreted one?

7.5. Which takes up the least memory space, a program that has been assembled from assembly language or a program that has been compiled from a high-level language?

7.6. What's a syntax error?

7.7. Write a brief explanation of the reason = takes the place of ⟵ in BASIC and FORTRAN.

7.8. When names like B, C, H, and L are used in a BASIC program, does that mean that the microprocessor in the computer has registers called B, C, H, and L, as the 8080 has?

7.9. Several items listed below are available in both the microprocessor hardware and in the virtual machine you see when you write a program in BASIC. Some of the items are part of only the virtual machine (called "primitives" in programming jargon), and others are part of only the microprocessor hardware. For parts (a)–(f), identify whether the item is part of the virtual machine, the real microprocessor hardware, or both.
   (a) Addition
   (b) Multiplication
   (c) Logical EXCLUSIVE OR
   (d) Registers
   (e) Variables
   (f) Logical AND

7.10. Do line numbers in BASIC have to follow one another in consecutive, numbering order, without gaps (0,1,2,3,4,5, . . .) as addresses do in machine language?

7.11. Is the insertion of BASIC line numbers between other line numbers part of the virtual machine, or is it something built into the hardware of the microprocessor?

7.12. Can the programmer check the microprocessor's parity flag directly in BASIC?

7.13. Why do BASIC and FORTRAN use the * symbol for multiplication, instead of ✕?

7.14. Define "algorithm" in your own words.

7.15. Explain why you might want to use BASIC to test out a diagnostic routine you intend to write later in machine code.

7.16. Look at the BASIC program for finding the impedance of a parallel RLC ac circuit. Is the number called PI stored in the computer as an integer or a floating-point number?

7.17. Is the impedance program an endless loop?

7.18. What is a prompt?

7.19. Write a BASIC statement that contains a chain computation.

7.20. Describe what a flag is in a high-level language.

7.21. Describe what a FOR . . . NEXT loop does.

7.22. What BASIC statement permits you to enter bytes of machine code directly into RAM?

7.23. What are some BASIC statements you might use to call or run a machine language routine in RAM?

8

Telecommunications

In previous chapters we looked at input and output devices that computers use to communicate with the outside world. In the examples we chose, the computer was part of a human-machine, document-machine, or machine-machine interface. When we described the machine-machine interface, we imagined that the computer was used for numerical control of some device like a "smart" drill or lathe. So far, we've never considered that the machine our computer outputs to or inputs from might be another computer. Why not? One computer's output can be another's input, and vice versa, provided that each one knows how to take turns with the other. In this chapter we'll look at the communication of data from one computer to another (data communication), and in particular, methods for transferring data from one computer to another over long distances (telecommunication).

Microprocessors are used in microcomputers, but can be made to imitate virtually any kind of digital network where extremely high speed is not an important consideration. We will often describe, in this chapter, how a microcomputer "talks" to another microcomputer over the telephone system or some other common carrier. Do not be misled by our choice of examples (in microcomputers) at each end of the data link. Microprocessors appear in all parts of the ESS (*electronic switching system*) between the source and destination of any long-distance communication. Many of our examples will use the telecommunications network as a glorified I/O device for a microcomputer (or two microcomputers). It's important to remember that that's not "all there is" to do with microprocessors in telecommunications, and we'll endeavor to show examples, from time to time, of the other "dedicated machine" aspects of microprocessor usage.

8.1 LONG-DISTANCE COMMUNICATION BETWEEN COMPUTERS

Suppose that there are two people with 8-bit computers in different cities. One person has a program that the other person would like to have. Instead of making a copy of the program on diskette or tape and sending it by mail, the people would like to have one computer "send" and the other "receive" 8-bit words between Chicago and Toronto.

How do they do it? If the computer in Chicago is sending and the computer in Toronto is receiving, the Chicago machine can be attached to an output port and the Toronto machine can be attached to an input port. Now all they need is a ribbon cable 500 miles long!

That's certainly not very practical. The cable would cost a fortune, and they'd have to get permission (or buy the right-of-way) to lay the cable. Someone has already done that. The telegraph company and telephone company have had conductors connected between Chicago and Toronto for over a century. The circuits are already there, and the cost of using them is not very high, compared to connecting their own circuits. Not only that, but in this case, they only intend to use this circuit one time. A *common carrier* is a communications network (like the telephone company) that is available to everybody, on a pay-for-time basis. The two people should connect their computers to one another via a common carrier.

8.1.1 A Parallel Communication System

In Figure 8-1, we see the most obvious way of carrying 8-bit data from the computer in Chicago to the one in Toronto. It seems simple enough, but there are several things wrong with it that are not evident in the diagram:

1. *Propagation delay.* There are eight separate telephone circuits. What are the chances that all of these circuits are equally long? Suppose that one path chosen to connect Chicago and Toronto is 100 miles longer than the others. Its data will arrive over 500 microseconds later than the other bits. That's not a long time to a human being, but it's "digital eternity" to a computer. A parallel output port can receive data hundreds of thousands of times a second, but if data are sent on this "cable" of unequal-length paths, if 2000 outputs are done per second, the bits will be out of phase when they arrive.

2. *Amplitude.* There's no guarantee that the logic pulses put into the telephone circuit (about 4 V peak to peak) will come out the other end exactly the same size. Nobody told Alexander, when he designed the system, that it would have to have unity gain (give or take less than 1 dB). "Can the

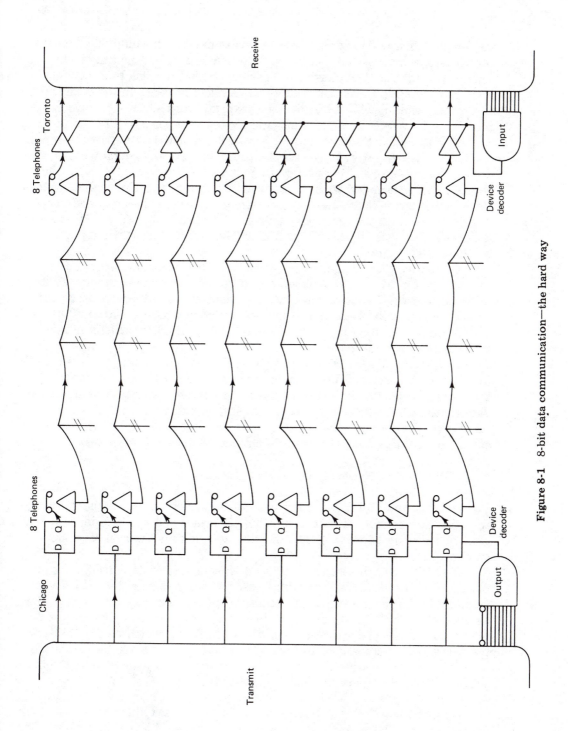

Figure 8-1 8-bit data communication—the hard way

guy on the other end hear me?" was the main concern. It wouldn't be unusual for the signals on the other end to be 6 dB higher or lower than the incoming signal. In one case, the voltage would swing about 1 V, peak to peak, and the logic gates wouldn't even know there was a signal present. In the other case, the voltage would swing 16 V, peak to peak, and turn all the 5-V logic in the receiver to "WAS GATES"(!) Not good for the well-being of TTL circuits.

3. *DC level.* Suppose there's a miracle, and a 4-V (p-p) wave input produces a 4-V (p-p) wave at every output. Is there any guarantee that the output doesn't have a LOW level of 18 V and a HIGH level of 22 V? No way! Nobody told Alexander, when he designed his system, that a wave that has the same shape, but is "centered" at a different dc level, makes any difference. "They both sound the same, don't they?" he might ask. True. But to the logic gates, 18 V is HIGH and 22 V is HIGH, and either one (if applied to a 5-V logic gate) is *goodbye.*

4. *Bandwidth.* While we're on the subject of what Alexander designed the system for, it was, you remember, designed for voice communications. The transmission-line characteristics and "repeater" amplifiers are designed to handle human voice frequencies (and not much more) from 300 to 3000 Hz. This is another limiting factor on the parallel output ports (which can handle *much* higher frequencies).

5. *Money.* Eight telephone calls to Toronto cost a bundle. Even if all the data are transmitted in a few seconds, the phone user will be charged for 3 minutes. If all the data could be sent on one circuit instead of eight, the data transmission would only cost an eighth as much. Even if transmission on one wire takes eight times as long as transmission on eight wires, money can be saved if the data are transmitted in less than (8 X 3) minutes.

8.1.2 Serial Data Transmission Using UARTs and Modems

Figure 8-2 shows how most computer "dial-up lines" work. In the diagram, the computer on the left is transmitting (Chicago) and the computer at the right is receiving (Toronto) by using the telephone system as its common carrier.

The CPU with information to send is using one of its output ports as a place where the data are kept while they are being transmitted. In this example, 8-bit words are being sent from the (8-bit, parallel) output port, the parallel logic levels of the port's output port. The parallel logic levels of the port's output are *space-division multiplexed* (SDM), which means that you can tell what bit is being transmitted by where it is. There is a 1-wire, a 2-wire, a 4-wire, an 8-wire, and so forth. The location of the wire on the bus tells you what the binary place value of the bit is.

The UART block. The second block in this block diagram is used to convert the parallel data into serial data. The serial logic levels of the UART's

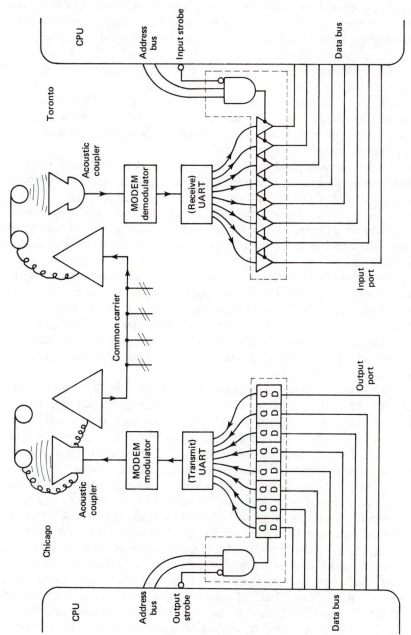

Figure 8-2 8-bit data communication—as it is really done

output are *time-division multiplexed* (TDM), which means that you can tell what bit is being transmitted by when it is transmitted. Only one wire is used for the output, but at one moment, it is 1-time, then it becomes 2-time, then 4-time, then 8-time, and so forth. From the timing of the signal, you can tell what its binary place value is.

We will briefly summarize how this UART block converts parallel data to serial data.

"UART" stands for universal asynchronous receiver-transmitter. When used in this sense, a receiver means a circuit that receives a serial data transmission and converts it into parallel form, while a transmitter converts parallel data to serial data before sending them.

In the circuits shown in Figure 8-3, the data are being transmitted. A parallel word is present at the input of each circuit, and each bit is separately "clocked" out of the circuit on a single serial output. The "clock" that coordinates the transmission of each bit is called a *baud rate generator*, and the frequency at which it clocks out bits at the output is called the *baud rate*. It measures the number of bits per second (also called bps) that are being transmitted.

In Figure 8-3(a), the input data word is clocked into an 8-bit latch in parallel (this is called a *broadside load*, because it resembles a "broadside" fired from a ship in the old pirate movies where all the cannons are fired at once). After the 8-bit word is transferred into the flip-flops of the 8-bit latch, the flip-flops are clocked for eight clock pulses as a shift register. At the end of eight clock pulses, the 8 bits latched into the register have been clocked out one at a time.

In Figure 8-3(b), the input data word is multiplexed onto a single output. We called this process time-division multiplexing, after all, so it shouldn't be any surprise that a multiplexer is part of one design for parallel-to-serial conversion. In this design, a mod-8 counter is needed to select the sequence of inputs that will be passed to the output. If an up-counter is used, data will be transmitted with the least significant binary places first and the most significant binary places last—1-time, then 2-time, then 4-time, and so on—while a down-counter could be used to transmit bits starting with the most significant and ending with the least significant. Unlike the shift register design in Figure 8-3(a), this circuit has the drawback that if its input data word changes in the middle of a transmission, the bits already transmitted will be from the first word, and the remaining half of the serial word transmitted will come from the second. With bits from the "front" half of one word and the "back" half of another, the serial word transmitted will be "garbage." There will have to be additional synchronization circuitry (not shown) to ensure that the input data change only when the counter is reset.

Figure 8-3(c) uses buffers to do the same thing as the multiplexer circuit. The buffers are enabled by a decoder driven by a mod-8 counter

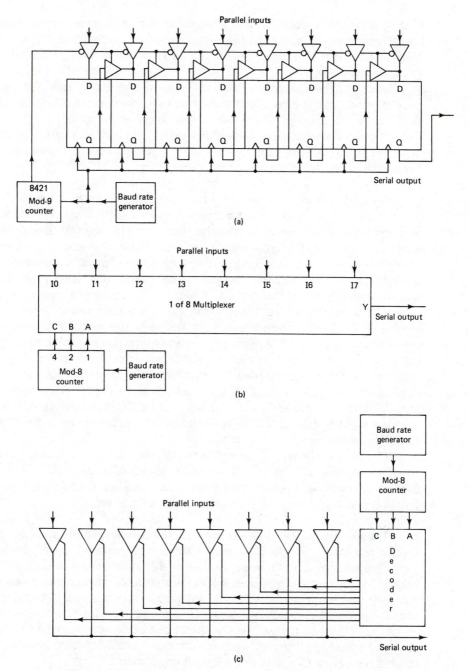

Figure 8-3 Transmitters (parallel-in, serial-out) (a) shift register; (b) multiplexer; (c) buffer

that selects which buffer's data is enabled onto the serial output wire. This design requires yet another block (the decoder) and still has the same drawback as the circuit in Figure 8-3(b). It can be "messed up" if its data change in midtransmission.

Of the three designs, the first is the most commonly used for serial data transmission, and is virtually the only method used in UART design (for reasons which will become clear when we see receiver design).

It is the transmitter of the UART which converts the data from the output port from parallel data to serial data. In serial form, only one circuit is needed to carry the data instead of eight.

The modem block.   The next block in the diagram (Figure 8-2) is a modulator. It is part of a two way circuit called a modem (modulator-demodulator) that converts the dc logic levels (digital) from the serial output of the UART into a frequency-modulated audio output (analog). Since there are only two levels of voltage at the input, there are only two frequencies at the modem's output. The HIGH logic level produces a frequency called a *mark* and the LOW logic level produces a frequency called a *space*. The mark and the space are a 1 and a 0 encoded by *frequency shift keying* (FSK). The frequency shifts between the mark frequency and the space frequency give FSK its name. Modulation is accomplished by a circuit called a VCO (voltage-controlled oscillator), which converts voltage to frequency. In an earlier chapter, we described the so-called Kansas City Standard used for tape recording. This standard can be used for data transmission, too. If data are transmitted at 300 baud using KC standard transmission, the mark is eight cycles of 2400-Hz oscillation, and the space is four cycles of 1200-Hz oscillation.

Figure 8-4 shows the waveforms for the number 5 transmitted from the Chicago side of Figure 8-2 using KC standard audio FSK. The parallel data on the output port are not shown, but the serial output of the UART are, and beneath them, the FSK output of the modem.

The acoustic coupler.   The output of the modem is not attached directly to the telephone line as the parallel wires in Figure 8-1 were. Instead, the audio frequency output is converted from electrical energy to acoustic (sound) energy by an **acoustic coupler**, which is a speaker with suitable waveshaping circuitry and amplification for the telephone mouthpiece. The telephone is now being used exactly as Alexander Graham Bell had intended. Sound arrives at the mouthpiece through the air, and leaves the earpiece of the receiving telephone through the air, and no "foreign" circuitry ever touches the unspoiled beauty of the phone company's equipment.

The common carrier.   On both the sending and receiving end of the telephone system, the handset of the telephone fits into two rubber cups

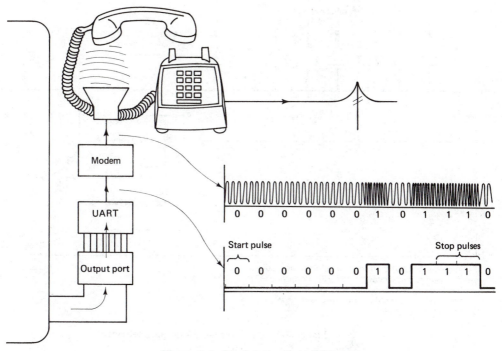

Figure 8-4   Modulation into FSK audio

with a microphone in the cup that holds the earpiece and a speaker in the cup that holds the mouthpiece. The indirect nonelectrical coupling of the signal into the transmitting phone is reversed at the receiving end. The acoustic signal at the receiving phone's earpiece is converted by a microphone and suitable waveshaping and amplifying circuits into an FSK audio signal at the acoustic coupler. The FSK audio output is transferred to the modem, which demodulates it into serial dc logic levels. The serial logic output of the modem is transferred to a UART (the receiver is used here) that converts its serial pulses back into parallel 8-bit logic words. The parallel logic levels are then input through the input port of the receiving computer.

A moment's digression on the subject of receivers is called for here. The transmitter part of the UART was shown in three variations; there is only one primary way of doing the receiver's job. That is shown in Figure 8-5. Data that arrive serially are clocked into the receiver shift register by the baud rate clock. The oscillations of the baud rate clock must be synchronized with the clock in the transmitter on the other end of the telephone system. Not only must the receiver clock have the same frequency but they must be in phase as well. The receiver clock's pulses must start at exactly the time the transmitter clock's pulses would arrive (if a clock pulse were included in the transmission—which it is not). To do this without transmitting clock

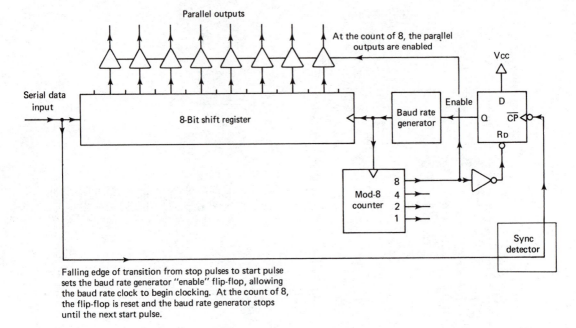

Falling edge of transition from stop pulses to start pulse
sets the baud rate generator "enable" flip-flop, allowing
the baud rate clock to begin clocking. At the count of 8,
the flip-flop is reset and the baud rate generator stops
until the next start pulse.

Figure 8-5   Receiver (serial-in, parallel-out)

pulses side by side with the data (which would require another circuit), we use the same approach a TV transmission uses to keep the horizontal oscillator of your TV synchronized with the horizontal scan in the transmitted TV signal. Sync pulses are sent at the end of each line of scan in a TV waveform, and the KC standard audio transmission includes a similar type of sync information at the end of each 8-bit serial word that's transmitted. The stop pulses at the end of a "word" and the start pulse at the beginning of the next word comprise a sync pulse whose rising edge can be used to trigger the baud rate generator and get it back in step if it has drifted slightly since the last word was received. This means that the baud rate generator could drift as much as 10 percent in the 11 clock pulses of a word like the one in Figure 8-4, and the stop bits and start bit will still get the receiver's baud rate clock back in step with the transmitter.

We have indicated this synchronization by a "magic" box in Figure 8-5 called "sync." It function is similar to the detector for the sync pulses in a TV receiver.

8.1.3 Analysis of Reasons for Serial Transmission

Let's look back at the five objections we had to parallel data transmission as it was done in Figure 8-1, and see how the circuit in Figure 8-2 answers these objections:

1. *Propagation delay*.   We now have only one telephone circuit. The bits are transmitted one after another, instead of all at once, so transmission is slower, but it's impossible for any bits to get ahead of any other bits. The wire that transmits the 1-bit has to be exactly as long as the wire that transmits the 2-bit, because they're exactly the same wire.

2. *Amplitude*.   We don't have to worry too much about the amplitude of the received waveform, because it's frequency modulated rather than amplitude modulated.   The only consideration in designing the transmitter-receiver combination is the "Can the guy on the other end hear me?" aspect. If the "guy" on the other end of the circuit is a microphone, the signal must be loud enough to operate the microphone reliably, but clipping and wave-shaping circuits at the receiving end will accept any audible signal and make it acceptable for the modem.

The lack of a direct electrical connection to the phone system eliminates the need to do 5-V-to-24-V interfacing and permits direct use of 5-V logic where it would not be possible in a direct-coupled system.   There are, however, direct-coupled modems that do not require an acoustic coupler. They use direct connection to telephone circuitry, and are more reliable than acoustic couplers because they are not affected by room noise.   The hardware, however, does require level shifters, and must pass type approval by the FCC, which regulates all interstate communications in the United States. The equivalent Canadian agency (at the Toronto end of our line) must approve the receiving circuit hookup.   The acoustic coupler, since it does not hookup directly to the communications network, does not require such approval, any more than a human voice does.

3. *DC level*.   As with our objections to amplitude shifts, the dc level shifts are unimportant to the circuit of Figure 8-2.   The acoustic coupler and use of frequency (rather than amplitude) to discriminate between a mark and a space input guarantee that "They both sound the same, don't they?" (despite different dc levels) is the only consideration that is needed for the FSK receiver.

4. *Bandwidth*.   Frequency response of the phone company's voice lines is still 300 to 3000 Hz, and there's nothing we can do about that.   There are, however, special lines that can be leased from the phone system, at added cost, that can handle 9000-, or even 19,000-band transmissions.   For most purposes, transmission at 300 baud (perhaps using 2.4 kHz and 1.2 kHz) will permit quite a bit of data to be transmitted at a reasonable cost (see below).

5. *Money*.   We now have just one telephone circuit, which is actually transmitting data 11 times as slow as parallel transmission.   We said before that there'd be a "break-even" point.   If the data could be transmitted in (8×3) minutes, we'd pay no more than the eight phone calls (and actually pay less because the next 3 minutes is cheaper than the first).   How much data can be transmitted in 24 minutes at 300 baud?   We worked it out and found 432,000 bits, or 54,000 bytes, could be transmitted in that time.

That's enough to fill the memory of most micros, or gobble up more than half of a diskette. Most microcomputer programs require less data than this.

8.2 DC AND AC SIGNALING AND BANDWIDTH

We're going to look at some examples of dc and ac transmission of data on transmission lines (wires) to see the dc and ac characteristics of common carriers that might be used for digital data transmission.

8.2.1 DC Attenuation

For our example, we're going to go back to the nineteenth century and look at how a telegraph works [Figure 8-6(a) and (b)]. The transmitter is a *key*, which is just a switch, and the receiver is an electromagnet which makes its moving armature produce a "click" when it's magnetized (this is called a *sounder*). Between them is a length of wire intended to carry the signal long distances, and a return path for the signal represented by a ground symbol at the transmitter and receiver. (To reduce the cost of copper wire, the ground return path was actually a metal stake driven into the ground in early telegraph transmitters and receivers. The ground is a reasonable conductor—if the stake is driven several feet deep—there is less than 100 Ω resistance between stakes several miles apart.) The resistance of the copper wire gets larger as the wire gets longer. To transmit a long distance, the sounder coil had to be made of enough windings of wire to get a majority of the source voltage; it had to have more resistance than the transmission line.

It was not the invention of the key and sounder—or even of the Morse code—that made Samuel F. B. Morse a rich man. All of those were invented by his predecessors in early telegraphs going back to the 1820s. What made Morse's system practical was the *repeater*, shown in Figure 8-6(b). Consider what happens if you want to send a signal to a sounder coil wound with 100 Ω of wire. Suppose that the transmission line is No. 18 copper conductor, the same size as household lamp cord. That gauge of wire has about 20 Ω per thousand meters. By the time we sent the signal down 5 km of wire, only half the original voltage would be delivered to the sounder coil. We need either a larger sounder coil to go farther, or thicker wire. To go 10 km using the same sounder at the end of the line, we'd need to use No. 15 wire (twice the cross-sectional area). To go as far as Toronto is from Chicago (about 800 km), you would need No. 0000 gauge wire (which is about 1 cm thick). The wire would be as thick as a finger, and mass just a tad over 3 billion kilograms for the entire conductor (over $61 billion worth of copper pennies!). This is obviously out of the question, and a wire from New York to San Francisco would be five times as long and five times as thick in cross-sectional area, so it would cost 25 times as much—if there's that much copper in the world!

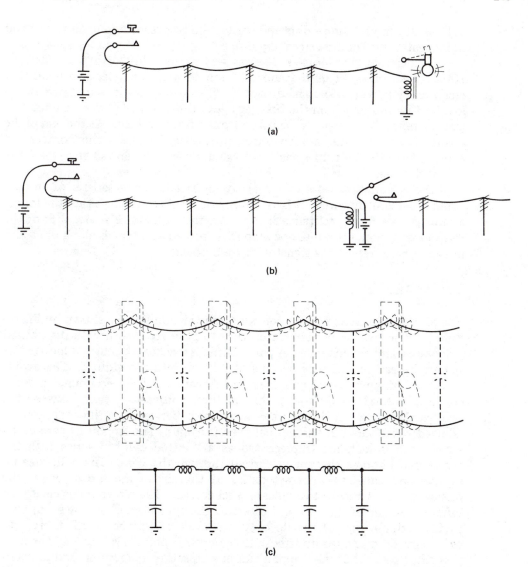

(a)

(b)

(c)

Figure 8-6   (a) Simple telegraph (b) with repeaters (c) equivalent circuit for parallel transmission line.

Yet the Morse telegraph system had linked New York with San Francisco by 1869. How?

What Morse invented was a way to keep the same thickness of wire over longer and longer distances by "refreshing" the signal with a fresh battery every few kilometers. Morse's repeater is what we would call a *relay* today. The telegraph system was the first *digital data transmission* network (using pulse-width modulation—dots and dashes—to represent two logic states) and the repeater was the first *signal amplifier*.

You can see that Morse's idea was very simple. Instead of a sounder, the 100-Ω electromagnet at the end of 5 km of wire is an electromagnet that closes a key (a pair of switch contacts). When it receives its signal (which has lost half its voltage) from the first segment of line, it completes a circuit that puts current into a second 5-km wire from a fresh battery. At the end of the second span of wire, a relay electromagnetically closes the contacts of another key after half the signal's voltage has been lost, and so on to the other end of the line.

DC attenuation (loss of signal strength) is a characteristic of all data communication by wires. It is an automatic result of the fact that the longer a wire is, the more resistance it has. Whether it's Morse's telegraph or the telephone system, there must be amplifiers placed at intervals along the transmission line to repeat the signal with fresh power.

8.2.2 AC Attenuation

The ac characteristics of an open-wire transmission line are shown by Figure 8-6(c). The two wires going from pole to pole are shown with distributed inductance and capacitance. A pair of lines is used for the current loop in this system instead of one wire and a stake driven into the ground. This avoids a certain "mixing" of signals that might occur if all voice circuits shared a common ground conductor. In the picture, you can see that, between the two parallel wires, a distributed capacitance between the lines appears as "dotted capacitors" in parallel between the lines. The lengths of wire themselves have inductance (represented as a "dotted coil" in series with the wires) that opposes changes in current through the wire. The collective inductive and capacitive characteristics of the circuit are shown below the picture of the wires on the poles as a schematic. The schematic is clearly an infinite number of "pi-section" filters of the type used in dc power supplies to filter ripple out of the dc output (the dc resistance is still there, but we've already discussed its effect). In a power supply, this is good. The low-pass filter gets rid of the "ripples" from a pulsating dc rectifier, and provides a steady, constant dc level. On a transmission line for digital data, or any kind of ac signal, this is bad news. The "ripple" is the information, and the longer the wire pair is, the more of a *low-pass filter* the circuit becomes. This means that there is more and more filtering of the ac signal as the line pair gets longer and longer.

Figure 8-7 shows the effect of this low-pass filtering on a digital square-wave transmission. At the top, a square wave is transmitted through a circuit with a negligible attenuation, because the RC and L/R times are very short compared to the wavelength. Traveling downward, we see the effects of in-

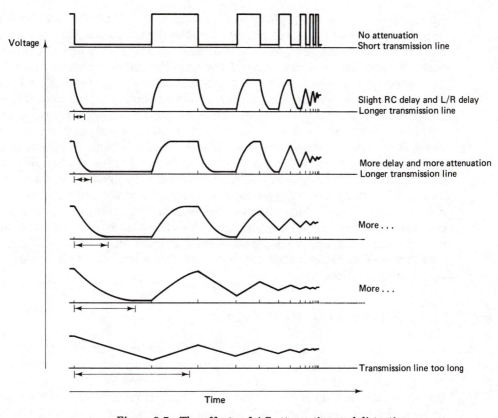

Figure 8-7   The effects of AC attenuation and distortion

creasing C and L. Both increases cause longer and longer time delays between the time the voltage starts to rise or fall and the time it gets there. By the fourth diagram down, the signal has been affected so much that its amount of rise and fall between waves is not enough for a digital gate to detect. The effect of differences in frequency is also shown. The pulses get closer and closer together as you go across the waveforms from left to right. This is equivalent to increasing the frequency. In the "short" transmission line at the top, the delay time only affects the very highest frequencies, but as the transmission line lengthens, serious attenuation of the signal happens at lower and lower frequencies. At the bottom, there's hardly anything left, even at the lower frequencies (pulses far apart). This is why we call the circuit characteristics of the open-wire line pair a low-pass filter. Only the low frequencies pass through; the higher frequencies are lost.

How much high-frequency attenuation is acceptable? What can we do about it?

Each repeater in an analog system like the phone company's voice lines amplifies the signal to replace lost power, and can also boost the high-frequency attenuation. This process is not perfect, and the 300- to 3000-Hz bandwidth of ordinary voice lines is a result of the length of lines between repeaters and the characteristics of the amplifier at each repeater junction. To answer the question "How much attenuation is acceptable?" we must say, "as much as we can have without making spoken words impossible to understand." Actually, a 300- to 3000-Hz bandwidth provides voice communication that can be easily understood, which is less attenuation than the worst case. It is not, however, anywhere close to covering the entire frequency range of human hearing. To get larger bandwidth and handle higher frequencies, shorter segments of wire between repeaters would be needed. The voice communication system was designed for the frequencies in the human voice. Leased lines that have better characteristics are more expensive because there are more repeaters, and the repeaters require higher-quality components. Circuits that permit data transmission at 9600 and 19,200 baud are not at all unusual, but you cannot transmit at these frequencies with ordinary voice lines.

8.3 TRANSMISSION MEDIA AND TECHNIQUES

When we used the word "transmitter" in describing part of a UART, you might have thought of a radio or television broadcast transmitter. That is certainly one kind of transmitter, although a "wireless" transmitter (as the British would call it) is hardly the only kind of transmitter that's possible. In fact, the telephone handset is also called a transmitter, when you're talking into the mouthpiece. In this section, we see some of the ways a transmitter can transmit.

8.3.1 Frequency-Division Multiplex

In an earlier section of this chapter we saw that space-division multiplexing (SDM) uses a separate wire for each signal being transmitted, and it is where the signal appears that tells you what it is. Time-division multiplexing (TDM) permits transmission of multibit numbers one bit at a time on the same channel. The time when a signal appears tells you what it is. Frequency-division multiplexing (FDM) is the technique used to separate channels of television or radio stations from one another. Radio transmitters use the same medium (the electromagnetic environment) to carry any different channels simultaneously.

There is absolutely no reason why this technique must be limited to "wireless" broadcast transmission. Electromagnetic broadcast allows you to use one antenna to transmit or receive many signals simultaneously. The total electromagnetic spectrum is divided into *bands* which are used by different types of transmitters, but there is really only one electromagnetic medium, and everyone shares it. If two channels want to transmit at the same frequency to someone in their vicinity, the receiver cannot separate the two channels of information. This problem can be solved by a combination of FDM and SDM. If wires or other conductors are used that confine the transmitter's signal into a "tight beam" so that it doesn't "slop over" into somebody else's signal, the two channels of information can be separated even though both are transmitted at the same frequency. In fact, if FDM is used, a single wire can carry many hundreds of channels with different signals on them, and another wire nearby can carry more hundreds of channels (using the same frequencies, if need be) without any conflict. Transmission of multiple channels across a single physical link can be done by TDM or FDM.

The amount of information that can be transmitted on a physical link depends on the variety of frequencies that can be used without confusion. This variety depends on the *bandwidth* of the link. Each channel requires a band of its own, so that information can be carried on the signal without overlapping another channel that can't be filtered out at the receiver. The total range of frequencies that can be transmitted on the link will determine how many bands will fit between the lowest and highest frequencies the link can handle.

8.3.2 Modulation and Demodulation

It's not fair to assume that everybody who's reading this already understands modulation. We've already mentioned modems as modulators and demodulators, without any real attempt to explain what those terms mean. Since this is a digital electronics book, we feel justified in "copping out" a bit and not going into detail on modulator and demodulator circuits—which are not digital circuits anyway—but we do feel a brief description of the various methods of modulation is in order.

We are not going to try to answer the question "Why modulate?" We'll assume from past examples in this chapter that you understand the problems that happen if you just "dump" voice or digital information onto a wire or other medium that's already carrying a signal.

Modulation combines the low-frequency information you want to transmit with a higher-frequency *carrier* signal. The idea of frequency-division multiplexing should already be familiar to you as a way of carrying more than one signal on the same medium. Now there is still the problem of how you combine the low-frequency information with the carrier. We see, in the modem for telephone communication, a shift in the carrier frequency when the level of the low-frequency signal changes.

There are three parameters that are part of the signal produced by a carrier-wave oscillator. The wave produced by the transmitting circuit has amplitude, frequency, and phase. Any one of these three items can be changed to represent a change in the level of the low-frequency information signal.

If the low-frequency changes cause a corresponding change in the amplitude (the peak-to-peak voltage) of the transmitting circuit's waveform, we call this **amplitude modulation** (AM). In a sense, the changes in the dc voltage of the voice or digital signal cause a corresponding change in the ac voltage being transmitted. The receiver demodulates by receiving an ac signal at the carrier frequency and converting it to dc.

Frequency modulation (which we already saw in an example) uses shifts in the dc voltage of the low-frequency signal to change the frequency that is transmitted. An FM (frequency modulation) modulator is a voltage-to-frequency converter. Frequency-shift keying (which we used in our modem) is just a specialized example of FM. To demodulate the FM signal, we do a frequency-to-voltage conversion, making variations in the frequency back into a changing dc level.

Phase-shift modulation (PSM) uses changes in the low-frequency audio or digital signal to shift the phase angle of the carrier wave. The amplitude and frequency of the transmitted wave do not change, but the phase angle shifts like the frequency shifts in FSK. A *phase-locked loop* (PLL) is one circuit that can be used to detect changes in the phase of the received signal and demodulate them by converting phase to a dc voltage.

In Figure 8-8, three diagrams show how a square-wave digital signal would affect the transmitted wave when the amplitude, frequency, and phase are modulated by the bits 1, 0, and 1 (transmitted serially).

Frequency modulation has supplanted amplitude modulation for most data transmissions because it is more noise-immune than AM. Phase-shift modulation is very similar to frequency modulation, but does not require as large a bandwidth to transmit the same digital information. This means that more channels of PSM can be transmitted on a band than would be possible

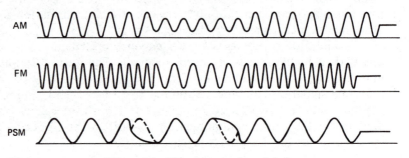

Figure 8-8   Three types of modulation

with FM. At the time of this writing, FM is still more popular than PSM, but we don't think that can last forever, with one-chip PLL circuits being produced cheaply.

8.3.3 Transmission Media

We have already determined that the number of simultaneous channels that can be carried on a physical link (a *medium*) depends on how far it is between the lowest frequency and the highest frequency that can be used (the bandwidth of the link). We'll look at some media to see what methods are used, and how the method relates to the number of channels.

   "Wireless" transmission. Radio broadcast (nonmicrowave) transmission (frequencies less than 1 GHz) spreads out like ripples on a pond. The number of frequencies possible is limited by the distance a transmitter can broadcast. Outside one transmitter's range, another can transmit at the same frequency. A receiver can't receive both transmissions, though, so only one channel can occupy each band. The number of messages that can be broadcast can be increased, though, if we transmit at higher frequencies, like . . .
   Microwave (frequencies in the gigahertz range). The microwave broadcast is a directional transmission, like a beam of light. It is possible for a receiver to pick up microwave "beams" from different directions at the same frequency. This is a little bit like combining frequency-division multiplex with space-division multiplex. As long as the transmitter is in a line of sight, the receiver can pick up its signal, and the communication to the receiving station can contain as many channels as the microwave transmitter can fit. Changing the direction of the receiving antenna can allow you to receive a whole new set of channels on the same frequencies. Since the microwave "beam" is like a beam of light—not "visible" beyond the horizon—the taller the tower is that carries the transmitting antenna, the farther the distance the transmission can carry. Microwave repeaters can relay the signal from one tower to another just as the repeaters on telephone and telegraph lines relay signals from one segment of transmission line to another. The number of repeater stations gets smaller as the towers get taller (and the signals can "see" farther and farther around the curve of the Earth). Ultimately, we can relay microwave signals using an *extremely* tall tower, like a . . .
   Satellite. If a satellite is placed in an orbit at an altitude of 37,000 km (23,000 miles), its orbital period is 24 hours. If placed in an orbit above the equator going in the same direction the earth is turning, the satellite will remain at the same point in the sky all the time, because the satellite will be in sync with the Earth's rotation (such a satellite is called *geosynchronous*). It will then serve as an "orbital platform" from which microwaves can be relayed just like any other microwave tower (except that it's a couple of hundred thousand times taller). Because it's extremely high, this "tower"

can "see" extremely far. With three satellites placed in the same circular orbit 120° apart, the whole earth can be covered, provided that one satellite can "talk" to another.

Early in the space program, passive satellites, which were nothing more than microwave "mirrors," were placed in *low earth orbit* (LEO). Radio signals were bounced off these satellites and picked up by ground stations as a way to "relay" information over long distances. The problem with this was that the satellite in LEO (450 miles up, or so) didn't stay in the sky very long. Like other microwave relay stations, the satellite was useless once it passed over the horizon. As many as 20 or 30 satellites would be needed in a LEO to keep one overhead all the time. Why didn't the users of these satellites use lower frequencies that could carry "over the horizon"? The answer is that a layer of the atmosphere called the *ionosphere* (or Kennelly-Heaviside layer) reflects low-frequency radio waves. High-frequency waves (like microwaves) penetrate the ionosphere. It's the reflection of the radio waves that enables them to "bounce" around the horizon. Unfortunately, the same reflection makes it hard for the radio waves to penetrate beyond the space between the ground and the ionosphere where they must go to reach the satellite.

Are the geosynchronous (24-hour orbit) satellites passive reflectors like the early ECHO I (which was just an aluminum-plated balloon)? The answer is "no," and in fact, the transmission to the satellite (*uplink*) is not the same frequency used to receive from the satellite (*downlink*). There's a very good reason for this—in the form of a natural satellite (the moon)—because reflected signals from a passive reflector come back at the same frequency they're transmitted. With the moon out there, there'll always be reflected signals coming back at the transmitting frequency. To separate these from the signals desired from the geosynchronous satellite (the moon does not go around the earth in 24 hours!), the satellite repeater's downlink frequency is different from the uplink frequency, and it's arranged so that nobody ever uses an uplink frequency for a downlink.

Wires and other conductors. Frequencies like those used for microwave transmission have characteristics like light waves. At these frequencies, the electromagnetic vibrations can be shaped into narrow beams and focused by reflectors, for instance. Like light waves, also, microwave beams are blocked by buildings, trees, and don't transmit well when an airplane is flying through the beam. Unlike light waves, microwaves and other radio frequencies can be carried through electrical conductors. For the lowest electromagnetic frequencies, ordinary wires may be used. At higher frequencies, significant amounts of energy radiate from the wires between the transmitter and receiver. The loss of power from the signal is bad enough, but that lost power gets into "the airwaves" and interferes with radio receivers near the wires, which is even worse.

Special geometries (shapes) for the conductors help to confine the signal within the conductor. A *coaxial* conductor [see Figure 8-9(a)] uses a hollow outer conductor with a wire in the center, separated by an insulator. Conductors with coaxial geometry can transmit much higher frequencies than a wire pair. Coaxial conductors do not radiate much power, and in a cable with many coaxial tubes, there is very little "crosstalk" between conductors. The current flowing in the coaxial tube is mostly on the inner surface of the hollow conductor and on the outside of the center wire. The outer part of the hollow conductor acts as a Faraday shield, and prevents radiation of signal and penetration of that signal into other conductors in the cable.

For even higher frequencies, especially microwave frequencies, *waveguides* with a rectangular cross section are used [see Figure 8-9(b)]. With higher frequencies and wider bandwidths comes a higher capacity for carrying information. Circular waveguides are available. One type has a helical geometry, with a conductor in the form of a spiral (a helix) forming the inner surface of the tube. These waveguides look like pipes (in some cases, square pipes), and are put together by techniques more akin to plumbing than electrical wiring. Any sharp bends in the waveguide become sites of severe power loss, so waveguides must follow gentle curves, or be connected around corners with special couplers. Although these conductors are much more expensive than ordinary wires, they can carry far more information, because they have more bandwidth (at the higher frequency) and can handle more channels.

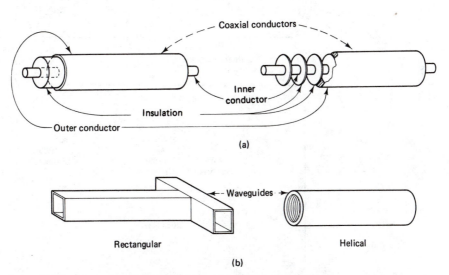

Figure 8-9   Coaxial cables and waveguides for microwave communication

Fiber-optics light pipe.   At higher and higher frequencies, the transmission of electromagnetic (radio) waves looks more and more like the propagation of light. Why not use light as the transmitting medium? For broadcast in the open air, this would not be a very good idea. Clouds, small birds, rain, and dust in the air all get in the way of light beams. The same problems (to a smaller degree) occur in microwave links, and the best solution is to use coaxial cables and waveguides (which don't allow things to block the beam and can go around corners). Light can be transmitted through a sort of "waveguide" called a **light pipe.** Its working principle is total internal reflection, which is something that happens at the boundary between two dissimilar transparent materials. The speed of light in glass or silica is slower than its speed in air (about two-thirds as fast in silica as air). When light traveling through silica strikes air, if it hits the boundary between the silica and the air at a shallow angle, all the light that strikes the boundary is reflected back into the silica, and none of it ends up as a beam in the air.

This is a better reflector than the best metal mirror that can be made. A pure silver shiny-metal reflector reflects about 93 percent of the light that strikes it, and absorbs the remaining 7 percent. Total internal reflection is necessary to "trap" a beam of light in a light pipe (see Figure 8-10). Suppose that we have a silica fiber 0.1 mm in diameter and 1 km long. If the

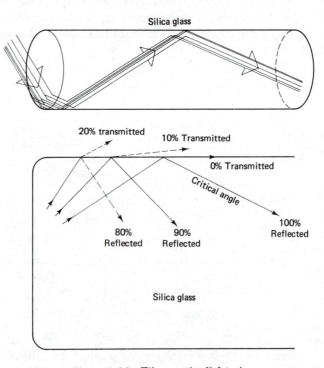

Figure 8-10   Fiber optics light-pipe

light loss at each reflection is 1 part per million, and the light strikes the silica–air boundary at a shallow angle so that it rebounds and strikes the other edge 1 mm down the fiber, there will be 1,000,000 reflections along 1 km of silica. At 1 part in a million loss per "bounce," there will be only 36 percent of the light left at the end of a kilometer. If 10 parts per million is lost at each bounce, only 45 millionths of the original light makes it to the far end of the fiber. Real mirrors lose 7 percent, at best. After 200 reflections (2 meters), less than half a millionth of the original light would remain. At the end of 1 km, nothing measurable would remain. Fiber light guides that use total internal reflection lose less than half the signal's power in 6 km. What loss there is happens because the silica isn't perfectly transparent, and has impurities in it. At the reflection, however, there must be 100 percent reflection—or at least 99.999999 . . . with more nines than we'd like to count—otherwise practically nothing would arrive at the far end of the fiber.

The silica used in optical fibers has exceptional transparency. To carry signals more than 1 km, the clarity of the silica must be better than (smoggy) city air.

Light frequencies are around 10^{15} Hz. This covers the range from infrared to visible light. Frequencies like this (10,000 times microwave frequencies) suggest a correspondingly higher capacity for multiple channels carried on a single fiber. Since the fibers are thin, and each thin fiber is quite flexible, a bundle of thousands of fibers can be made into a fiber-optic cable with flexibility as good as stranded-copper wire cables. One advantage of fiber-optic cables is that only one strand is needed for each "circuit," whereas copper-conductor cables need two wires for each line.

8.4 PULSE-CODE MODULATION

The modem was a device used to transmit digital signals in analog form, permitting multiple channels to use the same line by frequency-division multiplex. It is possible that one day in the future, the telecommunications industry may use a different method of transmission. Multiple channels will be combined on a single line using time-division multiplexing and transmitted as serial digital data instead of analog. In this case, analog signals will need to be converted to digital form using pulse-code modulation (PCM). Digital signals will not need to be converted to anything at all. They will be "ready to go" as they are.

Instead of the digital users having to convert their data over to analog form for transmission, analog users will have to convert their data to digital form. To do this, they will need a device called a codec (coder/decoder). This is a D/A and A/D device that will sample the analog waveform at some moment, convert its momentary voltage level to a digital number, insert the number into the bit stream "when its time comes" (time-division multiplexing) and return to sample the analog waveform another time. This is the "cod" part of the codec. The "dec" part reverses the process, reconstructing the channel's analog waveform from the digital numbers that come along in the receiver's time slot.

This method's strong point is the fact that digital repeater can reconstruct the data pulses it received, "cleaning up" noisy pulses or pulses which have degenerated due to line distortions. Analog repeaters amplify the noise along with the information, since they must be able to reproduce all of the waveform, and can't "decide" what part of the waveform is "unimportant." Digitally transmitted signals, since they are repeatedly reconstructed into clean pulses, can be transmitted through a signal path that distorts them badly, yet still be recognized by the repeater and reincarnated as fresh, clean pulses. Another advantage of PCM transmission is that a higher frequency of transmission can be used than with analog transmission, because the distortion at the higher frequency doesn't matter very much.

PCM is likely to take over from analog methods because of its higher reliability and the fact that there is continuing reduction of price-per-gate in digital systems. Multiplexing and switching of digital signals is simpler, and uses simpler and less expensive circuitry, than for analog signals.

8.5 IMPERFECTIONS

In this, the last section of the chapter, we'll define the main problems that "mess up" digital telecommunications. Since we are interested in communicating digital data, we might conclude after looking at the telecommunications system that exists today, that it wasn't designed for us. In a very real sense, that is true. The telecommunications system was designed for voice communications originally. As you can see in the section just concluded, this is changing, and will change more in the future. Eventually, someday, modems will be obsolete and codecs will be necessary in "old-fashioned" analog communications. In the meanwhile, there are some problems that are inherent in any system, digital or analog, and some problems that plague analog systems more than digital ones. There are even a few problems that cause more trouble in digital systems than analog ones (not very many).

Since analog systems will be with us for years to come, we'll look at analog system design features that have to be "corrected" by sneaky engineering, as well as authentic transmission problems that afflict all transmissions, digital or otherwise.

8.5.1 Noise

Noise is a term that refers to any electrical signal you don't want, that "creeps in" on top of the information that you're transmitting and superimposes itself on your signal.

RFI.   When a magnetic field moves across a conductor, it induces a voltage in the conductor.   Stray magnetic fields cross transmission wires all the time, and add noise to the signal on the wire.   As we already said, an analog system amplifies the noise with the signal at each repeater.   If a certain amount of noise is picked up randomly on each mile of wire, the noise added to the signal will get larger as the signal travels further and further.   Coaxial cable and waveguides are naturally shielded against this type of RFI (*radio-frequency interference*) noise, and are a much better choice than open-wire pairs for long-distance transmission.   Consequently, open-wire pairs are generally used only in the local area between the telephone user and the local office.   Trunk lines will be coax or waveguides (and now, some fiber-optic lines with repeaters are being used).   Since the silica used in fiber-optics light pipes is an electrical insulator, it is totally immune to RFI.

Thermal noise.   Another source of noise is the random motion (Brownian motion) of electrons in the wires themselves.   This is called **shot noise** or **white noise.**   There is also a similar type of noise caused by molecular and atomic vibrations within the semiconductor material.   It is produced by thermal energy in the crystal lattice, and since it's in the amplifier material, it gets amplified.   There's really nothing that can be done about it except to cool down the semiconductors (expensive) or tolerate a certain amount of it.   White noise or thermal noise can be heard as a hissing sound in the background of all electronically produced audio.

Crosstalk.   Signals on other lines or communications links that penetrate into your conductor and "walk" on your signal are called **crosstalk.**   If you have a neighbor with an overpowered and badly adjusted CB that "gets in" on top of your TV signal and messes up your reception, that's an example of crosstalk in the broadcast area, although you might think of other things to call it.

The clicks, beeps, and occasional snatches of someone else's conversation that you sometimes hear on the telephone are crosstalk.   Usually, the problem is caused by induction between one wire and another running alongside it, although a wire carrying multiple channels can have crosstalk if the channels are not effectively separated on the receiving end.

High-voltage spikes on lines caused by electromagnetic switching circuits or the ring voltage used to ring a phone are high-level signals that may penetrate into your circuit even though the lower-level voice signals do not.

Although the sources of noise on transmitted data may vary, the results are the same.   As the noise accumulates on the signal waveform, it becomes harder and harder to tell the signal from the noise, and eventually the data are lost in the noise. Digital transmission of data using digital repeaters remedies this problem, since repeaters can clean up small amounts of noise on a digital signal, and do not have to keep amplifying the noise along with the signal as it is passed from repeater to repeater.

8.5.2 Distortion

When the waveform transmitted down a line changes or loses its waveshape due to characteristics of the transmission line itself, we call the results **distortion**. One example of distortion was already discussed earlier in this chapter, when we saw how an uncompensated transmission line acts as a low-pass filter (attenuation distortion). Coils called *loading coils* are normally added to the transmission line at intervals of every few kilometers to compensate for this effect, but they may fail, or not be perfectly matched to the impedance of the transmitting and receiving equipment. Changes in phase or amplitude of the transmitted signal can arise in the amplifier (repeater) circuits along the line. Poor electrical contact can give a "noisy" character to signals transmitted down a wire.

Signals that contain a number of frequencies (and all digital signals do) may travel down lines that do not conduct all frequencies at the same speed. If parts of the signal arrive at a different time than others—for example, if the mark frequencies of an FSK signal get ahead of the spaces—total garbage is received. Equalizing the analog telephone circuit for this type of distortion is more complicated than equalizing it for frequency response, and the solution is to either convert to digital transmission and let closely spaced repeaters on the line correct the problem every time the signals begin to drift out of step, or else slow down the data transmission rate on an analog link to a rate where the differences in delay times are negligible compared with the time used to transmit each bit.

Intermodulation distortion is caused by "mixing" of two frequencies in a FDM multiplexed line to form a third frequency. If this frequency happens to be at or close to the frequency of another channel, IM distortion (actually a form of crosstalk or noise) gets into the "innocent bystander" channel.

8.5.3 Line Failure

This is one of the things that happens to cause the computer to "hang up" on you in the middle of a transmission. If it happens, another circuit will be needed. This is basically a reliability problem. Temporary loss of transmission capability is called a **dropout**. Loss of signal that lasts until a repair crew fixes the fault are called **line failures**. Failures in the modem, terminal, software, or power are not, strictly speaking, line failures, but they have the same effect. The computer you're talking to "hangs up" unexpectedly.

Suppose that an airplane flies through the microwave beam of a relay tower. This will cause a dropout that may be interpreted by your terminal as a "hangup" signal. It isn't good for the signal or the pilot of the plane, but the pilot knows this, and isn't likely to do it often unless he's a dropout or has bad hangups.

Outages are the long-term nasties that happen when the earthmoving vehicle plays pick-up-the-cable, or Mother Nature decides to use 10 MV of lightning for a bell voltage. The best thing to do in these cases is have an alternative path available—that's the common carrier's problem—which is usually the case when the failure is on an intertoll trunk. For the most part, though, the outages happen at the local loops, and there's not a lot that can be done until the repair crew is finished.

8.5.4 Data Errors

As the frequency of data transmission (baud rate) goes up, the chance that a short glitch will cause the loss of a bit—or several bits—goes up, too. We mentioned earlier that one way to handle losses of the one-bit variety was parity checking. For more-than-one bit losses, methods that take advantage of redundancy of information are more valuable. As far back as the old telegraph days, important information like dollars-and-cents figures was repeated twice, whereas alphabetic information could be read easily enough even if the odd letter here and there was wrong.

For the most part, the telegraph technique was "ignore the errors, but repeat the important stuff." Special error-detecting codes have been devised. The general approach to handling an error is to have the receiver say "Eh? How's that again?" and cause the transmitter to retransmit the data block that contained the error.

8.5.5 Delays and Blocking

Data are transmitted and received after a delay called the **propagation delay**. This is the time it takes the signal to travel from the transmitter to the receiver. If half-duplex transmission is used, each end of the line "takes its turn" and then the other end transmits. The propagation delay determines how fast this "turnaround" can take place.

On telephone lines, the speed of transmission is less than the speed of light. In the case of satellite communications, transmission is at nearly the speed of light, but has a long way to go. To uplink and downlink to a satellite in geosynchronous orbit takes 270 ms (74,000 km round-trip). To retransmit a block when an error has been detected, the satellite link is going to take a good deal longer than 270 ms to handle the "handshaking," and the receiver and transmitter will have to be able to "keep track" of what block of information was transmitted long after the transmission is over, so that if a "retransmit" request comes along after a long propagation delay, the transmitter will remember what block has to be retransmitted.

There aren't really any "magic" solutions to propagation delay time. The data transmitters and receivers will just have to be "smart" enough to work around the long delays involved in satellite communications and long cables.

CONCLUSION

The "digital invasion" is under way. Digital techniques are taking over from analog methods in almost every imaginable field of electronic communications. This book is dedicated to the technician who may someday service digital equipment in every guise from the "out-front" digital computer to the "hidden" VLSI chips in a fourth-generation television set. No textbook will ever keep you ahead of the game. The best you can hope for is to get the basic vocabulary and ideas, then keep abreast of the field by subscribing to trade magazines in your specialty. Learning—especially in the field of digital electronics—doesn't stop when you get your diploma. That's when the real learning, the OJT (on-the-job training) actually begins. Think of this text, and any course you take in digital electronics, as the "first-stage booster" you will need for a successful "launch" into the industry. *You* will have to supply the "sustainer engine" of your launch vehicle, and, unlike the ballistic missile from which this analogy is taken, you'll have very little time for "coasting flight." Good luck. Your adventure in the field of digital electronics promises to be as exciting as any astronaut's commitment to the space program.

QUESTIONS

8.1. What is a common carrier?

8.2. Which is more suitable for transmitting data from one 8-bit computer to another, parallel or serial data transmission?

8.3. Suppose that output signals from the data bus (outputs are placed on an 8080 data bus for 500 ns) of a computer are connected directly to the telephone system. The 500-ns pulses will not arrive at the other end of the telephone connection. Why not? What might happen to the logic devices in the data-bus buffer?

8.4. Describe what a UART does when it's transmitting, and what it does when it's receiving.

8.5. Describe what a modem does when it's transmitting, and what it does when it's receiving.

8.6. What is TDM, and how is it used in data communications?

8.7. Name three types of digital circuit that can be used for parallel-to-serial conversion.

8.8. What is a direct-connect modem? Do you think its 5-V logic (if it contains a 5-V logic) is directly connected to the telephone circuit?

8.9. Is level shifting and amplitude shifting important to a modem that uses an acoustic coupler?

8.10. What is attenuation? How does it affect pulses sent down a long transmission line?

8.11. What does a repeater do? How do repeaters make long-distance communication possible?

8.12. Briefly describe AM, FM, and PSM.

8.13. Why are satellites in a geosynchronous orbit better than those in low-earth orbit?

8.14. At various frequencies, different types of transmission lines are used to carry the signals. What types of conductors are used for transmitting electromagnetic waves at the following frequencies? (Choices at the right)
   (a) Audio (20 to 20,000 Hz)   (1) Silica fibers
   (b) Microwave (300 MHz to ? GHz)   (2) Open-wire pairs
   (c) Optical (400 to 800 THz)   (3) Waveguide

8.15. Approximately what percent of light is reflected at each "bounce" as light travels down a fiber in a light pipe?

8.16. What does a codec do when it's transmitting?

8.17. What does a codec do when it's receiving?

8.18. PCM is used in transmissions from the Space Shuttle. Do the astronauts' voices travel through a codec before transmission?

8.19. Does a telemetry transmission (already digital data) from the Space Shuttle to a ground station travel through a codec? Is it transmitted in PCM?

8.20. Does an analog repeater amplify distortion and noise as it amplifies the signal? Does a digital (PCM) repeater?

8.21. Describe "crosstalk" briefly.

8.22. What are dropouts in telecommunications? How do they differ from line failures? What would you do to transmit data reliably where periodic dropouts in the data stream are expected?

8.23. What is the factor that causes propagation delays in satellite transmission of data?

Appendix A:
Binary-Based Number Codes

Binary numbers are found in computer systems, stored in the memory device of the computer. There are several kinds of binary number codes that may be stored in the same memory device. The same pattern of 1s and 0s may have a completely different meaning in different places. A code may represent a number, pure and simple, in binary code. In another place, the same pattern of 1s and 0s may represent a letter of the alphabet, a punctuation mark, or even a numeral in the decimal system, rather than a binary value. In yet another application, the number stored in the computer's memory may be a binary-code number with a plus or minus sign and decimal point, or an exponent indicating where to shift the decimal point.

Each of these codes uses a combination of binary 1s and 0s in a different way. In some cases, the meaning of a 1 or 0 in a specific place changes according to the code being used. In this chapter we explore a number of these codes and how the 1s and 0s are given different meanings in each one.

A.1 BINARY, OCTAL, BCD, AND HEX NUMBERING

A1.1 Binary Code

The first application of binary numbers is . . . as numbers! In the interior of a computer memory, a group of binary bits occupy a common location called an **address**. Just how many bits there are at an address depends on the design of the computer, but the simplest way to use these bits is to assign one bit a place value of 1, another bit a place value of 2, another 4, another 8, another 16, and so on, giving each next bit double the value of the last. This is the simple binary code. For many microprocessors, a size of 8 bits is the natural word length of each memory address. A word with 8 bits will have binary place values from 1 to 128. A combination of these bits could stand for any binary number from 0 (no bits on) to 255 (all 8 bits on). This method of coding is called **simple unsigned binary**. Only positive, whole numbers (positive integers) are used in this system. If you want to represent a decimal number this way, all you have to do is convert it to binary, and if it comes out less than eight digits, "pad out" the remaining places with 0s. If the number has more than eight places, we have a problem. We either need a way to put together two 8-bit pieces (bytes), or a computer with a larger word length.

A.1.2 Octal Code

We know that the switches inside the computer memory are made from digital logic gates. This means that numbers must be composed of 1s and 0s, since digital gates are either ON or OFF. No matter what number system happens to be convenient for us (decimal, usually) the numbers inside computers (and any other digital logic circuit) are binary, really. Having said that, we still have good reasons for showing the contents of a computer's memory in number systems that are not binary. For example, if you want to print the number 127 on a sheet of paper in the binary system, it's 01111111. That takes up a lot of space, and a lot of ink, on a sheet of paper. In fact, binary numbers take up more space than any other number system, and that costs money. Worse, binary numbers are hard to read, just like decimal numbers with a lot of digits. Try reading eight-digit decimal numbers quickly, and keeping all the hundreds, thousands, and millions straight!

One thing we do with long decimal numbers is add commas to make reading more easy. Reading 12,345,678 is not as difficult as 12345678, since the millions, thousands, and units are separated. If we do the same thing with binary numbers, 127 becomes 01,111,111. Each group of three binary digits has a name (Table 8-1). We call 000 zero and 011 three, for instance. When we read 01111111 (127) as 01,111,111, we call the three groups of digits separated by commas one, seven, seven. The name of each group is the number you would read if the group stood alone as a binary number. Reading 01,111,111 as one, seven, seven—or 177, for short—is actually creating a shorter form of the binary number. This short form of binary is convenient for printing, because it takes only three symbols (1-7-7) to represent a number that's eight symbols long in binary. It's also better than the decimal 127 if you want to get the original binary back again. Converting the decimal number 127 to 01111111 is—to put it frankly—a headache, but

TABLE A-1   NAMES OF 3-BIT GROUPS

Digit name	3-Bit binary	Digit symbol
Zero	000	0
One	001	1
Two	010	2
Three	011	3
Four	100	4
Five	101	5
Six	110	6
Seven	111	7

converting the 177 short form back to 001,111,111 (the extra 0 makes no difference) means just having to know the three-digit binary number for things from zero through seven. If we only need to know the binary for eight different symbols, this means we're using a number system with the base eight, called **octal**.

Just for a little practice, let's use the binary form of the decimal number 56. It's 00111000. Breaking that up the way we break up long decimal numbers, the number becomes 00,111,000. You can see right away that we don't need the 00 at the front, but we want to keep the number in a form that "fits" an 8-bit computer. This means that we'll have a three-digit octal number every time we convert a byte of binary, whether we need all three digits or not. From 00,111,000 we get zero, seven, zero, by reading each group as a 4-2-1 binary code. Octal 070 takes more space than decimal 56, but is easier to reconstruct into binary if you need to. It also preserves the word size by showing that the 0 in front is a significant part of the number.

To go in the opposite direction, take the octal number 236. It's 010,011,110 according to Table A-1. Since this number has nine digits, and we're supposing that it is stored in a digital machine with a word size of 8 bits, let's chop off the front 0 of our binary number, leaving 10,011,110, an eight-digit binary number. We've reconstructed what the binary number with eight digits looks like from an octal number with only three digits. We've done it with a lot less work than the conversion from its decimal value would take, and the number (236) doesn't really take any more room to print than its decimal value (158) takes. (*Note:* octal numbers usually look a little "larger" than they do in decimal, but have about as many digits most of the time.)

A.1.3 Hexadecimal Code

The octal number is formed from the binary code by grouping bits by threes, then reading each group by itself as a number from 000 (zero) to 111 (seven). Since only eight groups are possible, the octal number is base-eight.

Octal numbers will never contain an 8 or a 9, since these digits cannot be written in 3 bits. Otherwise, octal numbers resemble decimal numbers pretty closely.

Now we ask whether there is an even more compact way to write the binary contents of a computer memory (or any digital device). The decimal system is a bit more compact than the octal system. Some three-digit octal numbers can be written with only two decimal digits, some four-digit octal numbers can be written with only three decimal digits, and so on . . . but *decimal* is awkward. To "see" what the binary for a decimal number is, we need a cumbersome conversion process, while octal is conveniently converted to binary by just looking up a 3-bit number for each octal digit. Is there another way to write binary that is as easy to convert as octal, but takes up less space?

Yes. The key is to change the way we break up the binary number using commas. When we took 00111000 and broke it apart into 00,111,000, we put a comma every third place. Suppose that we put a comma every fourth place, breaking the number up into 0011,1000—two groups of 4 *bits*. Each 4-bit group has a name. In this case, 0011 is called three, and 1000 is called eight, if we read the group as an 8-4-2-1 code. The number 0011,1000 can be written "38" using this form of notation. The names for all the 4-bit groups are given in Table A-2.

Notice that there are 16 possible groups of 4 bits. This makes it impossible to use a decimal symbol for every name, since there are only 10 decimal symbols. We had to use letters of the alphabet for numbers from 10 up to 15. This allows us to still use one symbol for each name, but the "numbers" formed this way will not always look like decimal numbers. Patterns like 3F and D1 are possible, and numbers like BE might not even look like numbers at all. This is one of the little sacrifices we have to make for the sake of compactness. Once we decide to use this system of writing binary numbers, every 8-bit byte becomes a two-digit **hexadecimal** (base sixteen) code that takes only two print characters to write. Since print shops have letters as well as numbers in their type cases, printing lists of binary information using

TABLE A-2 NAMES OF 4-BIT GROUPS

Digit name	4-Bit binary	Digit symbol	Digit name	4-Bit binary	Digit symbol
Zero	0000	0	Eight	1000	8
One	0001	1	Nine	1001	9
Two	0010	2	Ten	1010	A
Three	0011	3	Eleven	1011	B
Four	0100	4	Twelve	1100	C
Five	0101	5	Thirteen	1101	D
Six	0110	6	Fourteen	1110	E
Seven	0111	7	Fifteen	1111	F

the hexadecimal system is no hardship on the typesetters. Since every eight digits of binary is compressed into two digits of hexadecimal, there is a saving on printing cost over binary, decimal, and octal. The only inconvenience is for the person who must read the code, because numbers like BE are not "numbers" in our normal experience. Once we get over the shock of dealing with "funny" numbers like BE and D7, the two-symbol representation of each 8-bit byte is quite easy to work with. To "see" what binary code is "hidden" inside each *hex* (short for hexadecimal) pattern, the reader just looks up the 4-bit pattern for each symbol—the same process we use for octal, only with a larger lookup table.

We've used the number BE as an example of a hex number. Let's see what a BE is by looking up its symbols. B is the symbol for 1011 and E is the symbol for 1110. Putting these together, we get BE as 1011,1110. This is the decimal number 190. You can see that BE takes up less space than either its binary or decimal form. For this reason, and the fact that hex is more easily converted to binary than decimal is, most listings of numbers in computer memory are printed in hex. Whenever magazine articles or book chapters include listings of the code inside a computer memory, the code—which is really binary—is almost always printed in hex to save space. There are also a number of 8-bit small computers with hex keyboards for number entry. This means that loading code into the computer will take two key-strokes on the keyboard instead of eight switch operations for every byte of code.

One more example. What does the number 127 look like in the computer's memory? What does 127 look like when it's converted to hex?

If you're clever and sneaky, you'll remember that we gave you the binary value of 127 a few paragraphs back, and you won't have to convert it from decimal to binary. 127 is 01111111 in binary. Now, what do we do to make it hex? Right! We break it up every four places with a comma. 0111, 1111 is the result. Now, we must look up the names of these two 4-bit groups—0111 is seven (7) and 1111 is fifteen (F). The decimal number 127 comes out as 7F in hex. It doesn't look much like 127, but it takes up less space, and can be converted back to binary by anyone reading a listing a lot easier than decimal. Why convert it back to binary? Because in the computer, the numbers really are binary, and you might need to know just which bits are supposed to be ON or OFF when you're troubleshooting a sick computer—even though the printed listing in your hands is in hex.

A.1.4 BCD Numbers

Octal and hexadecimal codes as discussed in this chapter serve only one purpose. They are shorthand for the binary code that is really inside the digital logic circuit. In all cases, the 8-bit code inside the circuit is organized the same way; each position is twice the value of the place to its right, until you run out of places. All numbers are represented as a combination of 1s, 2s, 4s, 8s, 16s, and so on. This underlying *data structure* is the same whether we choose to represent it on paper using octal or hex symbols. The only basic inconvenience of the simple unsigned binary form of data is that simple binary and the decimal system of numbering really don't mix. Conversion between the decimal system we are all comfortable with, and the binary system natural to digital logic circuits, is awkward and clumsy. It's possible, though, to write two digits of hex in every byte of binary—shouldn't it be possible to write two digits of decimal in a byte instead?

Of course, the answer is yes. The two digits of a hex byte could be limited so that the numbers from 10 up are just never used. Some two-digit combinations like 38 (0011,1000) would still be around, but others like BE (1011,1110) would be gone. The last 4 bits (4-bit groups are called **nibbles**) would stand for the ones' place of decimal numbering, and the first 4 bits would be the tens' place. In this code, numbers with 8 bits (a byte) would be made of 1s, 2s, 4s, 8s, 10s, 20s, 40s, and 80s as shown below:

80s	40s	20s	10s	8s	4s	2s	1s
0	0	1	1,	1	0	0	0

In discussing this binary code, we said that the numbers 0011,1000 were 38. That's the same conversion we did in going from binary to hex, but in this case the 38 means thirty-eight in decimal. Notice that the 0011,1000 has one 20, and 10, and an 8. This adds up to decimal 38. The system described above is a different data structure from the simple binary described before, because it is **binary-coded decimal** (BCD). Each 4-bit group (nibble) is a separate decimal place. The number 1986, for example, would be encoded in this system as:

$$1 \qquad 9 \qquad 8 \qquad 6$$

$$0001,1001,1000,0110$$

where each nibble is read separately as one decimal digit, and numbers larger than 1001, although possible, are never used. In this BCD code, numbers like 1010, 1011, and 1111 are *illegal* code.

Most microprocessors, and all larger computers, contain circuitry for handling arithmetic in this code, or conversion from simple binary into this code. Such conversion is called a **decimal adjust** operation.

A.2 BCDIC AND HOLLERITH CODES

Numbers stored in the memory device of a computer may represent exactly what they look like—numbers—but they may also have other meanings to the user or designer of digital systems. Alphabetic information is needed for communication more often than pure numbers. As with numbers, there is not just one "right" way to represent an alphabetic symbol. Some of these methods derive from early data storage and communications media that were around before there were computers. One is used by IBM, and practically no one else—if IBM weren't such an important sector of the computer and digital industry, there would little reason to discuss this *alphameric* (*alpha*betic-nu*meric*) *code*. The BCDIC and EBCDIC (BCD Interchange Code and Expanded BCD Interchange Code) are used in various IBM machines and in IBM-compatible equipment made by other manufacturers. Their names include the BCD abbreviation, and they contain the one-nibble codes for the one-digit decimal numbers we called BCD codes. Unlike BCD nibbles stored in microprocessors, these BCD patterns include codes for letters and punctuation marks that really have nothing to do with the BCD code we talked about before. Both of these codes started with the punchcard, and the Hollerith code developed for it in the 1880s by Herman Hollerith. We normally call Hollerith punchcards "computer cards," because they have become associated with computing machines in the present day. Punchcards were around for a long time before computers, though, and were used with machines called *unit-record machines* decades before the first computer was built. They contain a code which works in the following way.

There are 80 columns on a punchard, in which one or more holes may be punched. If one hole is punched in a column, it is usually a number. There are 12 places where a hole may be punched. Nine of these are called *numeric punches*, and are indicated on most punchcards by having printed numbers in them from 1 to 9. If a hole is punched in one of these places in a column, that's the code for the decimal number indicated. Figure A-1 shows a "3" punched in its first (leftmost) column, and an "8" in the next column over. The remaining three rows are called *zone punches*. They contain a "0" and two positions at the top of the card which are usually unmarked, called the "11" and "12" rows. By themselves, these positions represent the number zero and two punctuation marks. They are usually used in combination with one of the numeric punches to make letters of the alphabet. When two holes are punched in a column, one a zone and one a numeric punch, the code is an *alphabetic symbol*. Three punches represent a punctuation mark or special character, usually a zone punch, a numeric punch from 1 to 7, and an "8" punch. Four or more punches were originally illegal in Hollerith code, because they were thought to weaken the card too much for it to pass safely through the card reader. This code follows a simple pattern, shown in the chart in Figure A-2.

The numeric punches alone are the codes for numbers and a few punctuation marks (&, -). The numeric + zone punches provide the first, second, and third nine letters of the alphabet. What's that, you say? There aren't that many letters in the alphabet? You're right, and Hollerith stuck the symbol "/" in the middle of his alphabet to round out the difference.

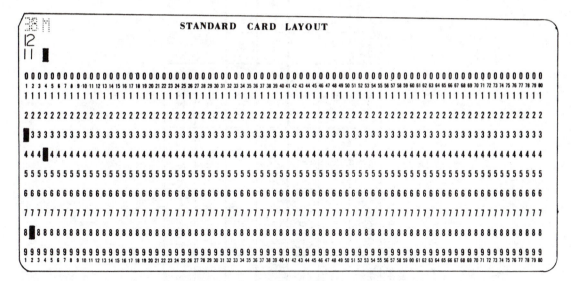

Figure A-1 Hollerith punchcard example

From this, we get the BCDIC and EBCDIC codes used in computers. The **BCD Interchange Code** (BCDIC) is a 6-bit code which uses 4-bit BCD code for the numeric punch (the 8-4-2-1 bits) and two bits (the B and A bits) for the zone punch. (A 6-bit code is sometimes called a *six-level code*.) The values of the numeric and zone bits for each character of the alphabet are found on the same chart as the Hollerith code. One example, to see how this chart is used: To find the Hollerith code for the letter M, search out the zone punch row and numeric punch column that cross where the M is. When you have them, you'll see that the numeric punch in an M is a "4" punch, and the zone punch is an "11" punch. To find the BCDIC code for M, find the zone bits and numeric bits listed at the opposite end of the row and column from the punches. The zone bits for the "11" zone are B = 1, A = 0; and the numeric bits for the "4" punch are 8 = 0, 4 = 1, 2 = 0, and 1 = 0. Put together, the BCDIC code looks like:

$$\begin{array}{cccccc} B & A & 8 & 4 & 2 & 1 \\ 1 & 0 & 0 & 1 & 0 & 0 \end{array}$$

for the letter M.

There is an **Expanded BCD Interchange Code** (EBCDIC) which uses all 8 bits of a byte (an eight-level code), and permits uppercase and lowercase letters as well as numbers and a variety of punctuation symbols and control characters. Its structure is basically similar to the BCDIC, containing zone and numeric bits, but with a greater variety of zone punch combinations in the expanded Hollerith code, four zone bits are used to represent the combinations of two, three (and even *four* using numeric "9" as a zone punch!)

Hollerith punchcode chart/BCDIC chart
numeric punches used in the symbol

No #	Numeric 1	Numeric 2	Numeric 3	Numeric 4	Numeric 5	Numeric 6	Numeric 7	Numeric 8	Numeric 9	Zone bits	Binary code
No zones ƀ	1	2	3	4	5	6	7	8	9	00	$\bar{B}\cdot\bar{A}$
12 zone &	A	B	C	D	E	F	G	H	I	11	$B\cdot A$
11 zone −	J	K	L	M	N	Ø	P	Q	R	10	$B\cdot\bar{A}$
0 zone 0	/	S	T	U	V	W	X	Y	Z	01	$\bar{B}\cdot A$
Numeric bits	0001	0010	0011	0100	0101	0110	0111	1000	1001		
Binary code	$\bar{8}\cdot\bar{4}\cdot\bar{2}\cdot1$	$\bar{8}\cdot\bar{4}\cdot2\cdot\bar{1}$	$\bar{8}\cdot\bar{4}\cdot2\cdot1$	$\bar{8}\cdot4\cdot\bar{2}\cdot\bar{1}$	$\bar{8}\cdot4\cdot\bar{2}\cdot1$	$\bar{8}\cdot4\cdot2\cdot\bar{1}$	$\bar{8}\cdot4\cdot2\cdot1$	$8\cdot\bar{4}\cdot\bar{2}\cdot\bar{1}$	$8\cdot\bar{4}\cdot\bar{2}\cdot1$		

In the symbol

Figure A-2   Hollerith/BCDIC code chart

Some characters of the expanded B.C.D. interchange code (EBCDIC)

No #	Numeric 1	Numeric 2	Numeric 3	Numeric 4	Numeric 5	Numeric 6	Numeric 7	Numeric 8	Numeric 9	Zone bits	Binary code
No zone ƀ	1	2	3	4	5	6	7	8	9	111	$D \cdot C \cdot B \cdot A$
12 zone &	A	B	C	D	E	F	G	H	I	1100	$D \cdot C \cdot \overline{B} \cdot \overline{A}$
11 zone −	J	K	L	M	N	O	P	Q	R	1101	$D \cdot C \cdot \overline{B} \cdot A$
0 zones 0	/	S	T	U	V	W	X	Y	Z	1110	$D \cdot C \cdot B \cdot \overline{A}$
12·0 zones	a	b	c	d	e	f	h	g	i	1000	$D \cdot \overline{C} \cdot \overline{B} \cdot \overline{A}$
12·11 zones	j	k	l	m	n	o	p	q	r	1001	$D \cdot \overline{C} \cdot \overline{B} \cdot A$
11·0 zones	?	s	t	u	v	w	x	y	z	1010	$D \cdot \overline{C} \cdot B \cdot \overline{A}$
Numeric bits	0001	0010	0011	0100	0101	0110	0111	1000	1001		
Binary code	$\overline{8} \cdot \overline{4} \cdot \overline{2} \cdot 1$	$\overline{8} \cdot \overline{4} \cdot 2 \cdot \overline{1}$	$\overline{8} \cdot \overline{4} \cdot 2 \cdot 1$	$\overline{8} \cdot 4 \cdot \overline{2} \cdot \overline{1}$	$\overline{8} \cdot 4 \cdot \overline{2} \cdot 1$	$\overline{8} \cdot 4 \cdot 2 \cdot \overline{1}$	$\overline{8} \cdot 4 \cdot 2 \cdot 1$	$8 \cdot \overline{4} \cdot \overline{2} \cdot \overline{1}$	$8 \cdot \overline{4} \cdot \overline{2} \cdot 1$		

Figure A-3 Hollerith/EBCDIC code chart

zone punches, providing a possible 16 "shifts" for each numeric punch code. (Maybe the Hollerith cards got *stronger* between 1890 and the development of EBCDIC, permitting more punches?)

A chart showing the EBCDIC code and its structure (related to the Hollerith punches on a punchcard) is given in Figure A-3.

The letter M, represented in EBCDIC code, is:

Zone Bits				Numeric Bits			
D	C	$\overline{B}$	$\overline{A}$	8	4	2	1
1	1	0	1	0	1	0	0

Note that the B and A bits are just exactly inverted in the EBCDIC code from BCDIC's B and A bits. This is the reason why they've been indicated in inverted Boolean form in this example.

BCDIC and EBCDIC codes are an improvement on the 12-bit punch codes used on cards. The card codes never use all 12 punch positions at once (for reasons of mechanical strength) and are inefficient (with 12 positions, 4096 different codes are possible, but fewer than 100 are actually used). In BCDIC, the four numeric and two zone bits are used to "compress" all the information available in one, two, or three punches of 12 possible punches. This reduces the number of circuits needed to store bits in the computer by half, if BCDIC is used instead of storing Hollerith directly. The EBCDIC code uses four numeric and four zone bits to compress the information available in one, two, three, or four punches. Again, reduction of the 12 bits of Hollerith (never all used) to 8 bits of EBCDIC is a considerable savings in circuit components (only two-thirds as many are needed for EBCDIC as for direct storage of Hollerith). Of course, this also makes computers that use these codes to store Hollerith information cheaper than they'd be otherwise, a fairly good reason for their use.

A.3 ASCII CODE

The **American Standard Code for Information Interchange** (ASCII) is a binary code for alphameric symbols that was defined by an agreement between most manufacturers of digital equipment in the United States. Practically everyone uses it for all data communication, with the exception of IBM (a rather outstanding exception!). It is not developed from Hollerith punchcard codes as BCDIC and EBCDIC are, but has some structural similarity to those codes. ASCII is a seven-level code (each symbol is represented by 7 bits). As with BCDIC and EBCDIC, the front bits of the ASCII character define different shifts or types of characters. There are four types of ASCII codes defined by the front 2 bits of the code: control characters, numerals/special characters, uppercase alphabetic characters, and lowercase alphabetic characters. Each of these four types contains 32 symbols defined

"back" 5 bits → / "front" 2 bits ↓	00000	00001	00010	00011	00100	00101	00110	00111	01000	01001	01010	01011	01100	01101	01110	01111	10000	10001	10010	10011	10100	10101	10110	10111	11000	11001	11010	11011	11100	11101	11110	11111
00	Control codes for typewriter control which don't print anything																															
01	␢	!	"	#	$	%	&	'	(	)	*	+	,	−	.	/	0	1	2	3	4	5	6	7	8	9	:	;	<	=	>	?
10	@	A	B	C	D	E	F	G	H	I	J	K	L	M	N	O	P	Q	R	S	T	U	V	W	X	Y	Z	[	/	]	∧	←
11	'	a	b	c	d	e	f	g	h	i	j	k	l	m	n	o	p	q	r	s	t	u	v	w	x	y	z	{	|	}	~	DEL

American Standard Code for Information Interchange (ASCII)

Figure A-4   ASCII code chart

by the back 5 bits of the character. A chart of the ASCII code is shown in Figure A-4. From this chart we can find the code for G. The front 2 bits are identified at the left end of the row G is in, and the back 5 bits at the top of the column G is in. For G, the front bits are 10 and the back bits are 00111, making the code:

$$G = 10 \underset{\uparrow}{} 00111 \qquad \begin{matrix} \text{uppercase type} \\ \text{seventh letter} \end{matrix}$$

whereas a lowercase letter g would have the code

$$g = 11 \underset{\uparrow}{} 00111 \qquad \begin{matrix} \text{lowercase type} \\ \text{seventh letter} \end{matrix}$$

and the number 7 would have the code

$$7 = 01 \underset{\uparrow}{} 00111 \qquad \begin{matrix} \text{numeric type} \\ \text{seventh number} \end{matrix}$$

Of course, if a parity bit is added to the ASCII code (usually in front of the rest of the bits), it becomes an eight-level code.

A.4 OTHER ALPHAMERIC CODES

A.4.1 Morse Code

Historically, the first code used commercially for data communications by ON and OFF digital signals, **Morse code** was (and is) used for telegraph messages. Devised by Samuel F. B. Morse, inventor of the first commercially practical telegraph system, it is really a trinary system, with signals sent using short ON, long ON, and OFF levels. Although still used in some places (wireless telegraphy, etc.), Morse code has no significant importance in the digital data communications field.

A.4.2 Baudot or Murray Code

Baudot was an inventor whose pioneering efforts led to the printing telegraph, forerunner of today's data terminals and Teletype machines. The **Baudot code** still used by older Teletype machines was not devised by Baudot, but by Murray. It's a five-level code which manages to represent the letters and the numbers by using a "figures shift" (numeric) and "letters shift" (alphabetic) symbol before each field of characters. Since numbers and letters are usually bunched in groups, this scheme works fairly well, using shift codes only once in a while. Sixty characters are possible in Murray (Baudot) code, but transmission becomes severely slowed down if data are transmitted containing both numbers and letters on each line, because many shift characters must also be sent.

Modern Teletype machines do not use Baudot code because of its inefficiency and limited number of characters—they use the ASCII code, instead. The only reason for knowing about Baudot code is the off chance that you might bump into one of the ancient "newsroom" Teletypes still chugging along at some remote location—they're noisy, but virtually indestructible.

A.5 NUMERIC CODES: TWO'S COMPLEMENT (SIGNED NUMBERS)

So far, we've looked at codes where a number represents a number, and where a number represents a letter. The numbers we looked at were all positive integers—whole numbers without a + or - sign in front of them—but a digital computer must have ways of handling negative numbers as well as positive ones. In the digital subtracters used in microprocessors, no answers are negative. Instead, the subtracter circuit, as it subtracts columns of binary digits from right to left, always assumes it can borrow a "1" from the next place over. When the subtracter runs out of places, the answer left is in two's complement code, rather than negative.

All microprocessor chips produce two's-complement code when they arrive at a negative answer. So do minicomputers, with ALU (arithmetic logic unit) chips made of TTL or ECL logic. The really big mainframes have hardware that can produce anything they darn well please—cost is no object—but even the biggest digital systems usually proceed to subtract numbers by one of the following three methods:

1. Add one number to the *one's complement** of the other number. Take the bit at the carry of the answer, and carry it around to the units' position, then add it on there. This is called the **end-around-carry method,** and it works. It's also easier to build with hardware than it is to explain in words. The answer is normal binary if it's positive and in one's-complement code if it's negative.

2. Add one number to the two's complement† of the other number. The answer is normal binary if it's positive, and in two's-complement code if it's negative.

3. Use a subtracter or adder/subtracter circuit. The answer is normal binary if it's positive and in two's-complement code if it's negative.

When numbers are subtracted by methods 1 or 2, the same adder used to add is also used to subtract. This isn't much of a savings, though, since circuits must be added to convert one of the two numbers into its one's- or two's-complement form whenever subtraction is desired. To do this, a *controlled inverter* (XOR) circuit must be added for each bit of the number. Method 3 has the controlled inverter circuits already built into the adder, if we use an adder/subtracter. It's really the same as method 2, when all the pieces of the circuit fall into place.

The one's complement is one way of representing negative numbers, and the two's complement is another different—but equally good—method. In methods 1 and 2, subtraction proceeds by adding a negative number. That's the same as subtracting a positive number, provided that we accept the fact that two's complement and one's complement numbers are negative.

Although we described how to convert a binary number to its two's complement in Chapter 7, we'll repeat the steps here, together with a description of the one's complement:

To convert a binary number to its one's complement:

1. Invert all the bits of the number.

To convert a binary number to its two's complement:

2. Add 1 to its one's complement.

And vice versa, to convert a two's complement to one's complement:

1. Subtract 1 from the two's complement.

---

*One's complement = invert all the bits.
†Two's complement = invert all bits and add 1.

To convert a one's complement to binary:

2. Invert all the bits of the number.

That was a little different from our description in Chapter 7, wasn't it?

Let's suppose that you're the designer of a digital system. Once you've settled on the method you'll use for showing negative numbers—let's use the two's complement—you still need a way to tell whether a number is a large positive one or a small negative one. Here's what we mean: Suppose that you have the binary code 11111000, and you know it's not a letter in ASCII or EBCDIC code—it's a number. You also know that the digital system you've designed uses two's complement numbers for negative values. Now, you have a problem: Is 11111000 a positive 120 or a negative 8? If you just add up the place values of the bits, assuming the number to be an unsigned binary integer, the number is 120 just as it appears. If you treat it as the two's complement of something (you assume it's negative), you subtract 1 from the number—getting 11110111—and invert all the bits—getting 00001000—which tells you this number is an 8, in two's-complement code, of course. Now, which is it?

There's no way to tell, just going on what you've got in the example. To know for sure, you need more information, which we're about to give you.

People who design computers that use signed binary numbers in the two's-complement system use the front bit to tell if the number is positive or negative. As long as the front bit is 0, the number's positive. If the front bit is 1, the number is negative, and it's in two's-complement form. The front bit of the number becomes its *sign bit*, and the rest of the bits give a signed value from 0 to 127 (positive) and -1 to -128 (negative).

Of course this limits the number of positive numbers you can write, because only numbers from 00000000 to 01111111 are positive. Anything from 10000000 to 11111111 is negative and in two's-complement code, so there are only 128 positive numbers and 128 negative numbers possible in this system. Unsigned numbers existed in 256 combinations, but they were all positive. We had to give something up in order to gain something. To get negative numbers as well as positive ones in one byte, we had to cut down on the number of positive codes possible. We chop them up half and half, giving half the values negative signs and the other half positive signs. The same idea is used in 16-bit machines—for numbers from $-32,768$ to $+32,767$—and in 32-bit machines—for numbers from $-2,147,483,648$ to $+2,147,483,647$.

A.6 MANTISSA AND EXPONENT (FLOATING-POINT NUMBERS)

With the two's-complement system, we have signed numbers, but they're still all integers. How does a computer handle numbers like $2\frac{1}{3}$ or 22.75 or 6.71×10^{-3}?

A.6.1 Binary Fractions

To write a *binary number* with a *fraction*, it's necessary to know what's on the other side of the *binary point*. Up to now, we've stayed on the left side of the binary point (a decimal point in a binary number) and used whole numbers. The place values on the right-hand side of the point are organized like this:

16	8	4	2	1	$\frac{1}{2}$	$\frac{1}{4}$	$\frac{1}{8}$	$\cdots$
1	0	1	1	0 .	1	1	0	

point

for the decimal number 22.75. Notice that as you go left each place value gets twice as big, and as you go right, each place value gets half as big. The only new thing we did is go past the "ones" place, finding the "halves," "quarters," and "eighths" places, and so on.

Any number can be converted from decimal to binary, even fractions—but a number like $2\frac{1}{3}$ takes an infinite number of decimal places to write. It also takes an infinite number of binary places. Writing this fraction (in either decimal or binary), we have to decide how many places we'll go before we stop. We could decide to have 8 bits of fraction and 8 bits of integer. Each number would take two bytes of storage space in a computer memory. There would be no need to store the "." point if we knew which byte was the integer part and which was the fraction part—an important advantage.

In real computer applications a one-byte integer can't be any larger than 255 (127, if it's signed). That limits the things we can do with the computer pretty severely. If our number is less than 0.004, decimal, it can't fit in the fraction byte either. Numbers are usually stored in computers using more than two bytes. Four bytes give a signed number whose decimal value has nine decimal places. This is about the same as a good pocket calculator.

Instead of using half the bytes for the integer part of a number and the other half for the fraction part, most schemes store a number in **binary scientific notation**. Rather than trying to explain every possible scheme used (there are many) we'll just look at one scheme: Four bytes contain a number called the **mantissa**. It has the signed value of the first 31 significant binary places of the number (nine decimal places), but doesn't say where to put the binary point. An additional byte contains a signed number called the ex-**ponent**. It says how many places to the left (if it's negative) or right (if it's positive) the binary point should be moved from the front of the number. Let's look at an example:

Mantissa	Exponent
11001111 00000000 00000000 00000000	00000111

First, we look at the front bit of the mantissa. This tells us that the number is negative. Then we convert from two's complement to binary to see what it is:

Step 1. Subtract 1.

$$11001111 \ 00000000 \ 00000000 \ 00000000$$
$$-1$$

$$11001110 \ 11111111 \ 11111111 \ 11111111$$

Step 2. Invert all bits.

$$00110001 \ 00000000 \ 00000000 \ 00000000$$

Now, we remember that the binary point is at the front of the number, and that it's negative:

$$-.00110001 \ 00000000 \ 00000000 \ 00000000$$

Right now, the number is "one-eighth" plus "one-sixteenth" plus "one-256th" (decimal value = −0.1914), but we remember that the exponent says that the binary point must be moved (unless it's 00000000). The exponent has a positive value (whew!) and is a seven in binary code. That means we should move the binary point seven places to the right.

$$-0011000.1 \ 00000000 \ 00000000 \ 00000000$$

This number has an integer part (binary 11000 = decimal 24) and a fraction part (binary .1 = decimal .5). Put together, the number is negative 24.5.

We'd like to point out three things before you worry too much about this. First, there are hundreds of variations on these codes, so don't bother to memorize this one—it's probably not the one you'll end up with, no matter what machine you work on. Second, this kind of number, called a **floating-point variable**, is about as complicated a beast as you'll find hiding inside a computer. Everything else is simpler than this. Third, if you are planning to become a technician who repairs the computer, it's not too likely that you'll have to know how floating-point numbers look inside the computer, until you have to troubleshoot everything in a memory bit by bit. By that time, you'll certainly have been trained enough on the system you're working with to know how its floating-point numbers are stored.

A.7 OCTAL BYTE CODE

It is common to represent binary numbers in 8-bit groups called *bytes*. This is done even for 16- and 32-bit computers. To write the **octal byte code** for a binary number:

1. Break the number up into groups of 8 bits.
2. Separate each 8-bit group, with commas, as you do with large decimal numbers.
3. "Digest" the groups between commas into octal digits. There should be three octal digits for each 8-bit group.

For example, the decimal number 32,767 will look different in octal byte code than it looks in simple octal code. If the number 32,767 is written in binary and converted directly to simple octal, it looks like this:

$$32,767 \text{ (decimal)} = 111111111111111 \qquad \text{(binary)}$$

$$111111111111111 = 111,111,111,111,111. \quad \text{(commas added)}$$

$$32,767 \text{ (decimal)} = \quad 7 \quad 7 \quad 7 \quad 7 \quad 7 \qquad \text{(simple octal code)}$$

But the number 77777 (octal) doesn't show how each byte of the number 32,767 (decimal) looks inside the machine. The number 32,767 is too big to fit inside one byte, and we can't see from the 77777 which 7s go into the front byte and which go into the back byte.

Converting the number 32,767 (decimal) into octal bytes proceeds like this:

$$32,767 \text{ (decimal)} = 1111111 \quad 11111111 \qquad \text{(binary bytes)}$$

$$1111111 \quad 11111111 = 1,111,111. \quad 11,111,111. \quad \text{(commas added)}$$

$$32,767 \text{ (decimal)} = 1 \quad 7 \quad 7 \qquad 3 \quad 7 \quad 7 \qquad \text{(octal byte code)}$$

which shows that in octal byte code, everything isn't 7s, and the front byte contains 177 (octal) while the back byte contains 377 (octal). A two-byte octal number like this may be written 177,377, with a comma to show the byte boundary between each 8-bit group.

A.8 HEXADECIMAL BYTE CODE

For reasons described above, numbers are also represented in hex according to bytes. To write the hexadecimal byte code for a binary number:

1. Break the number into groups of 8 bits.
2. Divide each byte produced by step 1 into groups of 4 bits with commas.
3. "Digest" the numbers between commas into hex digits. There should be two digits for each byte.

We'll do this for the number 32,767 again.

$$32,767 \text{ (decimal)} = 111111111111111 \qquad \text{(binary)}$$

$$111111111111111 = 1111111 \quad 11111111 \qquad \text{(separate bytes)}$$

$$1111111 \quad 11111111 = 111,1111. \quad 1111,1111. \quad \text{(add commas)}$$

$$32,767 \text{ (decimal)} = \quad 7 \quad F \qquad F \quad F \qquad \text{(hex byte code)}$$

We find that 32,767 (decimal) is 7F,FF (hex). Unlike the octal byte code, numbers in hex byte code look the same as hex numbers in general. 32,767 is 7FFF in hex even when it's not broken into bytes. Making hex into hex byte code is as simple as putting a comma every two digits. Maybe that's why hex is more popular than octal for writing listings of binary computer programs (the fact that it costs less to print hex is no handicap, either!).

Appendix B:
One-Byte Opcodes Used for
Both 8080 and Z-80

SINGLE-BYTE INSTRUCTIONS

(r = register code; B = 0; C = 1; D = 2; E = 3; H = 4; L = 5; M = 6; A = 7)
(Intel mnemonics are in capital letters; Zilog mnemonics are in lowercase letters.)

INR r inc r	0r4	INX B inc bc	003	POP B pop bc	301	RNZ ret nz	300	XCHG ex de,hl	353
DCR r dec r	0r5	INX D inc de	023	POP D pop de	321	RZ ret z	310	XTHL ex (sp),hl	343
		INX H inc hl	043	POP H pop hl	341	RNC ret nc	320	SPHL ld sp,hl	371
MOV r,r'1rr' ld r,r'		INX SP inc sp	063	POP PSW pop af	361	RC ret c	330	PCHL jp (hl)	351
						RPO ret po	340	HLT hlt	166
ADD r add a,r	20r	DCX B dec bc	013	PUSH B push bc	305	RPE ret pe	350	NOP nop	000
ADC r adc a,r	21r	DCX D dec de	033	PUSH D push de	325	RP ret p	360	DI di	363
SUB r sub a,r	22r	DCX H dec hl	053	PUSH H push hl	345	RM ret m	370	EI ei	373
SBB r sbc a,r	23r	DCX SP dec sp	073	PUSH PSW push af	365	RET ret	311		
ANA r and r	24r							DAA daa	047
XRA r xor r	25r	DAD B add bc	011	STAX B ld (bc),a	002	RLC rlca	007	CMA cpl	057
ORA r or r	26r	DAD D add de	031	STAX D ld (de),a	022	RRC rrca	017	STC scf	067
CMP r cp r	27r	DAD H add hl	051	LDAX B ld a,(bc)	012	RAL rla	027	CMC ccf	077
		DAD SP add sp	071	LDAX D ld a,(de)	032	RAR rra	037	RST # rst #	3#7

TWO-BYTE INSTRUCTIONS

(*** = any one-byte data number; ppp = device code for a port)

ADI ***	306, ***	IN ppp	333, ppp	MVI r ***	0r6, ***
add a,***		in a,(ppp)		ld r,***	
ACI ***	316, ***	OUT ppp	323, ppp		
adc a,***		out (ppp),a			
SUI ***	326, ***				
sub a,***					
SBI ***	336, ***				
sbc a,***					
ANI ***	346, ***				
and ***					
XRI ***	356, ***				
xor ***					
ORI ***	366, ***				
or ***					
CPI ***	376, ***				
cp ***					

THREE-BYTE INSTRUCTIONS

(? = an address in memory; L?, P? = line, page of address; % = a 16-bit data word)

JNZ ?	302, L?, P?	CNZ ?	304, L?, P?	LXI B %	001 %
jp nz, ?		call nz, ?		ld bc, %	
JZ ?	312, L?, P?	CZ ?	314, L?, P?	LXI D %	021 %
jp z, ?		call z, ?		ld de, %	
JNC ?	322, L?, P?	CNC ?	324, L?, P?	LXI H %	041 %
jp nc, ?		call nc, ?		ld hl, %	
JC ?	332, L?, P?	CC ?	334, L?, P?	LXI SP %	061 %
jp c, ?		call c, ?		ld sp, %	
JPO ?	342, L?, P?	CPO ?	344, L?, P?		
jp po, ?		call po, ?			
JPE ?	352, L?, P?	CPE ?	354, L?, P?	STA ?	062 ?
jp pe, ?		call pe, ?		ld (?),a	
JP ?	362, L?, P?	CP ?	364, L?, P?	LDA ?	072 ?
jp p, ?		call p, ?		ld a,(?)	
JM ?	372, L?, P?	CM ?	374, L?, P?	SHLD ?	042 ?
jp m, ?		call m, ?		ld (?),hl	
JMP ?	303, L?, P?	CALL ?	315, L?, P?	LHLD ?	052 ?
jp ?		call ?		ld hl, (?)	

DATA TRANSFER INSTRUCTIONS

(r = register-code; B = 0; C = 1; D = 2; E = 3; H = 4; L = 5; M(HL) = 6; A= 7; *** = any one-byte data number; ddd = any one-byte displacement added to IX or IY; % = a 16-bit data word; ? = an address in memory; ?L, ?H = Line, page of address)

LD r, (IX+d)	335, 1r6, ddd	LD r, (IY+d)	375, 1r6, ddd
LD (IX+d), r	335, 16r, ddd	LD (IY+d), r	375, 16r, ddd
LD (IX+d), ***	335, 066, ddd, ***	LD (IY+d), ***	375, 066, ddd, ***
LD IX, %	335, 041, %	LD IY, %	375, 041, %
LD IX, ?	335, 052, ?L, ?H	LD IY, ?	375, 052, ?L, ?H
LD ?, IX	335, 042, ?L, ?H	LD ?, IY	375, 042, ?L, ?H
LD SP, IX	335, 371	LD SP, IY	375, 371
PUSH IX	335, 345	PUSH IY	375, 345
POP IX	335, 341	POP IY	375, 341
EX (SP), IX	335, 343	EX (SP), IY	375, 343
LD a, i	355, 127	LD a, RFSH	355, 137
LD i, a	355, 107	LD RFSH, a	355, 117
LD BC, ?	355, 113, ?L, ?H	LD DE, ?	355, 133, ?L, ?H
LD HL, ?	355, 153, ?L, ?H	LD SP, ?	355, 175, ?L, ?H
LD ?, BC	355, 103, ?L, ?H	LD ?, DE	355, 123, ?L, ?H
LD ?, HL	355, 143, ?L, ?H	LD ?, SP	355, 165, ?L, ?H
EX AF, AF	010	EXX	331
LDI	355, 240	LDIR	355, 260
LDD	355, 250	LDDR	355, 270
CPI	355, 241	CPIR	355, 261
CPD	355, 251	CPDR	355, 271

ARITHMETIC/LOGIC

(r = register-code B = 0; C = 1; D = 2; E = 3; H = 4; L = 5; M(HL) = 6; A = 7; b = bit-position; 000 = 0; 001 = 1; 010 = 2 etc.; *** = any one-byte data number; ddd = any one-byte displacement added to IX or IY; % = a 16-bit data word; ? = an address in memory; ?L, ?H = Line, page of address)

ADD A, (IX+d)	335, 206, ddd	ADD A, (IY+d)	375, 206, ddd
ADC A, (IX+d)	335, 216, ddd	ADC A, (IY+d)	375, 216, ddd
SUB A, (IX+d)	335, 226, ddd	SUB A, (IY+d)	375, 226, ddd
SBC A, (IX+d)	335, 236, ddd	SBC A, (IY+d)	375, 236, ddd
AND (IX+d)	335, 246, ddd	AND (IY+d)	375, 246, ddd
XOR (IX+d)	335, 256, ddd	XOR (IY+d)	375, 256, ddd
OR (IX+d)	335, 266, ddd	OR (IY+d)	375, 266, ddd
CP (IX+d)	335, 276, ddd	CP (IY+d)	375, 276, ddd
INC (IX+d)	335, 064, ddd	INC (IY+d)	375, 064, ddd
DEC (IX+d)	335, 065, ddd	DEC (IY+d)	375, 065, ddd
ADD IX, BC	335, 011	ADD IY, BC	375, 011
ADD IX, DE	335, 031	ADD IY, DE	375, 031
ADD IX, HL	335, 051	ADD IY, HL	375, 051
ADD IX, SP	335, 071	ADD IY, SP	375, 071
INC IX	335, 043	INC IY	375, 043
DEC IX	335, 053	DEC IY	375, 043
RLC (IX+d)	335, 313, ddd, 006	RLC (IY+d)	375, 313, ddd, 006
RL (IX+d)	335, 313, ddd, 026	RL (IY+d)	375, 313, ddd, 026
RRC (IX+d)	335, 313, ddd, 016	RRC (IY+d)	375, 313, ddd, 016
RR (IX+d)	335, 313, ddd, 036	RR (IY+d)	375, 313, ddd, 036
SLA (IX+d)	335, 313, ddd, 046	SLA (IY+d)	375, 313, ddd, 046
SRA (IX+d)	335, 313, ddd, 056	SRA (IY+d)	375, 313, ddd, 056
SRL (IX+d)	335, 313, ddd, 076	SRL (IY+d)	375, 313, ddd, 076
BIT b, (IX+d)	335, 313, ddd, 1b6	BIT b, (IY+d)	375, 313, ddd, 1b6
SET b, (IX+d)	335, 313, ddd, 3b6	SET b, (IY+d)	375, 313, ddd, 1b6
RES b, (IX+d)	335, 313, ddd, 2b6	RES b, (IX+d)	375, 313, ddd, 2b6
ADC HL, BC	355, 112	SBC HL, BC	355, 102
ADC HL, DE	355, 132	SBC HL, DE	355, 122
ADC HL, HL	355, 152	SBC HL, HL	355, 142
ADC HL, SP	355, 172	SBC HL, SP	355, 162
NEG	355, 104		
IM 0	355, 106		
IM 1	355, 126		
IM 2	355, 136		

ARITHMETIC/LOGIC (continued)

RLC r	313, 00r	RL r	313, 02r
RRC r	313, 01r	RR r	313, 03r
SLA r	313, 04r	RLD	355, 157
SRA r	313, 05r	RRD	355, 147
BIT b,r	313, 1br		
SET b,r	313, 3br	RES b,r	313, 2br

CONTROL INSTRUCTIONS

(ddd = any one-byte displacement added to PC, IX or IY)

JR d	030, ddd	DJNZ d	020, ddd
JR C ,d	070, ddd	JR NC, d	060, ddd
JR Z ,d	050, ddd	JR NZ, d	040, ddd
JP (IX)	335, 351	JP (IY)	375, 351
RETI	355, 115	RETN	355, 105

I/O GROUP

(r = register-code B = 0; C = 1; D = 2; E = 3; H = 4; L = 5; M(HL) = 6; A = 7; b = bit-position; 000 = 0; 001 = 1; 010 = 2 etc.; *** = any one-byte data number; ddd = any one-byte displacement added to PC, IX or IY; % = a 16-bit data word).

IN r, (C)	355, 1r0		
INI	355, 242	INIR	355, 262
IND	355, 252	INDR	355, 272
OUT (C), r	355, 1r1		
OUTI	355, 243	OTIR	355, 263
OUTD	355, 253	OTDR	355, 273

Index